MW01079329

Hell under the Rising Sun

TEXAS A&M UNIVERSITY
116
MILITARY HISTORY SERIES

Hell under the Rising Sun

Texan POWs and the Building of the Burma-Thailand Death Railway

KELLY E. CRAGER

TEXAS A&M UNIVERSITY PRESS | COLLEGE STATION

Copyright © 2008 Kelly E. Crager
Manufactured in the United States of America
All rights reserved
First edition
This paper meets the requirements of ANSI/NISO Z39.48-992
(Permanence of Paper). Binding materials have been
chosen for durability.

Library of Congress Cataloging-in-Publication Data

Crager, Kelly E., 1968–
    Hell under the rising sun : Texan POWs and the building of the
Burma-Thailand death railway / Kelly E. Crager. — 1st ed.
        p.   cm.
    Includes bibliographical references and index.
    ISBN-13: 978-1-58544-635-3 (cloth : alk. paper)
    ISBN-10: 1-58544-635-1 (cloth : alk. paper)
    1. World War, 1939–1945—Prisoners and prisons, Japanese.
2. Burma-Siam Railroad. 3. World War, 1939–1945—Conscript
labor—Burma. 4. World War, 1939–1945—Conscript labor—
Thailand 5. Prisoners of war—Japan. 6. Prisoners of war—Texas.
7. Texas—History—20th century. 8. Oral history. I. Title.
    D805.B9C73 2008
    940.54'725209591—dc22
                                                          2007022276

Dedicated to the men of the 2nd Battalion,
131st Field Artillery Regiment,
and to the sailors and marines of the
USS *Houston*, as well as to their families

Contents

Illustrations

Preface

IN MARCH 1942, THE 2ND BATTALION, 131ST FIELD ARTILLERY REGI-
ment, 36th Division, formerly of the Texas National Guard, surrendered to
the Imperial Japanese Army on Java in the Dutch East Indies. Shortly after
the surrender, the men of the 2nd Battalion were joined as prisoners of war
by the sailors and marines who survived the sinking of the heavy cruiser
USS *Houston*. From March 1942 until the end of World War II, these men
lived in various Japanese prison camps throughout the Dutch East Indies,
in Southeast Asia, and in the Japanese home islands. Forced to labor for
their captors for the duration of the conflict, they performed grueling tasks,
including working in industrial plants and mining coal in Japan, and, most
notably, constructing the infamous Burma-Thailand "Death Railway."

During their three and one-half years of captivity, these prisoners experienced appalling brutality at the hands of the Japanese. Enduring prolonged
malnutrition and extreme overwork, they suffered from numerous tropical
and dietary diseases while receiving almost no medical care. Each day, these
men lived in fear of being beaten and tortured, and for months at a time
they witnessed the agonizing deaths of their friends and countrymen. In
spite of the conditions they faced, most survived to return to the United
States at war's end.

This book is not a history of the Burma-Thailand railway. Numerous
Australian, British, Dutch, and Japanese authors have written valuable studies on that topic, and attempting to add yet another work is not necessary
at this point. If the reader is interested in the building of the railway, labor
allocation, Asian *romusha* laborers, or any other issues related to the railway,
there is a wealth of books and articles to which they can look. Instead,
this is a study of the American experience on the railway. In many ways,

their experiences do not differ significantly from those of the other Allied POWs; they suffered from the same diseases, received the same poor food and medical treatment, and were abused as were the rest of the laborers. But as a distinct minority within the POW community on the railway, the Americans have not received the scholarly attention that is their due. How did the Americans view their captors, other Allied POWs, each other, and themselves? What does their understanding about their time on the railway reveal about these men? This study examines the experiences of these former prisoners from 1940 to 1945 and attempts to explain how they survived Japanese captivity.

I have relied heavily on oral history interviews as primary sources for this study. The 2nd Battalion surrendered virtually intact in March 1942, and its whereabouts were largely unknown for the entire war. The Japanese did not allow prisoners of war to keep records of their captivity, so traditional sources concerning these men between 1942 and 1945, such as unit records and after-action reports, are scarce. Even those official sources that are available do not adequately reflect the former prisoners' thoughts and feelings regarding their experiences. Therefore, oral history interviews provide the framework for this study. Where necessary, I have supported individuals' testimony with corroborating evidence from a number of others' recollections, as well as with personal memoirs and supporting documentary evidence gathered by the U.S. government in the immediate aftermath of World War II.

Throughout this study, I refer to cities and countries by the names by which they were known at the time. For example, I refer to Burma rather than Myanmar, and the Dutch East Indies rather than Indonesia. Also, I have chosen not to make extensive editorial changes to the direct quotes from the transcribed interviews. These direct statements by the survivors provide a quality and flavor that cannot be replicated by my writing, and they help provide an understanding of the men that heavily edited language cannot. Most of these men were from Depression-era Texas, and their grammar and expressions should express that. By sanitizing their statements, I would be telling a story that is only partly true. Therefore, I provide exact quotes, even when the words used may be offensive to readers in the twenty-first century, because that is the language these men used.

I am deeply indebted to many people for their assistance during the researching and writing of this work. First, I must thank Ronald Marcello of the University of North Texas for his devoted and tireless efforts in conducting the invaluable oral history interviews with the survivors of the railway, as well as for his advice in the preparation of this book. I must also thank

Mike Campbell, also of the University of North Texas, for all the professional direction he has provided for me over the years; Eric Van Slander, of the National Archives, made my research in the archives productive, efficient, and even enjoyable; numerous members of the Lost Battalion Association and CA-30 USS *Houston* Survivors Association have provided much assistance, as well as Christopher Koontz at the Center for Military History.

Finally, I offer the most heartfelt thanks to my family. My children, Becca and Ben, often reminded me that no matter how deeply involved in my work I may have been, nothing is as important as devoting as much time to them as possible. My wife, Jennifer, has been so generous, supportive, and caring that any attempt to list the ways in which she helped me would simply be incomplete and insufficient. Thank you, Jen. Once again, I want to thank all those who have assisted me, without whose help this work would not be possible. Of course, any errors of omission or commission are solely my responsibility.

Hell under the Rising Sun

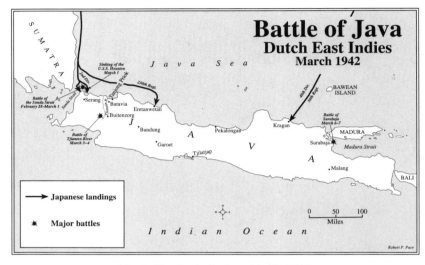

Map 1 The Battle for Java, March 1942.

Chapter 1

Becoming Soldiers

AS THEY LOADED THEIR GEAR INTO TRUCKS AND PREPARED TO MOVE to Camp Bowie in Brownwood, Texas, the young soldiers from Jacksboro, Texas, had little reason to fear the future. In fact, they were excited. These men belonged to a field artillery unit in the Texas National Guard—F Battery of the 2nd Battalion, 131st Field Artillery Regiment, to be precise. All these soldiers had spent most of their lives in and around Jacksboro, and they looked forward to the move to Brownwood. Being mobilized into the U.S. Army in late 1940 did not bother these young men. Most were in their late teens and early twenties—an age when men tend to think they are invincible—and few of them gave a second thought to their country's relations with the empire of Japan. A little more than a year later, things changed dramatically, however, and these young, happy-go-lucky men found themselves facing a horror that they could not have imagined growing up in Jacksboro.

The Texas National Guard's 131st Field Artillery Regiment came into being on May 5, 1917, and the unit entered federal service as part of the 61st Brigade, 36th Division, in August 1917. Upon receiving orders to leave for France in the fall of 1917, the 131st received its issue of 75-mm fieldpieces and took the long voyage across the Atlantic to join the American Expeditionary Force in France. Glory on the battlefield eluded the 131st in the First

World War, however, as the unit saw no combat and instead served only in a reserve capacity throughout the conflict. When the U.S. Army demobilized following the war, it released the 131st from federal service in April 1919, and the artillery outfit spent the interwar years training to maintain effectiveness should it be called upon to help defend the country again.[1]

The 131st, as part of the 36th Division, Texas National Guard, consisted mainly of officers and men from North and West Texas. The 2nd Battalion consisted of firing batteries D, E, and F based in Wichita Falls, Abilene, and Jacksboro, respectively. Rounding out the 2nd Battalion were Service Batteries from Plainview and Lubbock, a Medical Detachment from Plainview, and Headquarters Battery located in Decatur.[2] The men of the 2nd Battalion continued to drill and conduct small-scale maneuvers in North and West Texas on a regular basis, maintaining not just military readiness but their regional ties as well.

The soldiers of this unit joined the National Guard between the two world wars for a variety of reasons. Lt. Ilo Hard of Itasca, Texas, chose the National Guard because he had always had an inclination toward the military and thought he could make the military a career.[3] Lt. Huddleston Wright of F Battery, who entered the service in the days of horse-drawn artillery, joined because he had always liked horses and believed that through the National Guard he could get paid to work with them.[4] Amarillo native Lt. Col. Blucher S. Tharp, commanding officer of the 2nd Battalion, had been in the military for a considerable time and served with Gen. John J. Pershing on the border with Mexico in the 1910s.

Most of the enlisted men entered the National Guard for different reasons. They did not necessarily believe that the military would be a lifetime commitment but thought the service could provide them with things that were in short supply at home: money and excitement. During the economic hard times of the Great Depression, many of the farmers and ranchers in this part of Texas felt the financial squeeze especially hard. Creditors foreclosed on private homesteads by the thousands during the Depression, with North and West Texans being especially susceptible, and the farming conditions of the Dust Bowl made an agricultural way of life exceedingly difficult. Luther Prunty joined F Battery while he was in high school in Jacksboro because he and his family needed the extra income that National Guard service brought in; Prunty had to lie about his age before he could be admitted.[5] Service Battery's Clark Taylor enlisted at the age of fourteen for the same reasons and had to stretch his age even more.[6] Jess Stanbrough of Headquarters Battery joined the Guard while attending junior college because he needed the money to help pay his way through school.[7]

Another important reason these young men enlisted in the National Guard was that it promised some excitement in their rural, small-town lives. Frank Ficklin, who joined Headquarters Battery at seventeen in 1939, did so to break the monotony of his usual routine.[8] Uell Carter and George Killian, both of E Battery, became guardsmen because it might provide them with "a little fun."[9] Eddie Fung, who as a youth in San Francisco, California, ran away from home to become a cowboy, joined C Battery in the 1st Battalion in May 1940, hoping to be assigned to a cavalry unit.[10] According to Kelly Bob Bramlett of Headquarters Battery, "[Joining the National Guard] was something to do, you know, for young people around there."[11] The National Guard, with its uniforms, discipline, weapons, and travel, seemed a welcome departure from the sometimes dreary environment of North and West Texas, so it was especially appealing to these men, many of whom were still in their teens.

Since these units were based out of small Texas towns, the men who joined shared similar socioeconomic backgrounds, and many had known one another for their entire lives before joining the Guard. D Battery from Wichita Falls consisted mainly of men from that town or from the surrounding area; E Battery from Abilene followed the same pattern; and the men of F Battery, better known as "the Jacksboro Boys," were especially well known for their comradeship and for the small-town ties that held them together during the immensely trying times they faced later in the war. Comradeship, as well as peer pressure, encouraged some of the men of the 2nd Battalion to join their friends in the service. Roy ("Max") Offerle said that he joined D Battery at age sixteen mainly because his older brother, Oscar, had already joined and had attained the rank of sergeant.[12] Roger White of E Battery and Headquarters Battery's Dan Buzzo claimed that their friends in the unit talked them into joining.[13] Crayton ("Quaty") Gordon, who attended Texas Tech University at the time, joined Service Battery because his three roommates joined, and they looked "sharp" in their uniforms.[14]

Those who joined for the extra money and those who joined because they were looking for some excitement certainly were not members of a mutually exclusive list. Most shared the desire for the money and excitement, but there were myriad other reasons why these men chose to serve in the National Guard. Some, like Lester Rasbury and Alf Brown, both of Headquarters Battery, joined in part because they believed they would get drafted through the Selective Service sooner or later, and they would rather serve with people they knew from their hometowns than be sent away to serve with strangers.[15] Houston ("Slug") Wright worked in California for the Standard Oil Company but left his job to join F Battery because his brother had served in the outfit during World War I.[16] Others, such as Thurman Capps of Headquarters Battery, had no choice in the matter; they were drafted.[17] Whatever their reasons for joining, one common theme is clear: the men of the 2nd Battalion, 131st Field Artillery, joined because they believed their service would provide them with something they lacked. Very few claimed that they had more than a passing interest in world affairs in the late 1930s and early 1940s, and most did not believe that war was imminent for the United States. Stanbrough said that the thought of patriotic motivation and having to fight for his country on foreign soil "never occurred to me."[18]

Prior to the unit's federal mobilization in November 1940, service in the National Guard did not seriously disrupt the lives of these Texans. Once a month the guardsmen reported to their batteries and participated in the mandatory training and drilling. In some cases this meant holding small-scale maneuvers in the countryside around their hometowns for a weekend. They would roll out early on a Saturday morning with orders to set up their artillery pieces, practice firing only rarely due to a chronic shortage of ammunition, and then leave these positions to set up in another prearranged site and practice again. After two days of such training, they returned their equipment to the armories and went back to their civilian lives. In other cases these citizen-soldiers did not go on maneuvers but instead stayed at their armories and practiced servicing their equipment and attended training courses before returning home.[19]

These young Texans became familiar with the rudiments of military life, easing into their roles whether they were paymasters, cooks, or sergeants of firing batteries. Based on their early experiences in the National Guard, a large number believed that it was more a social organization than an actual military outfit. Kelly Bob Bramlett compared his service in the Guard to "summer camp."[20] Eddie Fung and Crayton Gordon believed that many men in the unit did not take their training too seriously and compared their experience to that of a social club.[21] Luther Prunty, who also joined F Battery in the days of horse-drawn artillery, remembered that "it was a vacation to go into National Guard camp."[22]

Although most members of the 2nd Battalion recalled their early days in the Guard in such a way, others took their service more seriously. Clark Taylor, who joined the Guard in 1927, enjoyed his time in the military and worked his way up through the ranks, receiving a lieutenant's commission in 1940.[23] Ilo Hard and Huddleston Wright also saw in the National Guard an opportunity for personal advancement. Wright advanced from the rank of private when he joined the Guard in 1932 to first lieutenant prior to mobilization. Hard completed the U.S. Army's Ten Series and Twenty Series training courses during his time in the Guard, courses that allowed noncommissioned officers to work toward a commission, which he received in August 1940.[24] Max Offerle, who served as a gunnery sergeant in D Battery, took training quite seriously and lamented the substandard quality and quantity of equipment, as well as the undermanned units in the 2nd Battalion.[25]

The somewhat leisurely pace of National Guard life quickly came to an end in November 1940, however, and these Texans soon received their first real taste of life in the military. As World War II raged on in Europe and in Asia, the U.S. government and Pres. Franklin D. Roosevelt took steps to prepare the country militarily should the United States enter the war. The Selective Service Act of September 1940, which established the first peacetime draft in the country's history, was soon followed by Roosevelt's announcement that certain elements of the National Guard would also be called into federal service. The president ordered the 36th Division to be mobilized on November 25, 1940.[26] The 36th spent the next two months traveling to and setting up facilities at Camp Bowie in preparation for duty in the army.[27]

Mobilization into the Regular Army certainly affected the lives of these Texans, as they were asked to leave their homes and families and to devote the next year in service to their country. Predictably, they reacted to mobilization in a variety of ways. Some believed that mobilization brought about a total change of lifestyle and that they were now more responsible for the security of the country.[28] Ilo Hard greeted mobilization with enthusiasm.[29] He anticipated that training would intensify, equipment would improve, and draftees would have to be trained to make their units effective in battle, should war come. Uell Carter described his reaction to mobilization as "a shock."[30]

For most of the 2nd Battalion, however, mobilization meant a year-long respite from their normal life. Max Offerle believed that becoming part of the army simply meant that he would be a full-time rather than a part-time soldier.[31] Lawrence Brown and Lester Rasbury of Headquarters Battery did not worry much about what mobilization could mean and did not take the news too seriously.[32] Wade Webb of Service Battery interpreted the mobilization in terms of dollars and cents: as a sergeant in Service Battery, he would now earn twenty-one dollars a month rather than the low salary he earned in the National Guard.[33] College student Quaty Gordon described his reaction: "To me, a year's mobilization was a type of relief from the grind of studying . . . I thought it'd be a real big relief and something different—a change, a relaxation—from schoolwork."[34] Perhaps George Killian best summarized the overall reaction of the 2nd Battalion: "Well, I'm going to have a ball, you know, like always."[35]

The fact that most of the men responded to mobilization in this way suggests that they still did not grasp the seriousness of the state of international affairs in 1940 or the role played by the United States in the world. Few of the men professed to have much knowledge about affairs outside the country or to have been following the ongoing war very closely.[36] Those who did follow world events thought that if the United States were dragged into the war, they would be sent to fight in the European theater against Germany rather than in the Pacific theater against Japan.[37] Everyday life in Texas seemed to be more pressing for these men, with the war being just a distant conflict that did not involve the United States. Kyle Thompson, who had been part of Headquarters Battery since 1938 and who was only eighteen years old in November 1940, claimed that he was preoccupied with big-band music and the girls of Wichita Falls and therefore paid little attention to the war.[38] Offerle said that "I was more interested in the top tunes of the 'Hit Parade' . . . We had no idea really what was going on in the world."[39]

Regardless of their views on mobilization and their knowledge of world affairs, the men of the 2nd Battalion made their way to Camp Bowie between December 1940 and February 1941 to undergo further training. The army had not finished construction of Camp Bowie by the time the first elements of the 36th Division arrived, so the first duty many of these soldiers performed was completing the building of the camp's facilities. The troops labored during the winter digging drainage ditches, building roads and sidewalks, setting up cooking and bathing facilities, and erecting pyramidal tents with wooden floors to house the men.[40]

Weather conditions at Camp Bowie hampered the construction's progress, as the Brownwood area received day after day of rain, turning the ground there into a quagmire. Wade Webb remembered that the generally desolate and sandy conditions of Brownwood quickly became characterized by the mud and slop caused by the heavy rains.[41] Roger White recalled Camp Bowie as being "the muddiest place I had ever seen in my life."[42] One of the local Brownwood newspapers continually reported on the sloppy conditions in the camp and of the effect on the camp's construction, and the *Fort Worth Star-Telegram* referred to Camp Bowie as "Camp Gooey."[43]

Although the weather did not cooperate, military training at Camp Bowie went forward along with the construction. The soldiers participated in week-long field exercises typical of such training, including scouting forward positions to call in fire from the firing batteries, running lines of communication back to headquarters, supporting the forward batteries with ammunition and food, and carrying out various other activities they might encounter in combat. Specialists, such as those in radio and communications, attended schools to better prepare them for their jobs.[44] Close-order drill, which had been largely disregarded prior to mobilization, became an everyday fact of life for the artillerymen.[45] The ranks of the 36th Division, which had been undermanned, began to swell with draftees at Camp Bowie. These new soldiers required special attention and had to work harder than their more senior comrades, who took them in and worked to make them into effective soldiers.[46]

Despite their efforts at Camp Bowie, however, many men did not believe they received adequate training for combat while there. The poor quality and quantity of equipment were their primary concerns. Although equipped with the American model of the 1897 French 75-mm fieldpiece, men from the firing batteries had to attach 37-mm gun tubes on the top of the 75s for practice in an effort to save the more expensive 75-mm ammunition and therefore performed firing training of little real value.[47] Service Battery's P. J. Smallwood recalled that his outfit was not issued rifles until the men were shipped overseas in November 1941.[48] George Burns of Headquarters Battery observed that although the training at Camp Bowie was extensive, it was not nearly thorough enough to prepare them for combat.[49]

If there were questions about the unit's combat readiness during the time at Camp Bowie, these questions would soon be answered after they participated in the army's maneuvers in Louisiana in September 1941. As the likelihood of American entry into the war increased, the army stepped up its efforts to prepare for the conflict. So, in September 1941, the Second and Third Armies held large-scale maneuvers in Louisiana to experiment with different fighting formations under simulated combat conditions to test the effectiveness of their forces. The Louisiana Maneuvers were the largest of their type up to this point in the country's history. Throughout the month Gen. Ben Lear's Second Army faced off against Gen. Walter Krueger's Third Army in the unpredictable climate and terrain of western Louisiana as the generals judged their soldiers' performance.[50]

The Louisiana Maneuvers are largely remembered for two things. First, the U.S. Army lacked adequate weapons, ammunition, and vehicles to allow any meaningful simulation of battle conditions. Trucks with the word *tank* painted on their sides often took the place of real tanks that were in short supply. Stovepipes passed as mortars, and soldiers used wooden guns to make up for the lack of Springfield rifles and Garands. Trucks with loudspeakers from the Signal Corps lumbered about the "battlefields" playing the sounds of artillery and machine-gun fire to simulate the noise of combat. Army umpires judged the battles and determined when a tank had been destroyed by an antitank nest, or when soldiers had been "killed" or taken prisoner. Under such conditions, the Second and Third Armies prepared for war.[51]

Second, the Louisiana Maneuvers proved to be a testing ground for

National Guard officers who went into federal service with their units in 1940. In an effort to determine which officers should and should not be allowed to lead troops in combat, the army decided to test its citizen-officers in Louisiana. Largely, these part-time soldiers failed. U.S. Army Chief-of-Staff George C. Marshall did not approve of the performance of the recently federalized Guard units in Louisiana, in general, and he took special issue with the officers. As a result, following the maneuvers Marshall "mercilessly" cut hundreds of National Guard officers from the army. Under the pretext of removing officers who were too old for their pay grade, he replaced National Guard officers with officers from the Regular Army. The commanding general of the 36th Division, Claude V. Birkhead, a San Antonio lawyer, lost his command and was replaced by Gen. Fred L. Walker.[52]

For the men of the 2nd Battalion, the Louisiana Maneuvers provided simply another experience away from their regular daily lives in Texas. Most of the men recalled their time in Louisiana as having been filled with hard work, bad weather, snakes, and mosquitoes. P. J. Smallwood said the maneuvers were more of an endurance test than anything else because the army kept him constantly on the move.[53] Rain poured on the troops in Louisiana, making any sort of movement much more difficult. Luther Prunty recalled that he spent most of his time that September digging trucks out of the mud.[54] In general, the food was bad; the rain nonstop; the humidity oppressive; the training tough; the snakes, ticks, and mosquitoes maddening; and the experience one they could have lived without.[55] But it was a new experience for the young Texans, almost a precursor of what was to come in Southeast Asia.

With the maneuvers wrapped up by the end of September 1941, the 2nd Battalion moved back to Camp Bowie with the rest of the 36th Division, but it did not remain with the division for long. In the late 1930s the U.S. Army decided to revamp the structure of its divisions, making them smaller and more streamlined, like those of the German *Wehrmacht*. During World War I, the army used large "square" division structures, composed of two infantry brigades of two regiments each, in order to mass troops for heavy frontal assaults. As a result of the restructuring between the wars, the army created "triangular" divisions, composed of three infantry regiments, providing more flexibility and mobility in the age of fast-moving mechanized infantry. As part of this reorganization, each division was pared down from an authorized strength of twenty-two thousand men to around fifteen thousand. The extra troops would then be organized along with other detached units into additional triangular divisions. The smaller divisions required less artillery support, and, therefore, the army removed some field artillery battalions from the divisions. The army cut the 2nd Battalion, 131st Field Artillery Regiment, from the 36th Division.[56]

It is still a matter of debate among the survivors of the 2nd Battalion as to exactly why their unit was chosen to be detached and sent to fill out a new division. Many claimed that the 2nd Battalion rated the highest performance of all the field artillery battalions in the 36th Division and that the army wanted to use its best to help fill out the new divisions.[57] Others are not so sure that this was the reason. Jess Stanbrough said that his officers indicated that they were being separated because of their outstanding performance but that it could have been the result of some random process.[58] Cecil Minshew of E Battery believed that his battery performed well in Louisiana, but he doubted that was the reason they left the 36th Division.[59] Wade Webb of Service Battery claimed that the 2nd Battalion's performance was "sloppy," which could have been the reason they left the division.[60]

The truth of this matter may never be attained, but it is likely that neither of the extreme views of their performance is correct. The U.S. Army conducted a major reorganization in the years just prior to American entry into the war, and the record of any one field artillery battalion would have had little, if any, effect on the army's decision. At a time when it sought to replace the large, cumbersome square divisions with the smaller, more flexible triangular divisions, the army simply made the cuts where it was the most practicable. The 36th Division did not have its full complement of men by the time it participated in the Louisiana Maneuvers in 1941 and was therefore already nearer than full divisions to being a triangular division in terms of numbers of men. Therefore, the 36th became a triangular division, bringing about the loss of a field artillery battalion. The 2nd Battalion was almost certainly chosen at random to leave the division in the fall of 1941 to help fill out a new division to be located somewhere overseas.[61]

Upon receiving orders to leave the division, the 2nd Battalion underwent its own internal reorganization. Because the army slated the battalion for duty overseas, it allowed those in the unit who, because of age or marital status, did not wish to leave the country to remain behind. All men over the age of twenty-eight had the option to transfer from the 2nd Battalion to the 1st Battalion, 131st Field Artillery Regiment, and therefore avoid the new assignment. Married men also had this option. Volunteers from the 1st Battalion—A, B, and C Batteries—and draftees replaced the men of the 2nd Battalion who chose to stay behind. This reorganization contributed to lowering the average age of the men in the outfit, excluding commissioned and noncommissioned officers, to around twenty to twenty-two years of age.[62]

Considering the fate of the 2nd Battalion later in the war, the decision of the men in the 1st Battalion to transfer voluntarily into that unit was momentous. At the time, however, the decision to transfer into the 2nd Battalion did not seem to be of much importance. Lt. Ilo Hard, originally of C Battery, enjoyed life in the army, and he volunteered to join the 2nd Battalion and help create a new division.[63] Eddie Fung, also of C Battery, joined the 2nd Battalion because he felt attached to his sergeant and wanted to stay under his command.[64] Frank Ficklin left Regimental Headquarters for the 2nd Battalion out of devotion to his officers, Capt. Winthrop ("Windy") Rogers and Capt. Arch Fitzsimmons, who also volunteered.[65]

Others joined the 2nd Battalion without much thought. It must have seemed like something different to do for these young Texans.[66] Eldridge Rayburn of C Battery said, "There was no problem for them to get the volunteers. Everybody was looking for adventure or something different, you know. We had a year in Brownwood, and we was ready to go somewhere and do something."[67] Twenty-nine-year-old Luther Prunty could have transferred out of 2nd Battalion but stayed. He reasoned that if the United States got into the war, the fighting would be in Europe, and rumors indicated that the 2nd Battalion was going to the Pacific. He thought that his time in the Pacific would be "a Roosevelt Tour" anyway, and after a year he would be back in the States.[68] Max Offerle, who came back early from his thirty-day leave home to join his outfit, remembers that he looked forward to leaving because it "sounded adventurous."[69]

After filling out its ranks to its full complement, the 2nd Battalion began the first leg of its journey toward the final destination, known to most of the men only as "PLUM." All the artillerymen speculated what PLUM meant. Some had heard enough rumors and had spoken to enough officers to put together enough pieces of information to solve the riddle. PLUM was the acronym for the Philippines, Luzon, Manila. The 2nd Battalion was to form the vanguard of a new triangular division to help bolster the defense of the Philippines. Although most of these Texans understood that the United States had strained relations with Japan at the time, few believed they would see combat in the Philippines. In their minds, they would be sent to the other side of the world, a world apart from the fighting in Europe.[70]

The 2nd Battalion left Brownwood by train on November 11, 1941, bound for Angel Island in San Francisco Bay. This trip across the western part of the country took many of the men farther from home than they had ever been; some had never before left Texas. The men passed their time typically, speculating what their new duty would be, playing poker and dominoes, and some simply looking out of the windows and taking in the scenery of the American West.[71] Apparently not all of the Texans were so subdued, however, for some rowdy activities may have also occurred while they were on their way to the West Coast. Wade Webb recalled purchasing a bottle of whiskey at one of the train's stops and remembered that, with the aid of the liquor, they destroyed some windows and other property on the train.[72] Luther Prunty recalled, "We boarded a train on November 11, and there's things that happened along there that we don't need to put on this record."[73]

The world had gotten a lot bigger for the men of the 2nd Battalion in a very short time. They left their homes and lives in North and West Texas for training at Camp Bowie and then moved on to Louisiana to try their skills and abilities alongside the Second and Third Armies. After a short-lived homecoming in October 1941, they left again for the big city of San Francisco. After that, they started for the Philippines to keep that American possession safe from the country's potential enemy, Japan. Along the way they saw and experienced more of life than they ever could have in Decatur, Jacksboro, Wichita Falls, Lubbock, or Abilene, and they were grateful for the experience. The Second World War would not leave them to their idyllic lives anymore than it would the United States, however, and the war would soon engulf them in every imaginable aspect.

Chapter 2

Across the Pacific

THE YOUNG TEXANS FELT GOOD ABOUT LEAVING THE LONE STAR State and the United States. First, they did not seriously believe that they would participate in any fighting. Few of the enlisted men were old enough to remember World War I, and that conflict seemed as if it were one hundred years in the past. Second, they did not believe that the Japanese posed a threat to the United States. Like many Americans in that era, these men labored under the misconception that the Japanese were mentally and racially inferior to them and that Japan did not have the material and manpower resources to challenge the United States. These men were naïve, and they had no idea how ill-trained and ill-prepared they were for war.

The trip through the American West initiated the coming adventure for the men of the 2nd Battalion. After a brief stop in San Antonio, Texas, the outfit spent the next three days and nights aboard a westbound train, reaching San Francisco on November 14, 1941. They then moved out to Fort McDowell on Angel Island in the bay, and in the finest tradition of the U.S. Army, they waited. They waited for the orders to move on to the next phase of their military experience, which by then most understood to be duty in the Philippines. It would be easy duty in the Philippines, they thought, considering the distance of that archipelago from the fighting in Europe, and they could continue to see more of the world outside their hometowns in

Texas. Less than a month after the unit's arrival in San Francisco, however, the Japanese attack on Pearl Harbor, Hawaii, would dramatically alter the Texans' fate. But first there was San Francisco.

Army life on the West Coast had little appeal for the Texans. It seemed to many that when the men were not on KP—feeding and cleaning up after thousands of GIs in what Lt. Huddleston Wright described as the "biggest mess hall I ever saw"—they were busy drilling and performing calisthenics.[1] Then there were the shots. The army had no intention of sending its troops to the tropical lands of the western Pacific without taking the proper medical precautions. The men stood in line for what seemed like constant inoculations against any and all tropical diseases.[2] To make matters worse, for all the shots and KP duty, the troops received only part of their pay. Lt. Col. Blucher Tharp, commanding officer of the 2nd Battalion, did not allow his men to draw full pay while in San Francisco because—according to Wade Webb—they would waste their money.[3]

In contrast to the tedium of duty at Fort McDowell, San Francisco beckoned with the lights, sounds, and activities of a bustling and exciting port city, and the soldiers were eager to see it all. Slug Wright had spent time in San Francisco while employed by the Standard Oil Company, and being an "old hand," he acted as an unofficial tour guide for his companions.[4] Jess Stanbrough acted like a typical tourist in the "City by the Bay," seeing sights such as Chinatown and the International Settlement. He also witnessed his first burlesque show while there on leave.[5] Clark Taylor and other officers spent one night with local businessmen, who treated them to a night on the town, complete with a steak dinner at one of the city's finest hotels.[6] Eddie Fung, a native of San Francisco, avoided the typical tourist activities and instead spent time with his family in Chinatown.[7]

Not all of the men took in the sights of the city. Some, like Roy Armstrong of F Battery, and Huddleston Wright, spent their time stuck on KP duty and did not get into town the entire time.[8] Ilo Hard missed out on the San Francisco experience out of a sense of responsibility. The serious-minded Hard did not care to go on leave because he did not have the time, considering the organizational tasks facing him at Fort McDowell. He also may have been reticent to spend money unnecessarily while on the West Coast when his wife had already signed up for government assistance back home to make ends meet.[9] Regardless of the myriad experiences in San Francisco, Dan Buzzo probably spoke for the group when he said, "I thought it was a grand adventure."[10]

Then the orders to depart from San Francisco finally came through, and the men of the 2nd Battalion, joined by Headquarters Battery of the

26th Field Artillery Brigade out of Camp Roberts, California, prepared to leave the States. The soldiers boarded the transport USAT *Republic* and settled in for a journey that would, they thought, take them eventually to their new home in the Philippines. The 22nd Bomb Group also joined the Texans aboard the *Republic*, which would take them as far as Pearl Harbor. The *Republic* was a large and slow transport, carrying aircraft and ammunition to resupply American forces in the Philippines, and the men expressed some displeasure concerning their temporary home.[11] Roy Armstrong complained of the crowded conditions on the ship, and for many the navy's food did not meet their standards. On the first day out of San Francisco, for example, the ship's mess prepared a dinner of baked fish and boiled cabbage.[12]

Soon after the *Republic* left San Francisco, this small outfit of Texans went through an experience they would all like to forget. The groundswells of the Pacific Ocean outside San Francisco Bay, combined with the smell of fish and cabbage, resulted in violent seasickness for the majority of the 2nd Battalion.[13] One of the sailors aboard the *Republic* advised Frank Ficklin to go back to the ship's fantail to avoid being sick, but Ficklin soon found out that he had been taken for a fool when he discovered that the fantail was the worst place to be.[14] Slug Wright bought seasickness pills prior to embarking to help him through the ordeal, only to find out that he took them too late.[15] Eddie Fung stayed and even slept above deck at a machine-gun emplacement to get fresh air to avoid being sick; it did not help.[16] Max Offerle recalled that "this was the worst sickness I ever went through; you feel like you're going to die, and you are afraid you won't die."[17]

Eventually, most of the Texan landlubbers became accustomed to ocean travel and settled in for the remainder of the week-long voyage to Hawaii. The *Republic* docked at Pearl Harbor on November 28, 1941, and some of the men received a four-hour pass to visit Honolulu. Although, to the consternation of all the men, they still had not received their pay, they spent their time taking in the sights of yet another city.[18] Those who went ashore generally recall a state of military preparedness on the island.[19] Offerle observed sandbag barriers being built, barbed wire being laid down, and machine-gun emplacements being built while he visited Honolulu.[20] Kyle Thompson later claimed that "with Pearl Harbor's devastation and war still a week in the future, the Hawaiian Islands were already in a state of wartime readiness."[21] P. J. Smallwood remarked that it looked like Honolulu "was under martial law."[22] After receiving fresh water and supplies at Pearl Harbor, the 2nd Battalion—along with Headquarters Battery, 26th Field Artillery Brigade—joined a convoy heading for the Philippines.[23]

The voyage across the Pacific was relatively uneventful, for a time. Soldiers passed the time as usual, by gambling, grumbling, and trying to sneak food from the ship's galley.[24] This initial period of routine and boredom did not last for the entire voyage, however, for the soldiers soon learned a hard lesson about life on the sea. On December 6, 1941, the *Republic* crossed the equator, prompting the sailors to initiate the soldiers into a special fraternity. Crossing the equator meant that the "pollywogs," or those who had never crossed the equator in their lives, were to become "shellbacks" by enduring a more-than-spirited initiation ritual. The shellbacks forced the pollywogs to crawl through a length of canvas tubing while beating them with improvised paddles.

After this stage, the pollywogs then sat in a barber's chair on deck, had their faces painted with oil and kitchen slop, and were shaved with an electrified straight razor. After the shaving the initiates were then unceremoniously dumped into a large pool of water while the shellbacks continually pushed their heads under until they decided that they had had enough.[25] Quaty Gordon had been beaten so badly during this hazing that he suffered a separated shoulder and a concussion, so he spent the rest of the voyage in sick bay.[26]

As bad as the initiation proved to be for the artillerymen, it paled in comparison to the events of the following day. On the morning of December 7, 1941, the Japanese launched a massive attack on the U.S. naval base at Pearl Harbor and the other military installations on Oahu, inflicting an immense amount of damage to the American forces there. The United States responded the next day with a declaration of war against Japan. The *Republic*'s convoy was just east of the Gilbert Islands when it received official notification of the Japanese attack and of the state of war. Cdr. Guy Clark of the *Republic* then made the following announcement over the public address system: "Attention all hands, a state of war exists between Japan and the United States; Pearl Harbor has been attacked. Good luck."[27]

After hearing the news, the army and navy officers on the *Republic* ordered their men to prepare the ship for combat. The sailors brought ammunition out of the hold and readied their machine-gun emplacements. The soldiers of 2nd Battalion brought out their 75-mm fieldpieces and lashed them down on the deck, despite their having little ammunition to fire.[28] The crew and the soldiers practiced for aerial raids and participated in countless battle drills in preparation for possible combat. The soldiers and sailors painted the *Republic* gray to help conceal the ship in the event of an attack, and the ship's captain took a zigzagging course, not to the Philippines, however, which the Japanese had also attacked, but toward their new destination, Brisbane, Australia, by way of the Fiji Islands to procure supplies and fresh water.[29]

The commencement of war against Japan started a new chapter in the lives of the men of the 2nd Battalion. They were soldiers and had been trained for combat, and as such they were ready to help defend their country. On the other hand, these men were young, inexperienced, and a long way from their homes and lives in Texas. The Japanese attack on Pearl Harbor predictably affected them in a number of ways, and their reaction to the events of December 7 helps explain how unprepared, psychologically and emotionally, they were for the war. Some, like Max Offerle, experienced "tremendous shock" over the news of Pearl Harbor and tried to understand what that meant for them.[30] Slug Wright was playing cards below deck when he heard the news and "felt pretty disillusioned."[31] Kyle Thompson described "a new feeling of urgency [that] permeated the crew and their cargo of mostly young citizen-soldiers, all evidently steaming to war."[32] Many others expressed how the declaration of war similarly affected them.[33]

Other soldiers had different reactions to the news. George Killian remarked that he was not surprised by the attack on Pearl Harbor, while his friend Uell Carter said that he "didn't think the Japs were that crazy."[34] The news apparently did not surprise Thurman Capps because he had witnessed the military preparations in Honolulu, and he knew the United States was readying for war.[35] Ilo Hard experienced no change in his military routine as a result of the attack, only that "it [the war] had finally happened."[36] Some of the men, like Eddie Fung, simply did not grasp the significance of the attack and did not know how it would affect them.[37] Nearly all of the men, however, agreed on one point: the war with Japan would be over quickly, certainly within the span of one year.

Many, if not most, Americans held racially stereotypical beliefs about the Japanese in 1941, and the men of the 2nd Battalion were no different in their views. A long, drawn-out conflict with a nation of people they considered inferior in a variety of ways seemed unthinkable to these Texans. The Japanese inhabited small, resource-poor islands and were no match for the material resources of the United States. Furthermore, the racial differences between the Japanese and the Americans would ensure a quick American victory in the Pacific. The soldiers of the 2nd Battalion typically described their Japanese enemy in 1941 as being of small physical stature, with bucked teeth, and having eyesight so poor that they all required thick "Coke bottle" eyeglasses in order to see. Japanese military equipment, the Texans thought, was inferior to that of the Americans, even to the degree that many in the

2nd Battalion believed that Japanese fighter planes were made of bamboo and paper. Ilo Hard remarked that "we'd been thoroughly indoctrinated about the little, short, weakly, ignorant, stupid, spectacle-wearing Asian [who] wouldn't be any real problem."[38] George Burns expressed his confidence in a short war: "I thought we could whip them with a cornstalk."[39] Thus, they believed, the war would last no longer than one year, and probably closer to six months.[40]

Not all the men held these views, however, there being two important exceptions. Eddie Fung, who joined the "Jacksboro Boys" in F Battery prior to the unit's moving to San Francisco, was a Chinese American. Fung's parents were both Chinese, and they lived in San Francisco among that city's Chinese community. He left his family as a teenager and moved to Texas, where he joined the National Guard. Fung did not labor under the misconceptions about the Japanese that most of the Texans held, though his prejudice was just as clear. He said that being raised in San Francisco among the Asian community, he had come into contact with Japanese and knew that the stereotype was patently false. But growing up as a Chinese American, his family and friends passed their prejudice against the Japanese on to him. He said that although it was unfortunate, beginning in his childhood "it was always impressed upon us that the Japanese, of course, are possibly not even of the human race as far as the Chinese were concerned."[41]

The second exception was Frank Fujita. Fujita's father was Japanese and had come to the United States from Nagasaki, Japan, in 1914. Employed as a cook on the Texas and Pacific Railroad, the elder Fujita married Ida Pearl Elliott, an American girl, in Oklahoma and started a family. After convincing the enlistment officer of his American nationality, of his weight of 135 pounds—though he weighed only 105 pounds—and of his age of eighteen—though he was only seventeen—Frank Jr. joined Headquarters Battery and later transferred into E Battery at Abilene in 1941. Fujita naturally disregarded the typical myths about Japanese racial inferiority, but he fit in with the Texans nonetheless. "Foo," as he was known by his friends in E Battery, proved to be a very able soldier and rose to the rank of sergeant before leaving for the Pacific. He recalled receiving almost no trouble concerning his lineage when war broke out, and others in the outfit remember giving him only some good-natured ribbing.[42]

Regardless of their views toward the Japanese, the men of the 2nd Battalion now faced a war that many of them did not believe would occur. The Republic reached Brisbane on December 22, 1941, and the men began to unload the military cargo.[43] They were glad to set foot on solid ground again, especially after living with the threat of submarine attacks since Pearl Harbor. The 2nd Battalion set up camp at the Ascot Racetrack in Brisbane and awaited further orders. They enjoyed their surroundings in Brisbane and took part in little, if any, military training while stationed there. Although they had not yet felt the sting of war, they noticed that the war had already hit home for the Australians. There was an acute lack of Australian men of fighting age in Brisbane, since they had already been called upon to help defend the British Empire in the Mediterranean and in Southeast Asia. This fact seemed somewhat bewildering to the Texans, who still had little idea of the sacrifices that were necessary during the war.[44]

While the Australians fought for the empire against the Japanese and the Germans, the Texans thoroughly enjoyed themselves in Brisbane. The Australians were very generous and gracious hosts. Civilians would not allow the Americans to pay for drinks at the local pubs, and the Australian women enjoyed taking the "Yanks" to dances and to dinners.[45] Many Australian families invited the Americans to Christmas dinner and laid before them a bounty of food, centered on a main dish of mutton. Although the Texans fondly recall their days in Brisbane, none of them had a taste for mutton.[46] The Texans got along very well with the Australians and believed that there was a sense of kinship between those rough-and-ready people and themselves.[47] P. J. Smallwood explained why he believed the Australians treated them so well: "They realized that we were a bunch of dumb kids a long way from home."[48]

Their days as tourists in Brisbane lasted only a week, however, and on December 28 the 2nd Battalion boarded another ship as the adventure continued and they headed for a new destination. This time they traveled aboard the Dutch ship *Bloemfontein*, a fast diesel-motored vessel, along the northern coast of Australia toward their next stop at Java in the Dutch East Indies.[49] The reality of war began creeping up on the young men of the 2nd Battalion. En route to Java, their convoy experienced a submarine attack that, even though it did not directly affect the *Bloemfontein*, gave the soldiers a small taste of war.[50] P. J. Smallwood recalled seeing destroyers chasing submarines and dropping depth charges to sink them, and he said that "we had our hearts in our mouths."[51]

In spite of the submarine scare, however, the Texans still did not take the war or their position in it very seriously. J. W. ("Johnny") Buck of Headquarters Battery remembered the submarine scare but commented that it was not serious enough to him to interrupt his poker game.[52] Others commented on how beautiful the scenery was on the cruise.[53] Jess Stanbrough had a clearer memory of his first experience with a bidet on board the *Bloemfontein* than he did the Japanese submarines.[54] F Battery soldier Preston

Stone shrugged off the submarines, saying, "I really wasn't concerned about the war; I was just more or less carefree and taking things as they come, and I wasn't afraid about it."[55]

The *Bloemfontein* docked at Surabaja, on the northeastern tip of Java, on January 11, 1942, and the troops were slated to help the Dutch, British, and Australians defend the island from the imminent Japanese attack. The 2nd Battalion debarked from the ship and traveled by train from Surabaja to Malang, a city in the highlands about sixty miles to the south, and reported for duty at Camp Singosari, a Dutch airfield just outside Malang. The Dutch had built Singosari airfield very quickly, and it was not much of an airfield by American standards. The sodden runways were short, and the tropical weather and landing planes took a toll on them. Nonetheless, the 2nd Battalion went to work maintaining the facilities of the camp, posted guards around the area, and settled into a routine.[56]

A large part of this routine consisted of serving as the ground crew for the 19th Bomb Group, U.S. Army Air Corps, based out of Singosari. The 19th, under the command of Col. Eugene L. Eubank, had previously operated from Clark Field in the Philippines, but it moved to Java in December 1941 following the Japanese attack on those islands.[57] Since the 19th had no ground crew on Java, parts of the 2nd Battalion served in this capacity. Despite having no experience in airplane maintenance or in the other various aspects of ground crew duty, they quickly became adept at servicing airplane engines, loading bombs, and patching up damaged planes that returned from missions against the Japanese.[58] A few men of the artillery outfit transferred to the 19th Bomb Group and served as gunners on these B-17s. Two men of the 2nd Battalion, Don Barnes of F Battery and Jack Bingham of Headquarters Battery, were killed by the Japanese in aerial combat.[59]

In early February 1942, the Japanese initiated bombing and strafing raids against Java, trying to soften the island's defenses in preparation for the upcoming invasion. Beginning on February 3, Japanese bombers and fighters attacked Camp Singosari on a daily basis, continuing regularly for about a week. The raids usually commenced late in the morning and lasted between twenty minutes and half an hour. At first, the artillerymen took to their foxholes and slit trenches, some even heading for the jungle outside the camp, to avoid their attackers. Later, they set up the 75-mm guns, even digging out the ground beneath the guns' trails to provide higher elevation, and fired these artillery pieces as antiaircraft weapons.[60] It is highly doubtful that they downed any Japanese planes, but Frank Ficklin claimed, "It gave you a better feeling to be able to fire back at [the Japanese]."[61]

These air raids introduced the men of the 2nd Battalion to the realities of war, and they struggled to adjust to the new circumstances. The excitement of being a soldier began to ebb as the Japanese attacked, and fear and confusion took its place. The men recall being "scared to death" when the bombs started falling and when the fighters' bullets ripped along the airfield.[62] Frank Fujita observed that while lying on his back watching the bombers release their terrible cargo, "It all seemed fairylike and unreal." But as the bombs hit, "the noise was terrible, and the concussion from the bursting bombs and flying shrapnel and earth brought home the deadly reality of it all."[63] The chaos and noise left these young men shaken, and they finally realized that war was a deadly, serious business. Although they gradually adjusted to coping with the almost daily raids, they never got used to them.[64]

Despite the psychological toll taken on the Texans, the raids on Singosari airfield did little overall damage to the field and to the planes based there. The Japanese put a few planes out of commission, temporarily damaged the sodden runway, and destroyed the camp's post exchange, but most of the damage was quickly repaired. The Japanese inflicted no casualties upon the Americans, either, although some men injured themselves diving into slit trenches or machine-gun nests to avoid the attacks.[65] The men went to work filling in craters left from the bombs, repairing damaged buildings, and scavenging parts from the damaged planes to help repair others and generally went about their duties as defenders of Java.[66]

As the Japanese continually moved closer to the invasion of Java, American military planners decided to save the 19th Bomb Group. On February 27, 1942, Colonel Eubank began the withdrawal of his forces from Java to Australia, leaving the 2nd Battalion behind. The survivors of the 2nd Battalion remember that Eubank and his pilots offered to shuttle the artillerymen back to the relative safety of Australia but that they had orders to stand fast and help defend Java from Japanese invasion. At this time the men had little idea about how desperate their situation was on Java or that the Japanese would launch their invasion of the island the next day.[67]

When informed that the 19th Bomb Group had been evacuated, the artillerymen experienced a sense of loss and loneliness. Many assumed that they would go with the army air forces when they left, and now they had been abandoned on Java to face the Japanese.[68] Frank Ficklin said that he experienced a "sinking feeling" and that the bombers' departure was "like your best friend leaving you."[69] Others, like Wade Webb and Headquarters Battery's Granville Summerlin, were not too concerned about this development because they believed that either the United States would send reinforcements to help them defend the island or the heavy cruiser USS *Houston*, which was stationed near Java, would help them evacuate when the time came.[70] Others had no idea why they were left on the island and expressed resentment at being left to fend for themselves.[71]

The men of the 2nd Battalion now began to feel the pressures of war. They found themselves on Java—a place most of them had never heard of only a few months before—cut off from air and ground support, encircled by a relentless enemy, and apparently abandoned by their government. Having survived submarine scares and Japanese bombing and strafing raids, they now faced the prospect of defending foreign territory against an overwhelming Japanese army that, as they understood it, did not take prisoners. To a man, the survivors believe the U.S. government sacrificed their unit purely as a propaganda measure to help reassure America's panicking ally, the Netherlands. The naïveté professed by the youngsters from Texas finally began to fade as they took measure of their bleak situation. They now had to become fighting men in the hope of getting out alive.

Chapter 3

Defense of Java and Capitulation

WHEN THE WAR CAME TO JAVA IN LATE FEBRUARY 1942, THE INEX-perienced Texans, though preparing for combat, still did not comprehend the desperation of the military situation. When the Japanese invaded the island, the multinational force of Dutch, Australians, British, and Americans put up a short-lived resistance in the face of Japanese military superiority, and those who could not escape were taken prisoner by the Imperial Japanese Army.[1] As is the case in all armies and in all wars, no amount of military training could have fully prepared the 2nd Battalion for actual combat. The sights, sounds, and smells of fighting cannot be reproduced during training, and soldiers have to adjust quickly to the realities of combat or become casualties. By the time the fighting ended on Java—little more than a week after it began—the Texans had not become battle-hardened veterans but were instead young men trying to cope with their defeat in battle, as well as with their status as prisoners of war.

The Japanese coveted the Dutch East Indies, and especially Java, because of this island chain's abundance of natural resources. In order to supply their military with petroleum, rubber, tin, and other necessities available in the East Indies, the Japanese launched an offensive against these Dutch colonies in February 1942. The Japanese struck Java with a two-pronged attack on the night of February 28. The Japanese 2nd Division of the Sixteenth Army invaded at the island's western tip at Bantam Bay, driving eastward toward the capital of Batavia, and received support from the 230th Regiment, which landed east of the capital and drove southward. The second prong, led by the Japanese 48th Division, landed on Java at Kragan, ninety miles west of the port city of Surabaja on the eastern end of the island.[2]

The Allied defense of Java, which proved to be woefully inadequate to meet the invasion, suffered from a variety of problems. First, the multinational character of the island's defenders precluded successful defense. Following the Japanese attacks on December 7 and 8, 1941, the countries with direct interests in Southeast Asia and the surrounding islands had formed a joint military command, known as ABDACOM for the Australian, British, Dutch, and American forces in the region, and named Field Marshal Sir Archibald Wavell of the British army as the supreme commander.[3] National rivalries and interests split ABDACOM from the start. The Dutch believed the East Indies should be defended at all costs, while the British focused on the defense of Malaya and Singapore. The Australians wanted to devote troops and materiel to protect their home country, and the Americans pushed for a troop buildup in Australia prior to any military action. While the Allies labored to determine ABDACOM's priorities, the Japanese continued their drive through the region.[4]

Service rivalries, combined with the problem of national priorities, also hampered effective defense against the Japanese. In keeping with the multinational character of the command, ABDACOM divided areas of military responsibility according to nationality. Lt. Gen. George H. Brett of the U.S. Army Air Corps served as deputy commander of ABDACOM, and Adm. Thomas C. Hart received command of ABDAFLOAT, the combined naval forces in the region. British air marshal Richard Peirse commanded AB-DAIR, the combined air defenses, and Dutch general Hein ter Poorten was in charge of ABDARM, all the ground forces on Java.[5] This combination of nationalities only exacerbated interservice rivalries over areas of responsibility, military intelligence, and resources, and a constant shuffling of command within each area due to national prestige put severe strains on the defense of Java.[6]

The state of the Dutch East Indies army (KNIL) on Java also created problems for the island's defenders. The KNIL overwhelmingly depended on the home country for supplies by 1940, but the German conquest of the Netherlands in that year precluded any resupply or reinforcement of the Dutch colony.[7] Equally as problematic, the KNIL, with twenty-five thousand men, the largest Allied force on Java, was predominantly Javanese in 1942, with European Dutch serving largely as officers over the poorly trained and poorly equipped Javanese troops. Native resentment of centuries of Dutch imperialism became all too apparent when the Japanese invaded in February 1942, as the native soldiers deserted the Dutch army in droves and went back to their villages. Some Javanese took the Japanese at their word concerning "Asia for the Asians," greeting the Imperial Japanese Army as liberators who would deliver them from the yoke of white, Western oppression.[8]

In spite of these serious problems, the Allies prepared to fend off the Japanese invasion. Initial KNIL resistance to the invasion in western Java quickly faded, and as the Dutch army retreated eastward, the Australian contingent—largely the 2/2nd Australian Pioneer Battalion—took up the defense. The Australians, under the command of Brig. A. S. Blackburn, hoped to hold the cities of Batavia and Buitenzorg in the west while the British and Dutch slowed the Japanese advance on the island's eastern end.[9] Blackburn ordered the establishment of defensive positions along the Tjianten River west of Batavia and Buitenzorg, and on March 3, his forces made first contact with the advancing Japanese.[10]

While ABDACOM and the Allied forces struggled to prepare for combat, the Americans readied themselves for deployment. Shortly before the Japanese invasion on the night of February 28–March 1, Lieutenant Colonel Tharp ordered his men to evacuate Camp Singosari and the Malang area and to prepare to help defend the island. Tharp chose E Battery to help defend Surabaja, and the rest of the battalion moved toward the western end of Java. Contrary to standard practice in combat, the 2nd Battalion traveled during the day and rested at night and made a point of being seen during their long march. This seems to have been part of an ABDACOM plan to deceive the Japanese into believing that the American presence on Java was stronger than it actually was and that this would help stall the Japanese attack.[11]

The 2nd Battalion, less E Battery, reached the front lines on March 3, 1942, and immediately entered combat. A firing battery under the command of Capt. Winthrop Rogers came up with its artillery to support B and D Companies of the 2/2nd Pioneers on the eastern side of the Tjianten River that afternoon. Lt. Roy E. Stensland acted as forward observation post officer and, along with Eddie Fung, called in fire coordinates to the battery.[12] The Americans, according to an Australian historian, "opened very accurate and sustained fire on targets across the river" and helped prevent the Japanese from crossing.[13] The combined Australian and American efforts in western Java could not hold back the Japanese advance, however, and the Allies rapidly fell back. On March 4, General ter Poorten ordered that Batavia be abandoned in favor of defending the city of Bandung to the south, and from

March 4 through March 5, the 2nd Battalion moved with the Australians to cover the retreat.[14]

The battle on the Tjianten River is significant not only because it was the first experience of the 2nd Battalion in battle but also because it marked the appearance of Lieutenant Stensland. Stensland came to Java in mid-February 1942 and was assigned to the 2nd Battalion, serving with the Texans for the rest of the war. Surviving members of the battalion fondly recalled their experiences with Stensland, describing him as a courageous soldier who had "more nerve or had more guts than brains," but they knew little of his background.[15] Some believed that Stensland had been arrested for insubordination and drunkenness and was released from the stockade only to help defend Java against the Japanese.[16] Others, like Roy Armstrong, speculated that Stensland originally came from the 19th Bomb Group but that he stayed on Java when the B-17s left.[17] According to Slug Wright, Stensland was "Regular Army, a West Point man," who just happened to be on Java as part of his regular service.[18] All agree, however, that Stensland stood above the rest in terms of bravery.

Although recollections of his background are somewhat clouded, Stensland's story is nonetheless interesting. He originally took part in a secret mission—known as the Robenson Mission for its commander Col. John Robenson—to resupply Gen. Douglas MacArthur's forces in the Philippines. In January 1942, Robenson was given a large sum of money to purchase and ship supplies from Java and other Allied territories in the southwest Pacific to help the besieged American forces in the Philippines. Robenson chose Stensland, along with a dozen other young officers, because of his personal qualities, which included resourcefulness and the ability to exercise good judgment. Given responsibility to handle operations in Makassar on Celebes, Stensland spent little more than a week there before leaving the island just ahead of the arrival of the Japanese army. In early February, Stensland came to Java where Robenson, as a result the overall failure of the mission, released him to join the 2nd Battalion.[19]

While the Allies labored to slow the Japanese advance in the west, the Americans of E Battery battled the Japanese in the east. Separated from the rest of the unit just prior to the invasion, E Battery moved up to Surabaja and established its position south of the city at the municipal zoo. The Japanese 48th Division attacked Surabaja on March 7, giving E Battery its first and only taste of battle. The enemy troops quickly overwhelmed the outnumbered and outgunned American defenders, and late in the afternoon of March 7, E Battery received orders to abandon its positions. After destroying their trucks and artillery pieces to prevent their use by the Japanese, the men of E Battery left Surabaja, some moving into the surrounding hills and others going to the island of Madura, across a narrow strait from Surabaja.[20]

Despite the American and Australian efforts, the Japanese continued to advance across Java. The Imperial Japanese Navy had virtually destroyed the Allied naval forces around the island by March 1, 1942, and enjoyed total naval superiority in the area. Japanese bombers and fighters had taken control of the skies above Java, leaving ABDARM forces completely vulnerable to air attack. Faced with the combined naval and air problems, and believing that the Japanese invasion force numbered as many as two hundred thousand troops, General ter Poorten asked for a cease-fire. On March 8, 1942, he met with Gen. Imamura Hitoshi, commander of the Japanese Sixteenth Army, and agreed to surrender the island unconditionally. Java had fallen to the Japanese in less than a week.[21]

Upon receiving word of the surrender, American officers gave their men a short and discouraging list of options. First, they could choose to move into the mountains of Java and continue fighting the Japanese in guerrilla-style warfare. Given the military dominance of the Japanese, the lack of supplies, and the hostile attitude of the native Javanese toward the Allies, however, none of the 2nd Battalion chose to continue fighting. Next, they could have gone to the coast, hoping to hold out long enough to find a way to leave the island for Australia. Some, with Capt. Windy Rogers, decided to try their luck on the coast, but most turned back when they discovered no available ships and plenty of Japanese patrols.[22] The Japanese quickly discovered the men of E Battery who had found their way to Madura and forced them to return to Java.[23]

Last, they could accept the fact that they had been defeated and submit to the Japanese as prisoners of war. Although this option certainly did not appeal to them either, given the circumstances, it proved to be the only practical choice. Japanese control of the island precluded any serious thought of continuing the battle. Native hostility toward the Dutch and their allies became readily apparent when the island fell to the Japanese, and the Javanese proved quite willing to disclose the location of Allied soldiers in hiding.[24] The men simply had no other place to go. As bad as captivity might be, the officers and men of the 2nd Battalion—534 in total—believed that they could better look out for their welfare if they stayed together as a unit.[25] Besides, the Texans still believed it was going to be a short war, and they expected to be relieved and rescued at any time.[26]

The rapid loss of Java came as a shock to the Texans. Though they were not adequately trained or armed, at the time they did not believe that the military situation warranted surrender. They had only just joined the fight and had seen little combat overall, and they always held out hope that the U.S. Army would send reinforcements to save the island. At the very least, most believed that should the situation become dire, the U.S. Navy would evacuate them to Australia.[27] The soldiers believed that they had not been allowed to fight to their capabilities and that they could have held out longer if there had only been willingness to do so on the part of ABDACOM in general, and of the Dutch in particular.[28] They saw little reason for their being sent to Java if they would not be allowed to carry on the fight, and many suspected that they were only on the island to bolster Dutch morale. That being the case, they thought, the American government had sacrificed the 2nd Battalion for Allied propaganda purposes.[29]

Upon learning of the surrender, the Americans reacted with both disbelief and dismay. Frank Ficklin could not believe the news: "It never entered our minds that we would be prisoners of war of the Japanese, that we could lose to the Japanese."[30] Ilo Hard also did not believe that they could lose: "I guess I was an optimistic fool."[31] Jess Stanbrough was extremely frustrated over the surrender, feeling "absolute despair and dismay."[32] Most of the men felt shame at having given up so quickly, some admitting that they had not even seen the Japanese prior to the surrender.[33] Slug Wright, who had experienced combat during the retreat, "was a discouraged dadgummed soldier."[34] Lt. Huddleston Wright commented that he "was very disappointed, and one of the hardest things I ever had to do was to tell my men that we were prisoners-of-war."[35]

Having lost so quickly certainly had a demoralizing effect upon the men, but even more troubling to them was the fact that they were now prisoners of the Japanese. The Texans had little understanding of the Japanese and did not know what kind of treatment to expect at their hands. Inasmuch as they were aware of the Japanese, they understood that they were brutal captors who killed prisoners just for sport. The Americans were aware of the Japanese treatment of the Chinese and other Asians earlier in the war, and they feared the worst. Persistent rumors circulated that their captors took no prisoners and that they would kill all the defenders of Java.[36] Eddie Fung, a Chinese American, remembered that he tried to lighten his comrades' depressed spirits by telling them that "I was the only one that had a Chinaman's chance of getting through" the ordeal alive.[37] Ben Kelley of D Battery probably summed up their feelings the best: "I have had several incidents in my life that have been serious, but that tops them all. Number one, we didn't know what was going to happen . . . I had heard rumors about the Japanese, that they didn't take prisoners. I had heard about their cruelty. Just the thought of being a prisoner-of-war was bad. Just the unknown itself was overwhelming. It was the worst feeling I ever experienced in my life."[38]

After destroying as much of their equipment as possible, the somewhat scattered troops of the 2nd Battalion began to congregate in the Bandung area to await further instructions.[39] On March 9 the Japanese ordered the captured Americans to move down to Garoet, about thirty miles southeast of Bandung. The Americans arrived the following day and spent the next week in abandoned warehouses and camped in the infield of the city's horse-racing track, where they went through a very rudimentary processing as prisoners. The prisoners spent these days idly, most fighting boredom by playing cards and dominoes and waiting to see what the future would bring. Some of the men were taken to a nearby tea plantation for a short time, where they performed light physical duty loading tea onto trucks for the Japanese, while others performed various routine tasks for the Japanese in Garoet.[40]

Up to this point in their captivity, the men of the 2nd Battalion had suffered few hardships. Having expected the worst possible treatment at the hands of the enemy, they were surprised to find that they had very little contact at all with the Japanese. They were largely free to roam about Garoet, where many of the men took advantage of the somewhat chaotic wartime conditions to procure food and liquor, and their command structure remained intact. The Japanese issued their orders through the American officers, and in no cases at Garoet were these orders demanding of the American prisoners. Although the Japanese made no attempt to supply or feed the prisoners, the Americans still had ample stores of foodstuffs, clothing, blankets, toilet articles, and other items necessary for day-to-day living.[41]

Early in their captivity, the prisoners took measure of the first Japanese with whom they came into contact. Given the extraordinary circumstances in which they met for the first time, it is not surprising that the Americans' reaction to their captors varied widely. Some of the prisoners described the Japanese as being very small in stature, while others recalled that they were well over six feet tall.[42] Some, like Johnny Buck, remembered that the Japanese soldiers looked sloppy in their oversized uniforms, while Luther Prunty described them as being "good specimens of men."[43] But the troops they encountered treated the prisoners well and seemed to be curious about life in the United States. Some remembered that English-speaking Japanese soldiers commonly asked questions about America, especially about Hollywood. Lester Rasbury recalled, "If you told them you were from Texas, you was automatically a cowboy [to them]."[44] Japanese soldiers often gave the prisoners candy and cigarettes, and some helped the Americans acquire supplies in Garoet.[45]

There are a number of reasons for this type of treatment of the prisoners. First, and most important, the Japanese still faced the task of occupying and pacifying the entire island in the second week of March 1942, and they had little time and no interest in making life more difficult for the ragtag bunch of soldiers they had only briefly faced in battle. Second, the initial groups of Japanese soldiers the POWs encountered were highly trained and disciplined frontline troops who did not degenerate into a brutal occupying force. Next, the Imperial Japanese Army did not expect to encounter tens of thousands of prisoners of war, and it had no immediate use for their labor on Java. Also, the prisoners' behavior in general did not warrant any harsh treatment by the Japanese soldiers; the prisoners did as they were told and were left alone. Finally, these frontline Japanese troops showed empathy toward their captured enemies. They could identify with fellow soldiers and saw no reason to persecute or humiliate them. Later, the Pacific war devolved into a bitter, drawn-out conflict in which racism on both sides led to atrocities, but on Java in March 1942 this was not yet apparent.[46]

Much has been written about Japanese treatment of prisoners of war during World War II, and it still remains a controversial topic. Since the mid-nineteenth century, the Japanese government had followed international regulations relative to treatment of POWs, and the Japanese received much praise from international observers for their efforts. In the Sino-Japanese War of 1894–95, for example, the Japanese closely followed the regulations established in the Brussels Declaration of 1874 dealing with the treatment of prisoners. During the Russo-Japanese War of 1904–1905, the International Red Cross regarded Japanese treatment of prisoners as excellent and well within the bounds established by the Hague Convention of 1899 dealing with prisoners of war. The Japanese again won praise in World War I for their treatment of German prisoners, in accordance with the Hague Convention of 1907.[47]

In 1929, the international community gathered in Geneva once again to refine existing and establish further regulations dealing with prisoners of war, and once again the Japanese participated. The provisions of the Geneva Convention of 1929 extended the general regulations established at the aforementioned conferences, the most important of which are the following: prisoners must be treated in a humane manner as concerns medical care, shelter, clothing, and food, receiving no less than the soldiers of the capturing army; prisoners must not perform labor for their captors that will be excessive or hasten the captor's war effort; and captors must establish a Prisoner-of-War Information Bureau to receive and disseminate any information about prisoners of war.[48] The Japanese delegates to the convention, Isaburo Yoshida, Sadamu Shimomura, and Seizo Miura, representing the emperor of Japan, signed the Convention Relative to the Treatment of Prisoners of War in July 1929, implying that Japan would once again willingly be bound by international law as concerned treatment of prisoners of war.[49] Although the Japanese representatives assented to the regulations of the Geneva Convention, the Japanese government refused to ratify the agreement, thus relieving Japan of the obligation to meet its requirements.[50]

The Japanese military, which exercised much influence in the nation's government in the 1930s, discouraged ratification of the Geneva Convention of 1929. Both the army and the navy objected to the treaty for several reasons. First, and most important, Japanese soldiers and sailors did not expect to become prisoners of war. Throughout their military training Japanese soldiers were indoctrinated in the way of the warrior, known as the code of Bushido. According to the precepts of Bushido, sacrificing one's life in battle for the emperor was the highest of honors for a soldier. The Japanese viewed surrender as being utterly shameful, disgracing not only the soldier but his family, clan, and the empire as well.[51]

The Japanese military taught its soldiers to fight to the death, and if that were not possible, they were to commit suicide rather than be captured. Those who died for the emperor would have their remains interred at the Yasukuni Shrine, memorializing their sacrifice for the ages.[52] Believing that its soldiers would unquestioningly live up to the precepts of Bushido, the Japanese military naturally assumed that none of its soldiers would become prisoners of war. Therefore, any application of the Geneva Convention on the part of Japan would be unilateral, requiring obligations only on behalf of Japan.[53]

Also, the Japanese navy believed that the lenient treatment of prisoners prescribed by the Geneva Convention would encourage the Allies to undertake long-range air raids against Japan. If Allied pilots knew they would receive lenient treatment as prisoners, the navy reasoned, they could participate in one-way raids on Japan, knowing that they would not have to return to their bases. As prisoners, they could count on the Japanese to provide for their safety and care, and they could therefore double their range of operations.[54]

The military also objected to allowing representatives of third-party powers (or "protecting powers") to interview prisoners without Japanese observers being present as being "harmful from the military point of view." Last, the Japanese navy claimed that under the Geneva Convention, prisoners of war would receive better treatment in captivity than Japanese soldiers received in the country's military, especially as concerned punishment. The Naval Ministry argued that ratifying the agreement would require a drastic reform of Japanese codes for punishment within the navy, which would diminish that service's discipline within the ranks and would therefore weaken the empire's defenses. Thus, the Imperial Japanese Navy and Army discouraged the treaty's ratification.[55] By rejecting the Geneva Convention, the Japanese government believed it was under no obligation to uphold the agreement's principles during the Second World War.

After the early Japanese conquests of the Allied forces in Asia and in the Pacific, the governments of Great Britain, the Netherlands, Australia, and the United States petitioned the Japanese government, asking that the Japanese consent to the provisions of the Geneva Convention. Japanese foreign minister Togo Shigonori replied to the Allied governments that although Japan did not ratify the convention and was therefore not bound by it, the Japanese would apply the provisions of the convention mutatis mutandis.[56] The Japanese promised to follow as closely as practicable American national and racial customs regarding provisions, food, and clothing, as well as other convention restrictions on the treatment of prisoners.[57]

Thus, when the men of the 2nd Battalion surrendered to the Japanese in March 1942, they had the assurance of the Japanese government that they would be treated according to international regulations. Even had they been aware of this agreement, however, the Americans would have received little comfort. Having fought so briefly against an enemy so overwhelming and so completely foreign from their experiences in Texas, the prisoners were justified in their fear and uncertainty about the future. Had life as prisoners of war remained the same as it was in Garoet, and had the Japanese faithfully lived up to their obligations, perhaps the Americans could have survived captivity relatively unscathed. Events would soon take a turn for the worse, however, and the Texans learned what life in Japanese prisoner-of-war camps would really entail.

Chapter 4

Becoming Prisoners: The Learning Period

DURING THEIR FIRST FEW WEEKS IN CAPTIVITY, THE TEXAN POWS functioned largely as they had before the surrender. They had almost no contact with the Japanese, and what little contact there was did not result in harsh treatment or strenuous work. The American command structure remained intact, and food and other supplies were plentiful. The troops lived according to their own customs and rules to this point, and they enjoyed a large amount of freedom. At that time they had seen no barbed-wire fences, there were no inspections or roll calls, they provisioned and fed themselves, and they moved about the Garoet area freely. It did not seem as if they really were prisoners of war but rather were in a state of limbo. They certainly understood that the Japanese were in charge, and they had to deal with this fact, but the realities of being captives had not yet set in. In April 1942 this began to change, however, and there was no mistaking their status as prisoners. They learned to become soldiers in the years and months prior to the war, and now they had to learn how to perform as prisoners of war.

After the Japanese had completed their conquest of Java, they then turned to the myriad responsibilities of administering the island. Part of this task included finding a more permanent home, as well as a use, for the thousands of prisoners they had taken during the battle for the island. On March 31, 1942, they ordered the American POWs in Garoet to assemble at the city's train depot for shipment to Tanjong Priok, the port for the capital city of Batavia. Upon their arrival at the port, the prisoners learned that they would now work in the warehouses and on the docks of Tanjong Priok, performing whatever tasks the Japanese required of them.[1] This would be their first experience laboring for the Japanese, and it established a better understanding for the prisoners about the mind-set of their captors. At this point they learned how to act as POWs and began to adopt techniques that would enable them to survive their ordeal.

Many of the men recalled a chaotic march from Batavia's train depot to Tanjong Priok. Japanese guards constantly harassed the POWs along the way, pushing them and screaming at them to speed up while prodding them with bayonets. Prisoners who fell behind were beaten with bamboo poles or with rifle butts until they caught up with the group. Much of the local population also abused the prisoners during the forced march. The Javanese stood on the side of the road and hurled rocks, rotten fruit, and insults at the POWs as they passed, and some spat upon them.[2]

Under these circumstances, the POWs quickly discovered that they carried too much extra baggage. Although they left the bulk of their possessions back in Malang prior to the Japanese invasion, they still carried with them what proved to be an excessive amount of gear. Along the road to Tanjong Priok the prisoners discarded many of their possessions, such as clothing, mess gear, canteens, and other items that were quickly scavenged by the locals. If given the benefit of foresight, however, they would have kept as much of this gear as possible.[3]

Upon arriving in Tanjong Priok on April 1, the prisoners discovered that the living conditions there were far from ideal. The facilities were very primitive and not fit for human habitation. The camp was situated on the sandy, open plain between the docks and the city, and their quarters consisted of open barracks, each crowded with more than one hundred prisoners.[4] Wooden platforms served as beds in these quarters, and they were infested with bedbugs, lice, and other vermin. Some POWs went without beds and slept on straw mats outside their barracks to avoid overcrowding.[5] The Dutch-style latrine facilities, consisting simply of open slit trenches, were also substandard and vulnerable to innumerable flies.[6] A barbed-wire fence surrounded the entire area, and according to Dan Buzzo, the Japanese warned the prisoners that anyone who attempted to escape would be shot.[7]

The prisoners were shocked when they discovered these new facilities. Jess Stanbrough described the buildings as being filthy, rundown, and rife with tropical insects. He thought, "God, this is an April Fool's joke!"[8] Huddleston ("Hud") Wright described their quarters as being vermin-

ridden "coolie barracks," and according to Luther Prunty, "The sanitary facilities were just nil."[9] The Texans became aware of the harsh realities of
POW life at Tanjong Priok, and this is where they began to learn survival
techniques.[10]

As their personal caches of food and drinking water began to be de-
pleted, the need for nourishment quickly became a major concern for the
prisoners. The Japanese provided food, but it was lacking in both quality
and quantity. Rations consisted mainly of rice served three times a day, but
the rice was of a very poor grade. The rice fed to the prisoners was often
rotten and contained weevils and worms, as well as small pebbles from the
sweepings off the floors of warehouses where the rice was stored. Most of
the men at first could not force themselves to eat such rations, but as their
hunger grew, they managed to force down the food.

Initially, they picked out the insects and worms from their rice, but they
later learned to eat them as well, rationalizing that they badly needed even
that kind of "protein" in their diets.[11] Said medic Raymond Reed: "The rice
and stew was full of worms and weevils . . . I would pick every one out, but
by the time I got through picking them out, the food was cold and tasted
like hell. It didn't taste that good to start with, but when it was cold it was
really bad. Finally, it wasn't a matter of picking out anything. You just looked
that ol' worm in the eye and chewed him up and swallowed him. You're past
that picky stage."[12] Vegetables and meat were almost nonexistent at Tanjong
Priok, and the prisoners soon began to suffer the ill effects of the early stages
of malnutrition. By illegally trading with the Javanese on the outside of the
camp and by scrounging on the docks, they managed to supplement their
diets with fruit and other foods. By U.S. Army standards, however, they were
being starved.[13]

The Japanese sent the prisoners to Tanjong Priok to perform menial
labor on the docks and in the warehouses. Under orders from the Japanese,
American officers formed work details each morning, asking for volunteers
to meet the quota demanded by their captors. Service on these details was
not compulsory at this point, and there were no shortages of volunteers to
go out each day. Prisoners usually joined one detail or another because it
helped break up the monotonous routine of life in the camp, but mostly
because it allowed them the opportunity to trade or scrounge for food.[14]

A typical workday consisted of marching down to the docks or warehouses and loading Japanese ships with supplies, such as barrels of oil or
gasoline and sacks of rice, and cleaning the area of debris left from the Japanese bombing of the harbor. They worked under constant Japanese supervi-
sion, but an American officer accompanied each detail to direct the work

and to serve as a liaison between the Japanese guards and the enlisted men.[15] Ilo Hard explained: "The only time we would go out of our way—I guess you would say fraternize—to any extent with the guards would be on work parties. At this time, around Batavia, we would try to get a Jap boasting about their conquests, with us standing there open-mouthed and listening to give him a good audience. The purpose was to keep the Jap in a good humor and keep him distracted so he wasn't pushing the work detail. It also gave the good thieves a chance to sneak off and do a little scrounging."[16]

The prisoners also encountered Japanese military discipline for the first time while at Tanjong Priok. From the outset the Japanese set forth rules and regulations that they expected the prisoners to follow, including falling in for tenko, or roll call, and the various other standard regulations involved in prisoner-of-war camps. The rule most difficult for the Americans to follow was that requiring all prisoners to salute their captors, regardless of rank, whenever they came into contact with them; if a prisoner was caught without a hat, he was forced to bow to the guard until ordered to stand at ease.[17]

Men recalled that having to bow to the Japanese guards, who were physically smaller than the Americans, was the most humiliating thing they had experienced up to this point in their lives. Ben Dunn, who transferred to Headquarters Battery from the 26th Field Artillery Brigade, said, "Bowing to the Japanese guards was humiliating. I never got over it. I always felt like, when I saluted one, 'Same to you, you son-of-a-bitch!' That's what we thought when we saluted our own officers, and that's what we thought about the Japanese."[18] F Battery's Grover Reichle added: "Inwardly, you hated the Japs, but you had to bow and scrape. You had to salute a Jap anytime you met him if you had headwear on. Otherwise, you had to bow. Well, I always had something on my head because I didn't want to bow to them little yellow bastards."[19]

But the prisoners had to obey the rules to the letter because any infraction resulted in physical punishment. At Tanjong Priok they first encountered this kind of treatment, which normally consisted of open-hand slaps to the head. Often, however, the Japanese resorted to kicking with hobnailed boots or striking the helpless POWs with rifle butts or bamboo poles.[20]

This type of treatment unsettled the young Texans. They did not understand the Japanese language, yet they were expected to follow Japanese orders explicitly. If they faltered in any way, they were beaten; if they moved too slowly or too quickly, they were beaten; if they miscounted during tenko, when they were forced to count in Japanese, they were beaten. Luther Prunty discussed this topic: "[A guard] told somebody to count [during tenko], and they didn't count, and that's when they started doing a little fisticuff work. It was pretty bad. It was the first time in my life that I ever had a man slap me, and I didn't try to cut his throat . . . That was the hardest thing in the world. I just didn't think I could stand it at all."[21] Survival depended on learning how to cope with such emotions, however, and if they were to survive as prisoners, the men had to learn to control their behavior.

They came to better understand Japanese discipline toward prisoners of war when they witnessed firsthand the discipline within the Japanese army. The Japanese commonly used slapping and humiliation to instill discipline within their armed forces. Higher-ranking soldiers held the authority to beat those of lesser rank. Officers could beat noncommissioned officers; noncommissioned officers could beat privates. Being the last in the progression, privates chose to take out their frustrations on Korean conscripts serving in the Imperial Japanese Army. The Koreans held a very low standing with the Japanese and were often relegated to rear-echelon duties, such as guarding prisoners in camps. Since the Koreans were considered racially inferior by the Japanese, they were of the lowest order in the military hierarchy and were often abused. In order to take out their frustrations, the Koreans abused the Allied prisoners.[22]

This kind of treatment shocked the Americans, but they soon learned how to deal with their Japanese and Korean captors, some more successfully than others. Eddie Fung observed that there were three types of guards: "those who left you alone and let you work, those who were curious and wanted to know more about you, and those who beat you for no apparent reason."[23] Since each guard could fall into any category at any time, the best way to deal with all of them was to avoid contact and remain as inconspicuous as possible.[24] If a prisoner could not avoid the Japanese, which was all too often the case, he had to follow the rules as closely as possible. Hud Wright at first had trouble counting in Japanese during tenko, but he quickly learned because "[the guards would] teach you Japanese pretty quick with a bamboo pole."[25] Roy Armstrong said that in those conditions, "you just have to [adjust]. You know you're going to have to do it because if you don't do it, then they was going to be rough on you. I just made up my mind that if they tell me to do something, I'm going to try to do it . . . [the Japanese] don't bluff you at all . . . You don't know what [being slapped by a guard] does to you. I'll tell you, it's the hardest thing that a human has to do—to know you could grab him and eat him if you wanted to . . . They had a complex about being smaller than we were, so when they got a chance to get one of us tall boys, they worked on us. Oh, yes, they liked to humiliate you. You just had to grit your teeth and take it. That's all you could do."[26] The prisoners were at the mercy of their captors, and the sooner they recognized this fact, the better off they would be.

Dan Buzzo had more difficulty than some adjusting to life as a prisoner of war. In April 1942, the Japanese ordered a group of prisoners to erect a barbed-wire fence around part of the compound, and Buzzo worked on this detail. While completing the task on April 7, he recalled stretching the last strand of wire and tying it to the post at the gate of the camp. There was a tag at the end of the spool of wire that read "Made in the U.S.A." Buzzo [weeping] said, "I was very dejected. It was my twenty-first birthday."[27]

Dealing with the emotional impact of POW life was only one aspect of survival. Another important part was learning how to acquire extra food. Prisoners learned how to trade or scrounge to augment their increasingly scanty rations. They stood at the camp's fence and met with the Javanese, who, despite their initial attitudes toward the Allied prisoners, were interested in trading with them. Since the POWs had little in their possession, they often traded their watches and rings or spare clothing and stolen cloth to the natives for fresh fruit or canned goods. At other times, Dutch women came by the fence and gave them bananas and pineapples or cigarettes, then flashed the "V-for-victory" sign and ran off before they were discovered by the Japanese.[28] Slug Wright described the Dutch women: "Without a doubt, they're the most courageous people I have ever run into in my life."[29]

The Americans also maintained military discipline in the ranks to help ensure that the prisoners did not become a rabble. The military chain of command remained intact throughout the stay on Java, although the prisoners quickly dispensed with formalities such as saluting. Most officers still commanded the respect of their men, and the men willingly followed orders.[30] According to Ilo Hard, "[I]t was not 'by-the-numbers' discipline, but basic discipline, [and the officers would try to] do the right thing at the right time . . . All we expected, when we talked to a man, was that he give us his undivided attention, that he'd listen to us, you know, respectfully."[31] The officers played an essential role in keeping the prisoners organized for work details, and officers accompanying these details acted as buffers between the Japanese and the prisoners, protecting the latter from abusive guards.

Officers also oversaw the preparation and distribution of food. In an environment where food was becoming scarce, it was vital to ensure that all POWs received an equal share. The prisoners carefully watched the cooks and those handling the food to make sure that the distribution was equitable. Should any prisoner receive more than what others deemed proper, the POWs would protest loudly, and fistfights occasionally broke out. Donald Brain, who joined the 2nd Battalion as a prisoner in May 1942, described a typical scene: "I would say that probably 99 percent of all fights that broke out in prison camp were based on groceries . . . Somebody was always saying, 'Well, I bought this and I said I would share it with you, and you took a bigger bite,' and then it was 'You S.O.B.,' and then that's all it took. Tempers got pretty short there, too." When overseeing this process, the officers saw to it that the cooks gave each man an equal cupful of rice and ladleful of stew. Commenting on the cooks, Brain continued: "[The cooks] got abused something terrible later on . . . Why, hell, you know the cooks were always holding something back. There was no doubt in my mind that they did . . . I would assume that they probably took a little bit bigger chunk of meat than they were actually handing out there in the stew. But damn it, hell, it was under their custody and control . . . I'm not excluding myself when I said they were abused and accused."[32]

When practicable, the officers saw to it that the POWs followed strict procedures regarding hygiene. Climatic conditions on Java were conducive to the spread of a variety of diseases, especially in a camp with substandard sanitation facilities. Large black flies, drawn to the open latrines, swarmed the camp, moving from the latrines to the mess areas to the prisoners' mess gear and food. To help stave off disease and maintain the prisoners' health, the officers ordered all POWs to dip their mess gear in a barrel of boiling water prior to and following each meal. Also, the POWs always boiled their drinking water at Tanjong Priok to ensure that no dangerous microbes remained to cause them harm.[33]

Though many had trouble settling in to life as prisoners, the Americans did their best to adjust. In their spare time, the POWs tried to keep busy to keep their minds off their predicament. Many played cards or dominoes, while others read what few books they had.[34] At Tanjong Priok the prisoners, perhaps unconsciously, began forming the rudiments of a small-scale society in which each member, whether he was a cook, medical orderly, or just a comedian, played a part in the larger prisoner-of-war community.

The prisoners' stay at Tanjong Priok lasted only about six weeks, however, and on May 14, 1942, they left the facilities on the coast and moved twenty miles inland to Bicycle Camp in Batavia. This camp formerly housed the Dutch 10th Infantry Battalion in Batavia, which used bicycles as its major mode of transportation. Bicycle Camp served as the home to the Americans for the next five months, and there they settled into a routine and really learned how to be prisoners of war. Bicycle Camp measured roughly nine hundred feet by seven hundred feet, was surrounded by a high masonry wall, and housed between twenty-five hundred and three thousand Dutch, British, Australian, and American prisoners throughout the war.[35] At this camp the Americans completed their transformation into prisoners of war, learning how to deal with their captors to minimize abuse as well as learning techniques to help them survive.

The prisoners marched the twenty miles from Tanjong Priok to Bicycle Camp under the blazing Java sun. Most of the men still had in their possession extra uniforms, one or two pairs of shoes, blankets, mess gear, and other truck they could stuff into their duffel bags. They had personal items, such as books and some jewelry, photographs of their loved ones, cooking gear, and whatever money they could hide from the Japanese. Along the way they again jettisoned some of their extra gear and personal belongings to make the march less stressful.[36] Upon reaching the camp, the prisoners were herded into the first set of barracks by the front gate, and they took measure of their new surroundings.

The facilities at Bicycle Camp were the best the American POWs encountered during their captivity. The barracks consisted of two-story brick buildings with open balconies and walkways that allowed the flow of fresh air, and each barrack was wired for electricity. Each barrack floor was divided into smaller three-sided cubicles that housed from three to four prisoners, and the open side faced a central hallway. Each barrack held approximately three hundred prisoners. Although the barracks contained no beds, the prisoners soon improvised their own, with some sleeping on the balconies and verandas to enjoy the cooler flow of air.[37]

Food was always paramount in the minds of POWs and was certainly true of the Americans in Bicycle Camp. The kitchen facilities were deemed adequate in this camp, and the Japanese provided standard rations of rice—though of the same poor quality POWs received at Tanjong Priok—and occasionally they would divide small amounts of vegetables and some meat among the prisoners. The prisoners were responsible for their own cooking, and after an initial period of trial and error in which error seemed more common, the American cooks learned how to steam the rice in the native pans known as *wajans*. The prisoners ate three times a day, with steamed rice making up the principal component, and usually had a thin, watery vegetable stew occasionally flavored with meat or fish. As at Tanjong Priok, the officers kept a close watch on the distribution of food, ensuring that each POW received his cup of rice and ladleful of stew. This rice diet did not meet the nutritional or culinary requirements of the Texans, and there was never enough to satisfy their appetites.[38]

Bathing and sanitation facilities, considered adequate for the Dutch troops who once lived here, were not adequate for the nearly three thousand prisoners. The latrines were of the traditional Dutch type, consisting of a number of holes in the ground over which prisoners would squat, and they were covered by a wooden roof and surrounded by three walls. Water constantly ran through the latrine trench and carried away most of the waste, but there were too few of these latrines to meet demand. Some prisoners had difficulty adjusting to this type of facility, especially following the Dutch practice of cleaning one's backside with one's left hand and a bottle of water; no toilet paper was provided. P. J. Smallwood described Batavia as "the land of liquid toilet paper." Paul Papish offered the standard advice of the Americans when he said, "Don't shake hands with a Dutchman."[39] Fresh water was plentiful at this camp, however, and the prisoners took advantage of the bathing facilities.[40]

Medical facilities at Bicycle Camp were also substandard, but given the relatively good health of most prisoners at this time, care was adequate. Each nationality at Bicycle Camp maintained the health of its own prisoners, but one hut was set aside as the camp hospital. Lt. R. B. Ross, who contracted severe dysentery prior to his internment at Bicycle Camp, died in May 1942, and after two Australian POWs also succumbed to the disease, the Japanese provided some medicine and allowed POW doctors to go into Batavia to purchase necessary medicine and medical supplies.[41] These were the only reported deaths in this camp, and the prisoners described their health as being good.[42]

The Japanese also allowed the prisoners to open a camp canteen where prisoners could purchase various items, such as soap, tooth powder, and other personal items, although the quantity of such goods was often low. The canteen also sold much-needed food items, including eggs, sugar, cocoa, canned goods, nuts, and sweetened condensed milk. Most of the prisoners' money naturally went to buy food, although some traded food for cigarettes at this point. The Americans also built a bakery in June, and the POWs supplemented their rations with small amounts of baked goods.[43]

Upon entering Bicycle Camp, the Texans discovered they were not the only Americans held captive there. The survivors of the heavy cruiser USS *Houston*, which had been sunk by the Japanese during the Battle of Sunda Strait on the night of February 28–March 1, 1942, had arrived at Bicycle Camp in mid-April after spending over a month in captivity at Serang, Java (see figure 4.1).[44] Having swum away from the sinking *Houston*, the surviving sailors and marines endured up to twenty-four hours in the water before being taken captive by the Japanese on Java. Many of the survivors suffered from severe burns after swimming in fuel oil-laden waters caused by the sinking ship, and none had adequate clothing or any personal gear. After spending over a month in deplorable conditions in Serang, during

Figure 4.1 The heavy cruiser CA-30 USS *Houston*, 1940.
Courtesy of the USS *Houston* Survivors Association.

which time many contracted a variety of diseases and began suffering from malnutrition, the *Houston*'s survivors were taken to Bicycle Camp.[45]

The sailors' appearance shocked the men of the 2nd Battalion. The *Houston*'s men were underclothed—some were naked—and malnourished. Some suffered from dysentery and from third-degree burns. They had no gear, no plates or eating utensils, no medicine, and little food. Moved by what they saw, the Texans immediately, and voluntarily, shared their surplus with the sailors. They gave them their extra uniforms and shoes, their extra K rations, and their extra medicine.[46] Luther Prunty regretted that he discarded some of his equipment and clothing on the way to Bicycle Camp because he could have shared it with those desperate sailors he encountered.[47] Jess Stanbrough described the sailors: "They looked thinner and bushed and more tired [than the soldiers]. They'd seen a lot more of life than we had."[48] After witnessing the condition of the sailors, Ben Dunn recalled: "I was almost ashamed to tell them of my experiences."[49] One *Houston* survivor, J. O. ("Jack") Burge, remembered: "What gear the 131st could spare, they shared. I mean, they had to look out for theirselfs, you know. They didn't have too much. They weren't outfitted like a regular army, you know. They just had maybe one or two pairs of shoes and so on; they didn't have enough to go around."[50] Thus began a lifelong friendship between the soldiers and the survivors of the *Houston.*

Japanese administration over and policies toward the POWs became more systematic at Bicycle Camp, and the prisoners quickly learned how to live in this more consistent environment. The Imperial Japanese Army assigned noncommissioned officers, usually sergeants, as the commandants of the camp, who exercised wide discretion in operating the camp. The commandant was allowed to interpret general regulations according to personal whims and particular situations, especially in regard to physical punishment and feeding the POWs. Japanese noncommissioned officers likewise held much power over the day-to-day aspects of camp life and exercised much more power than their American counterparts.[51]

The guards left no question as to who was in command of the camp, and they expected prisoners to comply with their every demand. When prisoners broke the rules, they learned to expect immediate reprisals. Trading with civilians outside the camp was strictly forbidden, and the guards punished offenders by slapping and beating them. Failure to salute or bow to a guard resulted in a beating. If a guard caught a POW stealing from the Japanese, the prisoner was beaten severely.[52]

The Japanese proved to be quite creative in their punishment of prisoners. One type of punishment included forcing a prisoner to kneel back on his legs for hours at a time with a bamboo pole lodged behind his knees, a particularly excruciating punishment. Wade Webb described one incident: "The worst treatment that I saw in Bicycle Camp was taking a prisoner . . . they'd get a piece of stove wood and split it about so big [three to four inches in diameter]. It's got splinters and four or five edges to it. They'd put it behind a guy's knees and make him squat on it until he fainted. My friend [S. J.] Whatley got put through that, and I don't know for what reason. But as far as I know, that was the most inhumane—if that's the right word— thing that I saw at Bicycle Camp."[53] The Japanese also forced prisoners to drink massive amounts of water and would then jump on their stomachs.[54] Although the POWs still disobeyed many of the regulations, they learned to do so very carefully in order to avoid such punishment.

As one might expect, the guards responsible for enforcing the regulations varied in their treatment of the prisoners. Some dealt with the prisoners in a compassionate manner, not pushing them too hard on work details and ignoring minor infractions. One such guard, known as "Holy Joe" to the prisoners because he professed to be a Christian, treated the POWs with kindness.[55] Most of the guards were not so compassionate, however, and abused the prisoners at every opportunity. These guards, both Japanese and

Korean, also earned nicknames from the prisoners, usually due to some physical characteristic.[56]

The prisoners particularly despised a Korean guard they called the "Brown Bomber," who liked to catch prisoners unaware and beat them for little or no reason.[57] Quaty Gordon described this guard: "[H]e was short in stature, and apparently this was something that didn't set very well with him, you know. Goddamn, he equalized it with that rifle! He'd come up there, and, man, he'd smash you upside the head with that damn rifle in the bat of an eye. Had you known the Japanese language real good, I imagine every other breath would have been a cuss word at you . . . He probably was a very low-class coolie to begin with, but, damn, he wanted to make himself known, and he damn sure did . . . here's this little banty-legged devil talking to you and knocking you upside the damn head with a rifle butt, and there ain't a damn thing you can do about it. See, that's belittling to you. Your teeth *do* rattle."[58]

William Chapman recalled a specific incident during which the prisoners were being marched from Tanjong Priok to Bicycle Camp: "[Amarillo resident Sgt. John E.] Rogers and [Wichita Falls resident Sgt. Jewel L.] Sisk were at the rear of the column carrying a sick man. They got behind, and this [Korean] beat them very badly . . . The 'Brown Bomber' beat Rogers first with his rifle butt and knocked him down and kicked him in the ribs while he was on the ground, and also kicked him in the stomach, shins, and body about 15 to 20 times. Then he started beating Sisk. He slapped him around, kicked him on the shins, and knocked one of his false front teeth out. He also beat Sisk with his fists. The entire incident covered a period of 10 to 15 minutes while the column continued to move ahead."[59]

Charley Pryor, a marine from the *Houston*, described another guard called "Liver Lips": "'Liver Lips' will probably be the worst one that we ever ran onto, and he was turned loose there in Bicycle Camp. He just went through there from one end to the other bashing and hammering and clubbing with his silly rifle—[he was a] big rascal . . . [he got his nickname] from his prominent lips . . . Oh, I think he was just about the meanest and orneriest rascal that we'd ever run onto. You didn't have to provoke him. He'd just see you, and he was provoked."[60]

Although the administration and policies were more consistent at Bicycle Camp than at Tanjong Priok, the behavior of individual guards could vary widely. A particular guard might catch a POW violating a regulation at one moment and do nothing. Later, the same guard was likely to beat a prisoner for a minor infraction, such as not carrying an ash can while smoking a cigarette. Jess Stanbrough remembered that the Brown Bomber once caught him in the act of illegal trading, and Stanbrough expected to be severely beaten. The Korean chose instead to trade with the prisoner and then let him go on his way without being punished.[61] A Japanese guard once beat Hud Wright for a minor infraction, and then shared a cigar with him.[62] There seemed to be no rationality in the guards' behavior, leaving the prisoners confused and constantly on guard.

Like all aspects of POW life, the Americans had to adjust to their treatment by the camp's guards. The best way to deal with the guards, according to the prisoners, was to avoid them altogether. Most were not lucky enough enjoy this luxury, however, and they had to learn to deal with the regulations and the beatings. The guards liked to single out the biggest of the Americans for punishment, perhaps to show the Westerners who were truly the most powerful. Prisoners over six feet tall stood out in camp, and the guards often forced them to stand at attention while they beat them. Occasionally, a guard had to stand on a wooden box to reach a prisoner's head, and then he beat the American unmercifully. If a prisoner fell as a result of the beating, the guards beat and kicked him for falling. The Americans discovered it was best to "roll" with a punch delivered by a guard, depriving the guard of a solid blow to his head.[63]

The prisoners had to learn to deal with such treatment, and most came to terms with their place in the camp. They found the rules difficult to obey, especially those that concerned bowing and saluting the Japanese. Although the rules and enforcement of the rules were often galling to the POWs, the men had to accept the fact that the Japanese were in charge. According to officer Clark Taylor, "You could curse a little under your breath or something, but [saluting] was something you could live with. Hell, when you would come under their rule, by dang, you would live by their rules or take their punishment. If you wanted to be bull-headed about it and not salute or stand up when they came in, and you would rather have a slapping for it, all right, you could have that. They gave the rules, and we had to live with them or take the consequences."[64]

The Japanese continued to employ the prisoners on work details at Bicycle Camp. As before in Tanjong Priok, the Japanese requested a certain number of workers, and the American officers then asked for volunteers among the enlisted men to fulfill the quota. During a typical workday, the prisoners left camp around eight o'clock in the morning and marched or would be trucked to the job site, usually at the docks of Tanjong Priok. There they worked loading and unloading ships, while others labored in the warehouses. Some prisoners believed that the Japanese were looting Java of its valuables, and they remember loading barrels of oil, large amounts of railroad steel, locomotives, and boxcars, as well as items of art and precious metals.[65] Others spent their days working in Batavia, cleaning up war damage. Work in these details was not too physically strenuous, and after a nine- or ten-hour day, the guards escorted the prisoners back to camp. Once again, those who worked in these details did so voluntarily, hoping to trade with the natives and Dutch civilians for food.[66]

When they were not working for the Japanese around Batavia, the prisoners participated in a number of activities in Bicycle Camp. The compound contained a large open area in which the men could take part in various sporting activities, and the Americans gladly joined in. The prisoners enjoyed playing basketball here, but volleyball proved to be the sport of choice. A number of volleyball teams took shape, usually according to American or Australian nationality, and they took part in high-spirited tournaments. The Americans claimed to have gotten the better of the "Aussies" in these tournaments, but the Australians also laid claim to being the best.[67] The Japanese also encouraged the prisoners to take part in boxing tournaments, which they did with relish. Two Americans in particular, Ben ("Dynamite") Dunn and Vincent ("Zip") Zummo of Service Battery, both of whom had been amateur boxers in civilian life, stood out among the rest.[68]

Others chose to spend their time in more leisurely pursuits. Bicycle Camp contained a small theater, and the Australians and British put on shows and plays for all to enjoy. Although books were in short supply in the camp, many of the POWs read, and then reread, whatever books they could find. Others attended classes on history, languages, astronomy, or a variety of other topics. Lester Rasbury decided to make the most of his spare time by cooking and selling fudge, known as "Rasbury's Finer Fudge," to the other prisoners. He cornered the market on fudge in Bicycle Camp and turned a tidy profit that he reinvested into other lucrative avenues during his stay.[69]

The Americans spent most of their spare time in idle conversations, commonly called "bull sessions," in which they discussed all topics, from the back roads of West Texas to the progress of the war.[70] Rumors also played an important part in these discussions. The POWs still believed the war would be over soon, and they speculated on the timing of their liberation. Rumors were rife that American ships were coming to take them to Australia and that the U.S. Army would soon land fifty thousand troops and take the island back from the Japanese.[71] Early in their captivity, the prisoners also liked to talk about women. As time wore on and as rations became more scanty, however, they found that the main topic was food. The POWs often discussed their favorite recipes and their favorite meals. Some prisoners were so descriptive in their recipes that others claimed they could actually smell the food. Alf Brown said that his favorite topics were "T-bone steaks and women," but that he quickly became more interested in the steaks.[72]

During their bull sessions, the Americans and the Australians discovered their common interests, and the men from these two countries grew quite fond of each other.[73] Ilo Hard described the Australians as "the most resourceful individuals that we met anywhere."[74] Max Offerle offered this about the Australians: "If I ever had to go to war again—God forbid—I'd rather be with some Australians than anybody I know in the world."[75] Hud Wright paid them perhaps the highest compliment that a Texan could offer: "The Australians are more like Texans than anybody we ran into."[76] Part of this shared admiration certainly stemmed from a mutual distrust of the British in Bicycle Camp, whom both the Australians and Americans regarded as arrogant and not too concerned with hygiene.[77]

The Americans received news from the outside world about the conduct of the war through a radio constructed from parts sneaked into camp. Jess Stanbrough, who had operated a ham radio before the war and who served as chief of the battalion's radio section, built a small receiving set that he kept hidden from his captors throughout the war. The radio was broken when Stanbrough came into possession of it, but with the aid of other prisoners who scavenged radio parts and other odds and ends while on work details, he put the radio in working order.[78]

Stanbrough and his friend Frank Ficklin took great pains to keep the radio out of sight in the barracks, because having a radio in one's possession would result in execution by the Japanese. On one afternoon, Stanbrough was listening to the radio through its headset while lying on his upper bunk in the barrack when a Korean guard made a surprise inspection. Ficklin had no time to warn his friend, and he feared for Stanbrough's life. The guard paced down the walkway, unaware that Stanbrough was still in his bunk. He passed the frightened prisoner, who dared not to make a sound, and the bayonet of the guard's rifle touched the electrical wire hanging from the ceiling. Those around Stanbrough held their breath, knowing that the guard would look up and discover the prisoner and his contraband radio, and that would be the end of him. The guard did not notice, however, and left the barrack. Ficklin remembered that his friend became more cautious after this close call.[79]

Stanbrough and Ficklin took turns listening to radio broadcasts from station KGEI in San Francisco and from the British Broadcasting Corporation operating from India. The pair then slowly and cautiously released the news they received through their officers, who then leaked the information to the rest of the prisoners. Only a very few prisoners were aware of the location of the radio in order to keep it and its operators safe. Although most of the news they received early in the war reported setbacks for the Allies, this radio proved to be the only link the prisoners had to the outside world.[80]

Even more important than outside news was food—the prisoners had to find a way to supplement their rations with whatever food they could buy, acquire through trade, or steal from the Japanese. The officers established a company fund with which they purchased food from the locals or from the Dutch outside camp. The money in this fund came from a number of sources. First, as the men had not received their full pay since leaving the United States in November 1941, the unit still had thousands of dollars in its payroll coffers to contribute to the fund. Second, Clark Taylor, who served as supply officer before his capture, deposited the American equivalent of 150,000 Dutch guilders in banks on Java upon reaching the island. He withdrew this money just prior to the surrender and later added it to the fund. Roy Stensland still had thousands of dollars in his possession from the failed Robeson Mission, which he donated. Last, the POWs kept any profits made by the camp canteen, and this money went into the fund as well.[81]

Taylor allotted a certain amount of money to individual prisoners who left camp on work details, who would purchase supplies. Upon returning to camp, they turned over the food to the prisoners' common commissary, or they returned the money if they were unsuccessful. Although the Japanese discouraged fraternization with the Javanese, they often turned their heads to such activities. Getting the contraband into the camp always proved to be an adventure, however, because the guards stopped and searched the POWs as they returned to the camp at the end of each day.

The prisoners learned to conceal the food in their clothes, usually in the crotch of their pants, as they went through an inspection. When the guards found contraband food or other items, they naturally beat the guilty prisoner unmercifully.[82] On one occasion, guards discovered a dozen American prisoners sneaking contraband items—nails and candles—into camp and forced the bare-legged prisoners to kneel for several hours on sharp gravel. When the prisoners proved unable to walk when ordered to do so, their guards beat them. Herbert Morris witnessed this episode: "If a man's legs were so numb that he couldn't stand one of the Jap guards would beat him with a large bamboo pole about as thick as your wrist until he did manage to get up. I saw one particular time when an American could not get to his feet. The guard beat him for about five minutes with the bamboo pole and then yanked him to his feet and helped him to walk a couple of steps, then made him return to the same position."[83] This treatment lasted from early in the morning until after sunset.

When placed in an environment where food is so important, one can expect disputes to arise between prisoners, and there were such disputes in Bicycle Camp. The men of each nationality looked after their own concerning food, and theft did occur as Americans and Australians occasionally "liberated" food from the British and Dutch in the camp. Disputes also arose among the Americans, usually concerning second helpings, but a more important conflict took place between the officers and the enlisted men. The enlisted men claimed that their officers took advantage of the company funds and kept more of the food for themselves. The officers ate in segregated mess areas, and the enlisted men resented the fact that the officers "lived high on the hog" while the enlisted men subsisted largely on rice.[84] Clark Taylor claimed, on the other hand, that the officers ate the same food as the enlisted men, and that they enjoyed no special privileges.[85]

In one particular instance, the officers risked their lives for the enlisted men. In July 1942, the Japanese required POWs to sign a pledge that they would follow all orders and that they would not attempt to escape. Initially, the Americans refused to sign the pledge, and the Japanese retaliated by closing the camp canteen and placing restrictions on POW activities. When the Americans still refused to sign, the Japanese separated the officers from the rest of the POW population, held them in tight confinement, and even beat some of the officers as a way to force them to order their men to sign the pledge. When the Japanese explained that they would then beat the enlisted men—and did indeed beat a number of them and then inferred that they would shoot them—Colonel Tharp and the officers decided to allow the Americans to sign the pledge. The officers rationalized that they would be signing under duress and threat of physical punishment, so the pledge would not be binding upon the prisoners. The Americans signed the agreement on July 4, 1942.[86]

Leadership was a quality not unique to officers, however, and other prisoners, regardless of rank, earned the respect of their fellow POWs. Circumstances in Bicycle Camp often brought out the best and worst in the men, and those who reacted calmly and used common sense during a crisis often became leaders whom the men looked up to. The prisoners respected men who exemplified bravery, especially when they put themselves at risk to help another prisoner. These men won the respect of the others and placed them on par with the officers. Men admired fellow POWs who showed strong character, and the officers often had to work through them. According to Ilo Hard, "They set an example, and you couldn't ignore them."[87] Those like Charley Pryor, Eddie Fung, Jack Shaw, and Roy Stensland stood out among the others for their bravery, and men naturally gravitated toward them.

Lester Rasbury, in particular, held Stensland in high regard. He recalled an episode when a Dutch woman arrived outside the camp one day to bring bananas to the POWs. A Japanese guard spotted the woman and ordered her to stop. According to Rasbury, "There was a guard [who] came up behind her and hit her. She didn't see this guard, and he hit her and knocked her down . . . We were across a kind of just a ditch . . . and Lieutenant Stensland was standing there. Boy, before you knew what was happening, he was over there and he'd done knocked that Jap down. He went one way, and the rifle went the other way. [Stensland] was helping this lady up, and, boy, that Jap picked up his rifle and run . . . He didn't do a thing about it; he didn't do a thing."[88]

Overall, the Americans experienced an egalitarian-type relationship within their unit. Officers naturally had more authority than most of the men, but others exercised authority and influence they had earned in their dealings with the Japanese. Rank certainly had its privileges—officers were not required to perform manual labor, and they almost certainly ate better than the enlisted men—but there was no drastic caste structure within the unit. Enlisted men called their officers by their first names, and as mentioned earlier, saluting had been abandoned very early in captivity. This feeling of relative equality within the unit largely precluded an adversarial relationship with the officers, and the Americans understood that they were all facing the same challenges together. Unit cohesion, based on trust and equality, helped provide a more stable environment for the Americans at Bicycle Camp, and this allowed the prisoners to adapt and learn together.[89]

Learning to get along as prisoners required the ability and willingness to do what was necessary to fit in, and the Americans showed this ability in a number of areas. First, to make life easier for themselves, the POWs had to learn essential portions of the Japanese language. During tenko, the guards forced the prisoners to count off in Japanese. Since none of the Americans spoke the language, each tenko resulted in numerous "bashings" because the prisoners could never get the count correct. Nearly all orders were given in Japanese, and if prisoners did not respond to their guards quickly enough, they would be beaten.[90] The guards tolerated no misunderstandings.

The Americans also became accustomed to the predominantly rice diet. Although most did not find the rice palatable at first, they learned to force themselves to eat it to help them maintain their strength. Eating the rice became somewhat easier for them after the American cooks learned how to steam it correctly in the wajans, and the burned grains at the bottom of the pan proved especially tasty.[91]

Maintaining personal hygiene also helped the prisoners adjust to life in the camp. Although bathing and latrine facilities were nearly adequate at

Bicycle Camp, they were primitive by the Americans' standards. Dysentery also became a problem for some POWs in the camp. The Americans remained diligent in their sanitation procedures, however, and always boiled their water before drinking it. The officers and men of the 2nd Battalion also made sure that they all took advantage of the showers provided in the camp, and those who were reluctant to use the facilities were occasionally bathed by force.[92]

Perhaps the most important thing the prisoners did to help them survive at Bicycle Camp was to form small support groups, known as "cliques." A clique normally consisted of two to five men—usually three or four—who looked after the welfare of the others in the group. Men were not assigned to specific cliques—they came about quite naturally as friendships became stronger during captivity. If one member of a clique happened to acquire medicine or extra clothes or extra food, such as a tin of meat or a can of sweetened condensed milk, he took it back to his group and shared it with the others; the others would do likewise when they had the opportunity. The prisoners quickly discovered that it would be increasingly difficult for a man to survive alone and that with the support of others they could better survive the crisis. Thus, from early in their captivity the American prisoners learned to depend on others, helping to form a tightly knit unit.[93]

The adaptability exhibited by the prisoners helped them deal with the hardships of life in Bicycle Camp. Despite the difficulties they experienced there, however, the prisoners remembered this camp as being the best they encountered during the war. Certainly, the food was bad, and there was never enough of it, but the POWs had ways of acquiring more. Medical facilities were lacking by American standards, but some medicine was available and most of the prisoners were still in good health at this point. The Japanese did not force the prisoners to work, and when they did work, it was not too taxing on them. They enjoyed access to bathing facilities, and there was always plenty of water. The bashings and other punishments were a reality, but if the prisoners behaved carefully, they could avoid such treatment for the most part.

The men described their experiences at Bicycle Camp in very similar fashion. Hud Wright believed "it was a very comfortable camp," and Slug Wright described it as being "a gorgeous camp."[94] Dan Buzzo recalled that the prisoners were becoming "a family" at Bicycle Camp, especially as they formed the individual cliques to help share the burden of captivity. Buzzo feared that the Japanese would soon move them out of the camp and separate the POWs, thus destroying the community that helped keep them relatively safe.[95] Others similarly expressed their trepidation at having to leave the camp.[96] Max Offerle admitted that conditions in the camp were not ideal, but that if everything had stayed the same throughout the war, he could have survived in good physical shape.[97] In describing Bicycle Camp, Quaty Gordon spoke for the prisoners: "It was horrible enough, but, hell, it was like a Sunday school picnic compared to later, but we didn't know."[98]

The Americans had gotten used to the conditions and had grown comfortable at Bicycle Camp during their five-month stay. Had they been allowed to remain there for the duration of the war, perhaps life would not have been too difficult for them. Their fortunes again changed rather quickly, however, and they were forced to leave the camp that had been their home. Their new destination awaited them in the jungles of Burma and Thailand, where they would endure unimaginable hardships in the worst of conditions. Perhaps the American POWs looked back on Bicycle Camp rather fondly because of what they faced when they left this camp. Whatever the case, they soon left the stability of the camp for the docks at Tanjong Priok, and the torture that waited there for them.

Chapter 5

"Hell Ships" and Changi

IN OCTOBER 1942, MOST OF THE MEN OF THE 2ND BATTALION, along with the sailors and marines from the *Houston*, left Bicycle Camp bound for Singapore. The Japanese found a use for the Allied prisoners, so they sent these Americans to Changi prisoner-of-war camp—a clearinghouse camp of sorts—until they could marshal appropriate numbers of POWs and provide sufficient transportation to send them to their final destination, somewhere in the Japanese Empire. The Americans had learned to expect rapid changes in Japanese behavior, and being taken to the docks of Tanjong Priok on short notice in early October came as no surprise.

It was clear that they were leaving Java, but they still knew nothing of their destination. The Japanese provided no information as to where they were taking the prisoners, saying only that when they reached their destination, they would receive better food, facilities, and treatment. The prisoners had grown accustomed to life in Bicycle Camp, with its relative comforts, and if the Japanese were to be believed, life as POWs was about to get much better. As it turned out, however, conditions became immeasurably worse. The experience at Bicycle Camp prepared them for some aspects of being prisoners of the Japanese, but nothing could fully prepare them for what lay ahead.

On October 2, 1942, the Japanese ordered some eighteen hundred prisoners in Bicycle Camp to pack their gear and prepare to be taken to the docks.[1] The American POWs, under Colonel Tharp, gathered their few personal effects in preparation for the trip. Tharp told the men to take only what they could easily carry because the Japanese would not allow them to bring extra gear. Most of the men, and especially the *Houston* survivors, had very few possessions, but it was difficult to leave behind surplus clothes, cooking gear, books, or anything else that had made life more tolerable in camp. Clark Taylor, ever the diligent supply officer, divvied up the cache of food among all the prisoners, each receiving a can or two of bully beef, vegetables, or condensed milk. This small amount of food proved invaluable on their trip to Singapore.[2]

The men left their temporary home in Bicycle Camp, as well as their somewhat predictable lives as POWs, and were trucked down to Tanjong Priok to start a new phase of their captivity. Some were hopeful that the move would mean a better life for them. According to *Houston* survivor H. Robert Charles: "Every time there was any suggestion even of a move, there was something that happened to you almost biologically. You became so excited and so hopeful that something of great benefit was going to occur; it was going to be better than this is here. I remember that rising feeling of: 'Oh, boy! This is going to be fantastic!'"[3] Others believed that leaving the relative safety of Java to venture into a war zone in Japanese ships would invite disaster. They feared that American bombers and submarines might be lurking in the area and that the unmarked Japanese ships transporting the prisoners would be easy targets.[4]

The Japanese divided the POWs into two groups in Tanjong Priok, and the groups left Java separately. The first group, under the command of Lt. Col. C. M. Black from Australia, consisted of about 1,500 men of different nationalities. The senior American officer in this group was Capt. Arch Fitzsimmons of the 2nd Battalion, and he commanded the 191 soldiers, sailors, and marines who accompanied him. On October 4, the Japanese loaded these prisoners on the forty-five hundred–ton transport *Kinkon Maru*. The ship sat in the dock for three days until it finally got under way on October 7, headed for Singapore.[5]

Conditions aboard the *Kinkon Maru* were awful. The ship's hold, within which the POWs were to spend the next seven days, was divided into two sections, and each section was subdivided into three tiers by three wooden platforms. Space aboard the ship was extremely limited, the Japanese having built these platforms with that fact in mind. Each tier was only about thirty inches below the next, allowing the prisoners only enough room to sit during the voyage. Prior to taking on its human cargo in Java, the *Kinkon*

Maru served the Japanese by hauling sacks of rice and other grains. Over the months some grain had spilled, and it combined with the water that seeped in through leaks in the ship's hold and began to rot. The stench of the rotting grain was nearly unbearable for the prisoners, and there was no way to get fresh air in the hold. Rodents feeding on the rotting grain infested the ship. A single bare light bulb lowered into the compartment illuminated each section of the hold, and it swayed with the waves, eerily lighting this prison hulk but never reaching the far corners of the hold.[6]

Although the hold was not fit for human habitation, the Japanese made the conditions worse through overcrowding. The prisoners lowered themselves into the hold on a ladder, and then crawled to the back of their respective platforms until they reached the ship's hull. Once each platform was filled, the guards forced more prisoners into the hold by yelling, kicking, and beating the prisoners until they yielded and crowded on top of each other. According to author Gregory Michno, each POW had a space of about two feet by five feet in which to live for the trip to Singapore.[7] The overcrowding and the lack of fresh air, combined with the equatorial heat, the steel hull of the ship, and the rotting grain, made the temperature in the *Kinkon Maru* virtually unbearable; prisoners estimated the temperature in the hold to have been at least 120 degrees Fahrenheit.[8] Eddie Fung recalled: "I have never read about Dante's Hell, but that comes to mind. There we were—damned near 200 of us—stuffed in that ship's hold with horse manure and fermented rice on the deck. The feeling of claustrophobia and the heat was intense. I swore to God if I ever got out of there, I would never complain about the heat again."[9]

The POWs on the *Kinkon Maru* also suffered from insufficient food and water. The Japanese supplied cooked rice to be distributed among the prisoners, but it always proved inadequate. The food the prisoners brought aboard the ship was quickly consumed, and they scrounged what little they could to add to their diet. Donald Brain described how they were fed: "[The Japanese] would pass wooden buckets of rice down to us. The first day we were fed aboard there, when the first bucket of rice was sent down, not everybody got some. A portion of the guys got a pretty good ration of rice, and we thought there would be another bucket coming down. There wasn't. Come to find out that was it. In the end, if everyone had gotten a share, you would probably have gotten maybe a tablespoon-and-a-half of rice. That was all, and that was if everyone had some rice doled out to them."[10]

Fung and others managed to find a store of onions intended for the Japanese, and they distributed them among the prisoners. Fung was so hungry that he ate the onions like they were apples.[11] The Japanese provided no water for the prisoners, only occasional allotments of tea. *Houston* survivor James ("Packrat") McCone—who earned his nickname by becoming a voracious scrounger while at Bicycle Camp—managed to bring aboard a five-gallon can filled with water that he shared during the trip, while others had to find what little water they could. Some, like Fung, caught dripping condensation from the ship's steam pipes.[12]

Sanitation facilities on the *Kinkon Maru* were predictably deplorable. The Japanese built a jerry-rigged *benjo*, or latrine, on the deck of the ship. This contraption was made of wood and looked very unstable, but to make matters worse, it was built hanging off the ship's deck. To use this "two-holer," a prisoner had to work his way out of the hold and convince the guards that it was an emergency. Once on deck and in the *benjo*, the POW could look down as he defecated and see the ocean passing below.[13] The Japanese made no effort to provide medicine or otherwise tend to the sick on this prison ship, and those suffering from dysentery made innumerable trips to the *benjo*, if they could get out of the hold.[14] Finally, after three days sitting in Tanjong Priok and four days on the ocean, the *Kinkon Maru* docked at Singapore and offloaded its miserable cargo.

The second and more numerous group of Americans left Java on October 11, on the *Dai Nichi Maru*, along with several hundred other Allied prisoners. This group of Americans, under the command of Colonel Tharp, encountered conditions quite similar to those on the *Kinkon Maru*. The hold of this ship was also divided into two compartments, each with wooden platforms dividing the compartments into three tiers. Space between each tier measured about thirty inches, again enough room to sit but not to stand. The Japanese jammed the prisoners into the hold, filling the bottom level first, with the prisoners moving to the back of their respective tiers until they filled each level. Lt. Julius Heinen of F Battery described this process: "[The guards] started the people down in there. They made them take up their places and lay down. Now as they filled up the bottom, then they started filling up the center, and then they started filling up the top. Now when all of that was full and you thought you were cramped, there were still men with no place to put their body that had to get down that hold. So they made space. They just took a rifle butt and jammed it at the guy who was closest. Well, of course, his reaction was to try to get away from the rifle butt that was coming at him, and he moved backwards with as much force as he could, and that left an area where another man could get in. So you were jammed into that hold as jammed as you can possibly put people. There was just no way to put anybody else [in the hold]."[15]

The prisoners were so crowded on the *Dai Nichi Maru* that they had no choice but to sit between each other's legs from the front of each tier to the back against the ship's hull. The POWs slept in shifts because there was no room for all the men to lie down at one time. When one man wanted to roll over, all those near him had to roll over as well to keep from being lain upon.[16] Ilo Hard believed that each prisoner would have had more room if he were in a coffin.[17]

Sanitary conditions aboard the *Dai Nichi Maru* were appalling. In order to make space to haul more prisoners, the Japanese removed the latrine facilities from the hold and built a makeshift *benjo*, similar to the one on the *Kinkon Maru*, hanging off the ship's deck. Prisoners were required to ask permission from the guards to make a trip to the *benjo*, and if it was granted, they had to crawl over the men in front of them and up the ladder to the deck to use the facilities. Those who had contracted diarrhea or dysentery in Bicycle Camp would make up to twenty such trips each day. Not all those who were in this condition made it out of the hold before they lost control of their bowels, however, and they defecated in the hold. Many others who could not get topside urinated in buckets designated for that purpose. The smell of human excrement, urine, and body odor combined with the oppressive heat in the hold to make a sickening atmosphere in which to live.[18]

The *Dai Nichi Maru* also lacked adequate food and water for the prisoners. The Japanese removed the water storage tanks on the ship to make more room in the hold, and they limited the prisoners to a canteen of water per man per day. Julius Heinen observed, "Everybody got completely dehydrated . . . it got to where nobody could urinate because there was nothing in the body to urinate . . . There was just no fluid."[19] As happened on the *Kinkon Maru*, prisoners resorted to capturing condensation and dripping hot water from the ship's steam pipes to quench their thirst. Alf Brown risked a severe bashing by stealing tea from a guard's unattended boiling pot. He explained: "I went over there, and I was about to die for something to drink, and that damned stuff was hot. It was strong tea, and it was so hot it was pitiful. But I sat there and drank that whole damned thing."[20]

Once again, the shortage of food became a major concern aboard the ship. The Japanese cooked rice for the POWs, and they either lowered buckets of it into the hold twice a day or the prisoners came on deck to receive their rations. The officers carefully kept watch over the distribution of the rice, making sure that each prisoner received a level cupful of the dirty, gelatinous slop. Naturally, the amount of rice provided did not satisfy the appetites of the POWs, especially those who contracted illnesses on the ship, and they searched for other ways to augment their rations. They shared and quickly devoured the canned goods they sneaked aboard the ship and searched for food to steal from the Japanese. Some of the more intrepid prisoners broke into a Japanese storeroom and discovered large quantities of dried potatoes, which they shared with the others. Kyle Thompson called this gift "a God-sent treasure."[21]

The conditions aboard the *Dai Nichi Maru* were like nothing the prisoners had ever imagined. The lack of sufficient food, the insufferable heat, the sickening stench in the hold, and the severe overcrowding, combined with the dire lack of fluids in the prisoners' bodies and the rough treatment by the guards made this a trip many of the men would like to forget.[22] Sailor Paul Papish described his experience: "It's a horror story . . . It was a living hell. You lived in your own filth, you ate in your own filth and the filth around you. I don't know. It's man's inhumanity to man. I can't understand and will never understand how a living human being can treat another living human being the way that we were treated on those ships."[23]

The conditions on the *Dai Nichi Maru* reminded Max Offerle of the pirate books he read in school: "It's almost beyond imagination to think that you were actually in this situation when you look back on it."[24] According to sailor Seldon Reese, "Aboard the *Dai Nichi Maru* conditions were pure hell . . . It was hotter than holy hell, and it stunk! God, that place stunk! I can't for the life of me remember how we were fed or when. All I remember is that that ship was hell!"[25]

Most of the prisoners were in reasonably good health at this point, however, and survived the trip in good condition. Having been in captivity for only six months and having spent the previous five months in Bicycle Camp, few suffered from serious illnesses. Many contracted dysentery, for sure, and others may have suffered from seasickness and malaria on the *Dai Nichi Maru*, but the prisoners maintained most of their weight and strength, and they still had limited quantities of medicine available with which to treat minor ailments. No men died on the *Dai Nichi Maru* during the short, but hellish, voyage to Singapore, which they reached on October 14, 1942.[26]

Upon arriving in Singapore, the American POWs left their ships and were sent by truck to the Changi prisoner-of-war camp. Changi, located on the northeastern tip of the island, was a large complex built by the British to house their troops defending Singapore. When the Japanese took Singapore in February 1942, the British surrendered more than fifty thousand soldiers on the island, most of which the Japanese interned at Changi. The Japanese ordered that the British be responsible for the administration of the camp, which included feeding and medical care, as well as the maintenance of discipline among the prisoners. Although the Japanese prisoner-of-war administration oversaw the British, and although Japanese and Korean guards patrolled the camp, for all practical purposes the British were in charge of all prisoners regardless of nationality.[27]

Conditions at Changi were similar to those at Bicycle Camp. British designed and built, the camp contained large, three-story masonry barracks, each wired for electricity. The barracks had long, open breezeways, and there was no glass in the permanently open windows, which allowed fresh air to flow freely throughout the buildings. British and Australian prisoners erected shower facilities in camp and dug deep antimalarial trenches and bore-hole latrines to help keep insect-borne diseases to a minimum. A high barbed-wire fence surrounded Changi on three sides, and the fourth side was open to the ocean; if a prisoner were to escape, he would have to swim through the shark-infested waters to gain his freedom. The Japanese segregated the prisoners according to nationality, and in March 1942 barbed-wire fences were built to fully separate the British, the Australians, the Scots, and the other prisoners in Changi; prisoners were required to possess a pass to move from one section of the camp to another. The most imposing feature of the Changi camp was the concrete-and-steel civilian jail, Changi Gaol, located just outside the camp.[28]

When the Americans arrived in Singapore, they had already learned the rudiments of how to survive in a Japanese prison camp, and they honed their survival skills here at Changi. The POWs who arrived aboard the *Kinkon Maru*, under Captain Fitzsimmons, spent only two weeks at Changi before they were shipped to Burma, but most of the Americans under Colonel Tharp remained here until January 1943. The Americans inhabited the area known as Roberts Barracks in the camp, where they tried to make life as comfortable as possible.[29]

The POWs' quarters at Changi were similar to those in Batavia. Hundreds of prisoners lived in each of the large three-story barracks, but overcrowding was not a serious problem. The Japanese provided no beds for the prisoners, and the Americans became adept at scrounging materials to build their own bunks. Service Battery's Herbert Morris found and repaired a discarded British medical stretcher that served as his bed during his stay at Changi.[30] Others improvised sleeping facilities as best they could, including stealing wood from the Japanese to make their own bunks. Some collected pieces of scrap metal that they formed into bed frames and then covered the frames with blankets or improvised mattresses. Packrat McCone somehow managed to acquire enough pipe and plumbing supplies to build a shower, for American use only.[31]

Despite their ingenuity, most of the POWs still were deprived of a good night's sleep by the ever-present bedbugs in Changi. The insects tormented the men as they crawled into the beds and feasted on the blood of the POWs. Herbert Morris described his battle with these parasites: "When you got everything cleared out, you could walk over, and you could see those darned bedbugs traveling up the wall . . . It was just like you had almost taken a bucket of paint or something. It looked sort of [like] dark brown paint. If you was lucky enough to get something to sleep on, like, an ol' piece of a cot or an ol' piece of a stretcher or something, those bedbugs would get down on that darned thing, and, man, after a while it looked like somebody had been murdered on that [bed] where you would roll over and mash them. Your own blood was all over the darned thing where they had sucked it out and then you had mashed them. They liked to drove me up the wall."[32]

Morris and others tried with varying degrees of success to combat the bedbugs. They found that if they placed cans of water or oil under all four of a bed's legs, the bedbugs would not cross through the liquid and would then leave them alone. After one particularly difficult night, Quaty Gordon took his bed out of the barracks and bounced it on the ground to dislodge the critters. Recalling the number of bedbugs that fell from his bed, he remarked, "My God, it looked like I'd poured peppercorns on the floor."[33]

Many of the prisoners began to suffer from a variety of illnesses while at Changi. Nutritional deficiencies caused by a lack of vitamins in their predominantly rice diet brought on a number of diseases, such as beriberi and pellagra. Others contracted dysentery, which was spread by the innumerable flies that lived off the human waste. Sick prisoners were sent to the camp hospital, where they received only the most basic treatment. Frank Ficklin developed stomach ulcers in Changi and spent over three months in the hospital while doctors treated him. Quaty Gordon grudgingly assented to undergo surgery in the hospital, and the surgeons removed a growth from his head. The Japanese supplied very little in the way of medical supplies, so the doctors and orderlies in Changi made do with what they brought with them into the camp or with what they could procure through trading on the camp's thriving black market.[34]

Most of the Americans complained about the food they received while at Changi. As before, rice was the main staple of their diet, and they ate this three times a day. The morning meal consisted of what the Dutch called "pap," a porridge-like emulsion of ground rice and water that occasionally contained weevils and worms. The prisoners ate their rations of steamed rice and thin vegetable stew for lunch and dinner, accompanied by whatever they could find to flavor the fare. Eddie Fung remembered that they once received a ration of mutton while at Changi. Although the mutton was very old—Fung said that the butcher's stamp on the frozen lamb read

"1931"—and there was not enough meat for each of the prisoners to receive a portion, it did help flavor the stew.[35] The POWs would add most anything to their meals for flavor, but they especially enjoyed native chili peppers and peanuts with their rice, and sugar always proved to be a godsend.

As their hunger continued to grow, the Americans found new ways to supplement their rations. As they ran out of the canned goods they brought from Java, they traded with locals for extra food, as well as with the Australians and British in the camp. The British also ran a canteen at Changi, and the Americans bought foodstuffs there with their dwindling supply of funds.[36] Sailor Paul Papish became so desperate for vegetables and vitamins in his diet that he picked through his own feces to retrieve seeds from a cherry tomato he had eaten so he could plant the seeds and grow more tomatoes.[37] According to Papish, "To be really hungry is just indescribable. It's just the idea that, 'By God, here I am! I'm a human being! I need food, and there's nobody that's going to give it to me!'"[38]

During their short stay in Changi, the American prisoners labored for the Japanese on a variety of work details. As was the case with all work details to this point, the men relished the opportunity to leave the boredom and routine of the camp, and they took advantage of this time to acquire more food. The men worked for the Japanese in warehouses and built military fortifications on Singapore, but most either worked cutting firewood to be used in camp or labored clearing rubber trees in an area that, the Japanese explained, would be turned into a large vegetable garden allegedly to feed the prisoners. The work details operated much as they did on Java, with the POWs leaving camp in the morning, accompanied by an officer and Japanese or Korean guards. The prisoners cleared trees at a slow pace, only fast enough to keep the guards from beating them, and when the guards were distracted, a prisoner would sneak off into the jungle to make contact with native civilians to trade. A typical workday lasted until about four or five o'clock in the afternoon, at which time the work party marched back into camp.[39]

The Americans made the most of these work parties, not just trading for food or stealing from the Japanese on the docks but also in lightening their mood and building a POW community. They viewed these details as an opportunity to work alongside each other in the open air, to tell jokes and stories about their past, and to collectively deceive their captors at every opportunity. Working together in this way built a sense of camaraderie among the POWs; they grew to know and understand each other. They discovered others who shared common interests and backgrounds and became friends. Conversely, they also became aware of other POWs whom they did not care to be around for one reason or another, and they learned to avoid them. The cliques that they started in Bicycle Camp grew and became stronger in Changi.

The Japanese did not understand the way the Americans, who in their eyes had disgraced themselves by surrendering, approached and carried out their work. These prisoners continually laughed and joked and did not take things too seriously. For instance, on the woodcutting and gardening details, the prisoners loaded the wood or produce on trucks the Japanese had taken from the British on Singapore. The Japanese scavenged the engines, the transmissions, and even the cabs and sheet metal from these vehicles, leaving only the frames, steering wheels, and tires and wheels. After filling the backs of these trucks, the Americans then pushed them into camp, with one prisoner at the wheel steering. If the work site was above the camp on a hill, the POWs pushed the trucks as fast as they could down the hill, racing each other to camp. The trucks had no brakes and very little steering, and they careened off trees and rocks and came rumbling into camp until they came to a stop. The cargo seldom made it to camp during one of these races. Despite the danger of the race, not to mention the surety of being beaten by their guards, the young Americans rolled with laughter at what they had done, while the Japanese could not understand what made them behave in such a manner. The Americans kept their sense of humor at a time when there was nothing amusing about their predicament.[40]

When they were not out on work parties or keeping up their section of the camp, the prisoners passed their time in the usual manner. The bull sessions continued apace, and although they still talked about the progress of the war and their hometowns, food remained the most important topic. They continued to swap recipes with each other, even inviting the Australians and the Scots who were in camp to join them in their culinary fantasy world. Those who could acquire reading material spent hours poring over the same lines they had read dozens of times. Lester Rasbury resumed his business of selling baked goods in Changi; this time he baked and sold cakes.[41] The prisoners played endless games of poker in Changi, the stakes being cigarettes or cans of food or, perhaps, one's next meal of rice and stew. The British held classes on a variety of subjects here, and many prisoners attended regularly; this school eventually garnered the nickname "Changi University." Changi also contained a makeshift theater in which British and Australian POWs performed shows for the entertainment of all.[42]

Although the British did much to improve life in Changi, their relations with the Americans were, at best, strained. The Americans often found themselves at odds with the British over any number of issues, and they constantly bickered with each other. The Americans did not resent the British for being in charge of the camp—the Americans could hardly have performed the task—but they resented the British for the manner in which they ran the camp. The British labored to maintain discipline in Changi, which to them meant standard British military discipline. They expected enlisted men to pay due respect to their officers, which included saluting them, as they tried to maintain the standard formalities of military life. The British naturally reasoned that in order to keep the POWs' spirits up, they had to keep them from degenerating into a rabble. Therefore, officers maintained the strict military caste system and separated themselves from the enlisted men. The men were expected to line up for roll call, to perform daily calisthenics, keep their barracks clean, and to behave like British soldiers.[43]

This did not sit well with the Americans. Since becoming prisoners in March 1942, they had dropped all military formalities and had adopted by common consent an unspoken and informal discipline within the ranks. The American POWs saw themselves as relatively equal to one another, regardless of rank, and saw no reason to behave as the British expected. The Americans thought that the British officers were smug and that they projected an air of superiority over other prisoners. American POWs were expected to salute British officers, which seemed demeaning. P. J. Smallwood said, "We didn't salute our own [officers]. I mean, why should we salute them?"[44] Johnny Buck believed the British officers "had a superiority complex."[45] Of the British officers, Ilo Hard commented: "They still didn't quite know they were prisoners, in a way."[46]

There were many specific, tangible issues that also broke down relations between the two groups. Early in their stay at Changi, British officers ordered American enlisted men to move the officers' possessions from one barrack to another, and the Americans naïvely complied. The next day the British ordered the Americans to perform more labor for them, and when this was finally relayed to Colonel Tharp, the American commander put an end to it by demanding that the British perform the work themselves.[47] The British also arranged the daily work details, and often the Americans received the less-than-choice jobs. The British controlled the distribution of hand tools that the prisoners used in a work party, and the Americans always seemed to receive the shovels and hoes with broken handles.[48]

The two groups also encountered problems over the most important issue: food. The British controlled the distribution of uncooked rice, and each day the American cooks lined up to receive their allotment from British officers. The Americans were convinced that the British were holding back on them, keeping more rice for themselves and getting fat while the Americans went hungry. All the American prisoners claimed that the British withheld the coveted Red Cross parcels and divided them among themselves, cheating the Americans out of the food, clothing, and cigarettes they believed was rightfully theirs.[49]

The issue of sanitation and personal hygiene was also a major point of contention between the Americans and British. Since early in their captivity, the Americans tried to maintain high standards of cleanliness. They bathed as often as possible and washed their clothes at every opportunity. At mealtime they dipped their mess gear in boiling water to kill any germs and to remove any food residue, lest it attract the ever-present flies. The Americans never drank water unless it had first been boiled to remove impurities. Because they adhered so closely to these standards, the Americans suffered less from illness than did other nationalities. The British, according to the Americans, took no such pains. They complained bitterly about the lack of cleanliness on the part of the British, who did not bathe frequently enough to satisfy the Americans, and they wore filthy clothes that carried a stench. According to Lawrence Brown, "You could smell [a British prisoner] coming from a mile away."[50]

The Americans did not like being subservient to the British officers and sought retribution in whatever small ways they could. Although the Americans are proud that they never stole from one another, the "Yanks" took a certain satisfaction from stealing from the "Limeys" whenever they got a chance. British officers maintained a number of chicken coops in Changi, which provided them with vital protein in the form of eggs and meat. The Americans often broke into these coops and stole eggs and, occasionally, chickens.[51]

Perhaps the most famous—or infamous—of the incidents between these two groups involved what were known as the "King's Coconuts." Since Singapore was part of the British Empire, British officers concluded that all things on the island belonged to their king. Monkeys were the king's monkeys; lizards were the king's lizards; trees were the king's trees. One evening while scrounging for food outside camp, some American POWs began chopping down a palm tree to harvest the coconuts that grew there. British MPs discovered the Americans' activity and immediately ordered them to stop. When the Americans asked why they should stop, the MPs replied that the coconuts they were taking belonged to the king and that the Americans were, therefore, stealing the king's coconuts. According to Max Offerle: "I don't know who it was, but some Limey hollered out, 'Quit cutting down that tree! That's the king's coconut tree and the king's coconuts!' If I'm not mistaken, [the Americans] said, 'To hell with the king! And to hell with his coconuts! We're going to cut it down, anyway!' They were typical British."[52]

Incidents like this one occurred regularly between the Americans and the British. National rivalries naturally developed in an environment like the one in Changi, and each group saw itself as being distinct from, and in many cases superior to, prisoners from other countries. It was important for the POWs, who had so much taken from them, to maintain their identity as individuals. An important part of that identity was the knowledge that they belonged to a larger community of like individuals. The Americans saw themselves as being distinct from others in the camp, and they were proud of their nationality. This pride in being American—and even more specifically for most of the POWs, the pride in being Texan—allowed them to differentiate themselves from others in the camp. They were not faceless, nameless prisoners skulking through the barracks; they were Americans.

Although the Americans maintained this pride—or outright chauvinism—they got along quite well with prisoners from other countries. They certainly disliked British officers, and they would condemn the British as a group, but many of the Americans forged friendships with individual British prisoners. As at Bicycle Camp, the Americans and the Australians got along famously, trading with each other, sharing food, gambling, and telling stories during their bull sessions. The Americans encountered a group of Scottish POWs at Changi, as well, and they held the Scots in very high regard. Ilo Hard said of the Scots: "They took us in as long-lost cousins."[53] Dan Buzzo explained why he believed the Americans enjoyed such good relations with the Scots: "They hated the British [English], too."[54] When the largest contingent of Americans left Changi in January 1943, the Scots played their bagpipes to honor them, "piping" them out of camp. The Scots reserved this honor only for the Americans, something the Americans remember with a great deal of pride.[55]

The voyages to and the time spent in Changi taught the men of the 2nd Battalion and their sailor and marine comrades a number of lessons. The time on the prison hulks, or "hell ships," gave the prisoners an indication of what little value the Japanese placed on their lives. They were treated like cattle on board those ships, and the Japanese felt no compunction to provide more than the most rudimentary care for them. They were lucky to survive the voyage. Once they arrived in Changi, they were again herded into a deplorable environment and were given little food and medical care.

It became clear that if they were going to survive captivity, they were going to have to use their survival skills to do so. American prisoners became better scroungers at Changi; they picked up parts of a variety of local languages to aid them in their trading; and they stuck close together to protect themselves from outsiders, whether they were Japanese, Korean, or British. They began to rely even more heavily on the others in their cliques to help them through each day, and these quasi-familial bonds brought them closer together. When the Americans left Changi, they had in place the most important mechanisms to aid their survival. When they left Changi, however, their new environment would challenge them in ways they could never have imagined.

Chapter 6

Into the Jungle

WHEN THE MAJORITY OF THE AMERICAN PRISONERS LEFT CHANGI between October 1942 and January 1943, the Japanese once again promised that their new destination would be a better place to live. The Japanese explained that the POWs would be involved in a very important project and that their participation in this would warrant better living conditions. Their captors promised better and more plentiful food, better quarters and medical care, and kinder treatment. The prisoners had heard rumors concerning their next move. Some said they were heading to Japan to work in the factories; others said the coal mines; some even held out hope that they would be repatriated in an exchange of prisoners between the United States and Japan. They soon learned that the promise of improved conditions was just a ruse, however, and that the Japanese intended to force them to labor on what was to be known as the infamous Burma-Thailand "Death Railway."

Their experience on this terrible stretch of wood and steel was, unfortunately, a defining one in the lives of the American prisoners. The conditions they faced were horrendous; the treatment they endured was ghastly. Only those who could quickly adjust to the miserable environment they encountered stood a chance of surviving, and adaptability was no guarantee they would live. The survival techniques the POWs learned and employed to this point helped them live through the trying months at Bicycle Camp and Changi, as well as the voyages on the "hell ships." Building the "Death Railway" would test these young men in unimaginable new ways, however, as they discovered that their struggle to live had just begun.[1]

In 1942, the Japanese began construction of the railway connecting the port city of Moulmein, Burma, to Bangkok, Thailand. This stretch of railway tied the existing rail system in Burma with the system running north from Singapore to Bangkok, which then turned northwest until it terminated at Ban Pong, Thailand. From Ban Pong, the proposed line followed the Mae Klong River northwest until it crossed the river at Kanburi (or Kanchanaburi). From this point the road paralleled the Kwae Noi River northwest across the Thailand plain and then through the mountains in western Thailand until it squeezed through Three Pagodas Pass near the Burmese border. The railway then snaked down through the mountains until it joined the Burmese rail line at Thanbyuzayat, south of Moulmein.[2]

Earlier in the century the British had surveyed this same route, hoping to make the railroad a reality to facilitate transportation in this part of the empire. They quickly abandoned the project, however, due to what they believed were construction factors impossible to overcome. The dense jungle characteristic of the area would have to be hacked away in order to lay out a right-of-way. Traversing the mountains in western Thailand and eastern Burma, the railway would cut through a region containing countless fast-flowing rivers and streams, especially during the six-month-long monsoon season. The terrain and jungle made supplying the workforce extremely problematic, since there were no passable roads, and it was difficult to employ enough workers to accomplish this task. Finally, this region was known to have been rife with tropical diseases that would inevitably take a toll on all those working on the line. Thus, the British gave up on the project because it was too costly in terms of money and lives.[3]

The Japanese were willing to accept this challenge in 1942, however, and they did so for a number of reasons. First, the railway was desirable from a military standpoint. The Japanese maintained a large army in Burma as they tried to wrest control of the country from the British, and they planned to ultimately launch an invasion of India from Burma. They wanted to improve communications and logistics between Japan and its forces in Burma, and the railway would serve such a purpose. Up to this point in the war, the Japanese supplied their forces in Burma by sea, which put a severe strain on the limited Japanese merchant marine. Also, in order to reach Burma by sea, Japanese ships had to sail around the Malay Peninsula past Singapore, then sail north up the coast through the Strait of Malacca and the Andaman Sea before reaching Moulmein. By mid-1942, Allied submarines and bombers were inflicting unacceptable losses on Japanese shipping in this area, so the sea route proved too costly. If they were able to supply Burma by rail, the Japanese could ease the pressure on their overextended merchant marine and avoid Allied attacks at sea. The Japanese also hoped to exploit the natural resources in this region and needed the railroad to expedite the process.[4]

The Japanese had an advantage denied the British: a large labor force. The Imperial Japanese Army took tens of thousands of prisoners during their conquest of Southeast Asia and saw no reason for them to live idly in prisoner-of-war camps. According to Japanese military beliefs, as expressed in the code of Bushido, the POWs had disgraced themselves, their families, and their country when they were captured. The prisoners were, therefore, not fit to live, but they might be put to some good use laboring for the emperor. Altogether, some 62,000 Allied prisoners of war worked on the Burma-Thailand railway.[5] The Japanese also conscripted more than 250,000 Asian workers for the project.[6] With these factors set in place, the Japanese ordered the prisoners to go to work.

The American POWs left Changi in two separate groups. The first group of 191 prisoners, under Capt. Arch Fitzsimmons of Headquarters Battery, spent only two weeks in Changi before leaving for Burma in October 1942.[7] They made up part of "Branch Party 3," which was a large contingent of POWs under the command of Lt. Col. C. M. Black. After a week's journey by sea on another of the "hell ships," the POWs arrived in Moulmein. Most of the men were still in fairly good physical condition at this point, although disease and malnutrition were beginning to sap the strength of the prisoners. *Houston* survivor Jimmie Gee described his arrival in Moulmein: "This particular night that we pulled in they dropped the anchor, and we were preparing to get off the ship. The moon was the most beautiful red that I have ever seen, with the palm trees and with the surrounding dense vegetation and all that you could see along the river . . . You could see these sparse, scattered lights and the jungle terrain and growth with this moon shining that lit the ground almost as though the sun was shining. And I shall never forget the beauty that surrounded us as we made our way by these small boats into the landing."[8]

After spending a week in a Moulmein jail, the prisoners marched to the city's train station for shipment to the railway. The POWs encountered Burmese civilians on the way to the station and were greeted with an outpouring of sympathy. The Japanese occupied Burma, and the country was under their rule, but the Burmese expressed their emotions toward the prisoners. Eddie Fung explained: "There I encountered an experience of humanity that I'll never forget . . . Here the whole population of Moulmein was along the route of our march from the prison to the railroad station tossing out cigarettes, bananas, candy, and all sorts of things . . . The Japanese tried to stop them, but it didn't do any good . . . I had never seen grown men break down and cry, but we did. I mean, it was just that kind of an experience. The Burmese were out there for only one purpose, and that was to try to give us something—fruit, cigarettes, candy. So by the time we got down to the station, why, all of us had something that they'd given to us."[9]

From the train station the POWs traveled to the railhead at Thanbyuzayat and began work on the railroad. Because of time constraints placed on the building of the railway, the Japanese started the construction of the line from both ends. On the Thailand side, Branch Parties 1, 2, 4, and 6 worked from Ban Pong toward Burma. Branch Parties 3 and 5, based out of Thanbyuzayat, worked southeastward toward Thailand. Thanbyuzayat served as a base camp on the Burma end of the railway, and all workers, tools, and materials were funneled through this camp.[10]

The Japanese welcomed the prisoners to Thanbyuzayat by informing them of the role they would play in the construction of the railroad. Because they had shamed themselves by surrendering, the prisoners' lives meant little to the Japanese. The Japanese did not wish to feed and care for their captives, but they would do so in return for their labor in the jungle. Lt. Col. Yoshitida Nagatomo, the commanding officer of the Burma branch of the railroad, delivered a speech to the men of Branch Party 3 when they arrived at the base camp in which he explained the work to be done, as well as the prisoners' place in this work: "You are only a few remaining skeletons after the invasion of East Asia for the past few centuries, and are pitiful victims . . . However, I shall not treat you badly for the sake of humanity as you have no fighting power left at all . . . The [Japanese emperor's] thoughts are unestimable and the Imperial Favors are infinite and, as such, you should weep with gratitude at the greatness of them . . . We will build the railroad if we have to build it over the white man's body. It gives me great pleasure to have a fast-moving defeated nation in my power. You are merely rubble . . . If you want anything you will have to come through me for same and there will be many of you who will not see your homes again. Work cheerfully at my command."[11] If the prisoners had any doubt concerning their place as captives of the Japanese, it was cleared away at Thanbyuzayat.[12]

Living conditions at Thanbyuzayat were typical of those camps all along the line. Prisoners were housed in bamboo huts with thatched atap roofs, roughly 150 feet long by 20 feet wide (see figures 6.1, 6.2, and 6.3). A long aisle bisected each hut, with bamboo platforms on either side of this aisle. The Japanese provided no beds for the POWs, so they slept on these

Figure 6.1 Typical bamboo and atap huts constructed in camps along the railway.
Courtesy of the USS *Houston* Survivors Association.

platforms, which were about one and one-half feet above the ground. Each prisoner received just enough space on a platform to lie down without touching those next to him. The walls of the huts were three feet high and were open to the outside, and the atap roofs overhung the walls to keep out most of the rain. Eddie Fung described his new quarters: "They would cram in as many men as they could . . . If you were lucky, you would be off the ground so that during the rainy season, if the water ran through the hut, you wouldn't get completely wet. Still, the atap roof might leak, but if it didn't, the wind would still drive the rain in, because the huts were open-sided, open-ended as a rule. It was difficult to get any restful sleep, because aside from the fact that there were bedbugs in the bamboo slats, just being out in the open was enough to be uncomfortable."[13]

One hut was set aside to serve as a hospital for the camp, but it was not sterile, and there was almost no medicine. Each camp housed between two thousand and four thousand POWs, although there were others large enough to hold up to twelve thousand prisoners.[14] There were no fences around any of these camps because escape was impossible. The Japanese

Figure 6.2 View of a typical jungle camp in Thailand.
Courtesy of the USS *Houston* Survivors Association.

placed bounties on escaped prisoners to encourage Burmese natives to turn them in or to provide information about escaped POWs, and white Allied prisoners were very conspicuous among the Asian population. Even if a prisoner could escape, which was highly unlikely, he had to find his way through hundreds of miles of dense jungle and then secure means to sail to Allied-occupied territory. According to Hud Wright, "We could have escaped anytime we wanted to, but where would you go?"[15]

The Japanese sent groups of POWs to various points along the line, where they stayed in camps that had been built in advance by Burmese natives. Each camp was identified according to its distance in kilometers from Thanbyuzayat, and after leaving the base camp the prisoners in Branch Party 3 initially walked to 40 Kilo Camp. Each day the Japanese sent out work parties of about fifty men, known as *kumis*; the senior Japanese noncommissioned officer in charge of each *kumi* was the *kumicho*. Two *kumis* made up a *han*, and the senior officer in charge was the *hancho*. The 191 Americans in the

Figure 6.3 Interior of hut at Wampo, Thailand.
Courtesy of the Australian War Memorial.

Fitzsimmons group served as an advance party on the rail line, clearing trees
and underbrush from the railroad right-of-way all along the Burma side of
the line. They also worked to maintain the camps, digging wells for drinking water and repairing huts. Jungle conditions quickly took a toll on all
structures, and the jungle rapidly reclaimed cleared land. The Fitzsimmons
group moved from 40 Kilo back to 25 Kilo in late November 1942, and they
were working at this camp when the rest of the Americans reached Burma
in January 1943.[16]

The second and more numerous group of Americans made up part
of Branch Party 5, which left Changi on January 9, 1943, under the command of Colonel Tharp. This group contained 463 Americans who, along
with Australian, British, and Dutch POWs, left Singapore by train bound for
the port city of Penang on the western coast of the Malay Peninsula. At the
train station in Singapore, the prisoners were loaded into small boxcars for
the journey to Penang. The boxcars measured approximately twenty feet by
eight feet, and the Japanese crowded between thirty and thirty-five prisoners in each car. The metal roofs and sides of the cars absorbed the intense
tropical sunshine, sending the temperatures in the cars soaring to well over
100 degrees (see figure 6.4). According to Kyle Thompson, "The tropical
sun transformed the cars into ovens, and we were forced to stay in them for
what seemed like hours. Sweat ran from every pore."[17]

Figure 6.4 Example of railway boxcars used to transport prisoners of war. Commonly, between thirty and forty POWs were transported in each car. Courtesy of the Australian War Memorial.

Because there was very little room in the boxcars, the POWs were forced to stand crowded together for the entire trip to Penang. The boxcars also lacked latrine facilities, so the prisoners relieved themselves out the side of the car. Those who could not make their way to the doors due to sickness or the overcrowding urinated and defecated where they stood. Some of the prisoners stricken with dysentery or malnutrition became so weak they fainted in the boxcars but remained upright because they had no room to fall to the floor. The Japanese stopped the train periodically to refuel the wood-burning locomotive, and they allowed the prisoners to tumble out of the cars for fresh air and fed them small balls of rice. When the train finished taking on fuel and water, the prisoners were jammed back into the boxcars at bayonet point, and the train lurched forward to Penang.[18]

Fortunately for the POWs, the trip up the Malay Peninsula lasted just one and one-half days, and they reached Penang on January 11, 1943. At Penang the Japanese herded the prisoners down to the docks for the next stage of the journey. Kyle Thompson remembered that when they reached the docks, one of his comrades exclaimed: "Oh, no! Not another ship trip! This is too much!"[19] This time the Japanese loaded the POWs into the *Dai Moji Maru*, a five thousand–ton freighter that would take them by sea to Moulmein along with two other prison ships in the convoy. Although the conditions aboard the *Dai Moji Maru* would be considered primitive and dangerous by most observers, those in Branch Party 5 described this ship as being much better than the *Dai Nichi Maru*. The prisoners had more room, and the captain of the ship seemed kind and reasonable. The Japanese allowed the prisoners to walk about the ship freely and spend as much time on the deck as they wished. Their captors still provided little food and water, and sanitary conditions were frightful, but the guards did not harass the prisoners, so they spent most of the trip playing cards and "batting the breeze."[20]

This relative calm was violently shattered when the *Dai Moji Maru* was one day out of Moulmein. On January 15, three American B-24 bombers attacked the convoy. Most of the prisoners were below decks playing cards or were enjoying the fresh air on the main deck when the attack began. They heard a low rumbling and began to speculate on the source of the sound. Garth Slate was on the deck washing himself when he heard the drone of the planes and knew they were American. He looked up to see one of the planes drop its bomb load over the last ship in the convoy, the *Nichimei Maru*, and stared openmouthed as the bombs struck their target. Slate said, "I could see one hitting the front [of the ship], and all of a sudden all you could see was big, black smoke back there."[21] The B-24s targeted this ship because it was the largest in the convoy, and they scored a number of direct hits. The ship sank in thirty minutes, killing most of the Japanese engineers and Dutch prisoners aboard and forcing the survivors into the Andaman Sea.[22]

The American bombers returned for a second bombing run on the rest of the convoy, and this time they targeted the *Dai Moji Maru*. The Japanese scrambled to defend the helpless ship from the attackers, and they ordered, forced, and beat the prisoners down in the ship's hold. Max Offerle remembered that the Japanese threatened them with machine guns if they tried to escape the hold. Japanese soldiers manned the ship's antiaircraft gun and fired on the B-24s but only managed to hit the ship's bridge, killing some of their own men. The Japanese captain turned the ship abruptly to avoid the bombs, hoping to zigzag through the danger. Some of the Americans kept as close to the action as possible, and a number of them peeked out the hatch to give a running commentary on the action to the rest of the prisoners. Bombs fell all around the ship, lifting the bow several yards out of the water before it crashed down, sending the prisoners sprawling through the hold. Luckily, the American bombers missed their mark on the *Dai Moji Maru* and headed back to their base.[23]

The bombing raid was quite literally a near-death experience for the POWs, and they responded in different ways. Some expressed elation that the Americans were disrupting Japanese shipping at this stage of the war and in this part of the world. They reasoned that if the Americans were

capable of this kind of action, the war would soon be over. *Houston* sailor
Seldon Reese cheered the American bombers, shouting from the hold: "Hit
the son-of-a-bitch! Sink the bastard!"[24] Others received a morale boost from
the American bombing, although they admitted that they hoped their ship
would emerge unscathed. Lester Rasbury had mixed emotions about the
bombing: "I was kind of hoping to take up for myself, if I could. But we
was glad to see it, and we weren't, either. We at least knew [the U.S. Army
Air Forces] were still doing something."[25] Kelly Bob Bramlett described his
reaction: "Well, you hate to get it from your own people, but you're glad to
see them out, too, you know."[26] To Johnny Buck, the reaction was simple:
"I guess I was partial toward the Americans, but I wasn't caring about them
hitting us."[27] Wade Webb spoke for many others: "I guess I had to pull for the
Japs, because I wanted to stay afloat. You know, you can't straddle the fence,
so I had to go with the Japs on this one."[28]

Regardless of whom they were rooting for, the common reaction among
the Americans was one of fear. They were packed down in the hold of the
ship with no chance to get out while the bombs rocked and pitched the
ship helplessly in the sea. The Japanese provided no life preservers or life
rafts for the prisoners, so if the bombs found their target, the POWs would
go down with the ship. The noise and the concussion caused by the bombs
rattled the men, and they were tossed throughout the hold. The air in the
hold was filled with dirt and rust as the ship repeatedly slammed down
in the water, and it was nearly impossible to see. Some of the men were
screaming and trying to escape the hold, only to trip over other POWs who
had been thrown to the deck. Dan Buzzo claimed that "[it was] near panic,
near chaos. There was a lot of scrambling."[29]

The bombing did nothing for Kyle Thompson's morale. It only frightened him. Thompson described his experience: "Japanese guards had kept
us in the holds at gunpoint, and we huddled there, gripped in fear. Being bombed at sea is one of the most helpless experiences imaginable. The
target is precisely and indisputably the very ship which is your temporary
shelter. I closed my eyes tightly and wrapped myself in a fetal position, my
arms entwined tightly about my head. Never had I known such fear. Being
bombed anywhere is bad enough, but at sea it is the worst of ordeals. There's
no running, no escape."[30]

Charley Pryor, a marine from the *Houston*, said, "Well, like I've told
people since, many times I've been scared—you might say 'scared out of
your wits'—but I would suspect that I was probably as scared that day, and
concerned that day, as I'll ever be in all my life."[31] As frightening as the experience was for the trapped prisoners, none of the Americans were killed,

and only a few suffered injuries from broken glass and shrapnel.[32] The POWs even recalled that some of the Japanese guards treated them more kindly in the aftermath of the bombing, probably brought on by the utter fear experienced by Japanese.[33] In Lester Rasbury's experience, however, the guards treated the men more roughly.[34]

After the planes left the badly damaged convoy, the captain of the *Dai Moji Maru* returned to pick up the survivors of the sunken *Nichimei Maru*. Hundreds of Dutch prisoners and Japanese technicians still clung to life, floating in the turbulent sea. The prisoners worked with the Japanese soldiers to pull the survivors from the water and, if possible, to give them medical treatment. Sailor Griff Douglas from the *Houston* scrambled with his medic's bag to tend to the badly injured prisoners. He encountered a Dutch prisoner lying on the deck whose wounds looked so bad that he passed him up for dead. Douglas described this scene: "The right side of his head . . . his ear was gone and an inch of the side of his head was gone like you'd taken an axe. I whirled around and looked at him, and I went on; there was a lot of other wounded laying around . . . Later that night, we was stacking the dead over to the side of the ship; I picked him up and he was alive . . . He had wood splinters in his brain, [and] bone splinters. It was the damnedest thing you ever seen for a man . . . he just laid, and after a while he got to hollering 'Oh!' in Malayan. That's what he hollered for three or four days."[35] Kyle Thompson witnessed a Dutch prisoner desperately climbing out of the water on the ship's rope ladder, only to reach the deck and die from stomach wounds.[36] Due to the influx of rescued survivors, conditions on the *Dai Moji Maru* worsened as the ship became much more crowded and rations declined accordingly.

Having survived the attack, the *Dai Moji Maru* arrived in Moulmein the next day, January 16. A tug then pulled the ship the short distance up the muddy Salaween River to the docks, where the prisoners disembarked and marched into Moulmein. The Japanese paraded the POWs through the city for the civilian population to see, finally leading them to Moulmein Prison. This prison served as the home for the POWs for the next several days, and it once again reinforced in their minds how little value their captors placed on human life. The prison was a large, three-story concrete fortress, dark and very imposing. The Japanese had established a puppet government in Burma, who sent its political opponents to rot in this filthy jail. The Americans reported seeing starving Burmese civilian prisoners, male and female alike, shuffling about the compound dragging large steel balls attached to their legs with chains. Darkness had fallen by the time the American POWs reached the prison, and the Japanese crammed them into small cells for the night. Upon waking the next morning, the Americans discovered they had spent the night in the prison's leper ward.[37]

After ten days in Moulmein Prison, the POWs again packed their few belongings and prepared to move out. This time they boarded a train bound for Thanbyuzayat and the jungle beyond. The train reached the base camp on January 27, and the prisoners then marched to their first camp at 18 Kilo. Although they had experienced some of the most dreadful conditions so far in their captivity, they were shocked at the primitiveness of their new surroundings. Like all jungle camps, 18 Kilo Camp was constructed by native Burmese laborers and consisted of the typical bamboo and atap huts built a foot off the ground. There was no running water or electricity, and the latrine facilities consisted of shallow holes in the ground, dug too near the living quarters. Flies and mosquitoes infested the camp, especially the huts in which the prisoners slept, and insect-borne diseases soon became rampant; of course, bedbugs were ever present. As with the other jungle camps, there were no fences because escape was impossible.[38]

Food at 18 Kilo was of predictably poor quality, and there was never enough to satisfy the prisoners' appetites. Twice each day the POWs lined up to receive their now-standard ration of a cup of steamed white rice, which contained maggots and worms, and a half-canteen cup of watery vegetable stew. Occasionally, the Japanese delivered a live steer or carabao to the camp—with the best cuts of meat going to the Japanese officers and guards—but one animal could not feed the twenty-five hundred prisoners here, and the meat only barely flavored their stew. Fresh well water was not available at 18 Kilo, and those prisoners lucky enough to work in the camp kitchens hauled water from nearby streams. Two prisoners would carry a cut-off fifty-five-gallon drum between them from the river to the camp, and then the water had to be boiled thoroughly before it was deemed safe to drink. Others constantly hauled firewood into the camp to fuel the ever-present fires necessary to boil water and to sanitize cooking and mess gear.[39]

To supplement their meager diet at 18 Kilo, the POWs employed the techniques they learned in Bicycle Camp and at Changi. They traded for food with each other, swapping a can of milk here for a can of beef or vegetables there, and they did the same with the Australians and others in the camp. Once again, they clandestinely traded with locals on the outside of camp, exchanging their few valuables, pieces of cloth, or their hard-earned pay for fresh fruits or blocks of native sugar, known as *gula*.[40] A kilogram of this sugar typically cost four dollars, which amounted to a half-month's wages for a POW. Protein-rich duck eggs proved to be especially valuable, although they often fetched up to two dollars apiece. When a hapless python occasionally found its way into camp, it was certain never to leave, as the hungry POWs had learned to catch, kill, and cook these serpents. They used nearly anything to flavor the bland diet of white rice and continued to prize the native chili peppers. The prisoners considered any food belonging to the Japanese to be fair game for stealing, but they attest that they never stole from one another.[41]

Tobacco was another precious commodity in camp, and the Americans discovered means to support their habit. Manufactured cigarettes, either American or Japanese, were unattainable for all practical purposes. The POWs consumed a coarse, native tobacco—known as "wog" tobacco—purchased in the form of bricks from Burmese civilians. After buying this weed in bulk, prisoners washed it and let it dry in the sun before rolling their own cigarettes. Rolling paper was also scarce, so the smokers learned to improvise by using thin banana leaves or sheets of paper from the books they kept. Eventually, they tore pages from their pocket-sized New Testaments that they were issued before leaving the States, allegedly read the Gospel on each sheet, and then rolled their tobacco in it.[42] The Americans found these wog cigarettes to be quite harsh and very strong. Kyle Thompson described smoking such a cigarette: "I recall inhaling that strong, dark brown bulk tobacco rolled up in a banana leaf and experiencing a sharp stab in my lungs that seemed to ricochet upwards in my throat and bounce off the top of my skull. It was wicked stuff, but we clung to it like a baby clings to a blanket."[43]

Medical facilities at 18 Kilo were typically substandard. The Japanese delegated one barrack as the hospital hut, and the seriously ill were "treated" here. Medicine in the jungle camps was almost nonexistent. The Japanese routinely ignored requests for medicine and supplies, forcing the POW doctors and their staffs to improvise with native cures learned from the Dutch, who had been in the East Indies for hundreds of years. Most prisoners were stricken with malaria while in the jungle, but the Japanese provided no quinine to combat the illness. If a prisoner were to survive a bout with malaria, his doctor usually had to procure precious and costly quinine tablets on the black market, or the sick man had to "sweat it out." Sweating out malaria could take over a week, during which time a prisoner ran a very high fever and became dehydrated. If a prisoner survived a bout with malaria, he could count on suffering a relapse every few months.[44]

Dysentery, caused by the unsanitary conditions in the camps, became prevalent early on in the jungle. Eventually, this affliction became epidemic as sanitary conditions worsened and as prisoners' immune systems broke down. Those suffering from dysentery routinely made twenty to thirty trips to the latrine each day. Medical officers advised prisoners to eat burned crusts of rice from the bottom of *wajans*, which they claimed contained higher amounts of vitamins, especially vitamin B. In many cases, prisoners ate plain charcoal from campfires to combat the disease; apparently, the charcoal absorbed the microbes causing dysentery, allowing the sick to pass them from their digestive systems. Diseases associated with malnutrition, such as beriberi and pellagra, typically went untreated; the only cure was nutritious, vitamin-rich food, which the Japanese were of no mind to provide.[45] Korean guards once hanged P. J. Smallwood by his thumbs on a barbed-wire fence for a day—his offense: stealing medicine from the Japanese to help treat sick POWs.[46]

At first, each nationality cared for its own sick POWs, but as the number of sick increased, the medical officers and orderlies looked after all prisoners, regardless of their country of origin. Capt. Hugh Lumpkin of the 2nd Battalion, who served as the Americans' senior medical officer, worked with Cdr. William Epstein, senior medical officer from the *Houston*, to treat the POWs. Enlisted men like Slug Wright assisted the medical officers, cleaning wounds, washing bandages for reuse, and tending to the dysentery ward (see figure 6.5). These were thankless jobs, and the Japanese made their efforts immeasurably more difficult through poor and careless administration. According to medical historian Allan Walker, "Even in these earliest episodes of Japanese railway construction camps can be seen evidence of lack of reasonable organization. The efforts of the medical officers were hindered by inefficiency and indifference, which were matched only by a complete disregard for truth and reliability [on the part of the Japanese]."[47] The medical officers and orderlies labored day and night attempting to ease the worst of the POWs' suffering, but their best efforts could not keep pace with the growing illnesses.[48]

Perhaps the most successful doctor to treat the Americans was Henri Hekking, a Dutch physician captured in the East Indies. Hekking had practiced medicine throughout these Dutch colonies prior to the war and had extensive knowledge of native plants and treatments for tropical maladies. The Japanese sent Hekking with the Fitzsimmons group in Branch Party 3, and he earned a legendary reputation among the prisoners for being able to help them when British, Australian, or American doctors could not. Hekking treated POWs through traditional native practices, such as applying certain herbs to wounds, and achieved a large degree of success. Slug Wright, who worked as Hekking's orderly, ascribed the physician's success to the fact that he cured the mind and body together; Hekking worked to keep a man's

Figure 6.5 Sketch by *Houston* survivor John W. Wisecup of conditions in dysentery ward in Kanchanaburi, Thailand. Courtesy of the Oral History Program, University of North Texas.

morale strong so he would want to survive. Wright recalled that Hekking often slipped out of camp at night to procure medicine and plants and that he would treat people in local villages on these forays.[49]

Part of maintaining good health was preserving adequate clothing, and in the jungle clothing became a major issue for the prisoners. Throughout their months in captivity, the Americans' uniforms began to wear out, and the Japanese did not bother to supply them with new clothes. By the time they reached the jungle at 18 Kilo or 40 Kilo, the Americans were down to the bare essentials in clothing. Most wore only shorts, and if they were lucky, they still had the remnants of a torn, filthy shirt hanging on their backs. Others were not so fortunate—their wardrobe consisted only of a length of cloth wrapped around their waists and up around their crotch. The Americans called this loincloth a "G-string," whereas the Australians referred to it more colorfully as a "Jap happy." Whatever one called it, this improvisation provided little protection from the insects, rocks, and vegetation of the jungle.[50]

Shoes were another concern for the prisoners, and many had none. Those without shoes improvised. Some fashioned footwear out of old tires, and others carved wooden clogs from the hard native lumber in the jungle. Even the best-quality clothes would not have lasted long in the jungle, as the humidity, mold and fungus, and highly acidic soil rapidly broke down clothing fibers. The prisoners' makeshift attire fell apart even more quickly.[51] Thomas Whitehead of Service Battery described his attire: "I had no shoes; I was going bareheaded. I had one pair of shorts that, honest to God, if I could have kept them, would have had about fifteen layers of patches. They were lice-infested. Naturally, there were lice in between some of those patches and down in some of the seams that even the strongest fumigation or boiling process for a week wouldn't have killed them all. But that's all I had, is a pair of shorts."[52]

Inadequate clothing notwithstanding, the Japanese intended to build a railroad in Burma, and they immediately put the prisoners to work. Each day the Japanese engineers and Korean guards led the kumis from camp to the construction site. At first, the prisoners felled large trees and cleared underbrush from the railroad's right-of-way; when this task was finished, they started building up the railroad bed. The railroad necessitated a level grade all along the line, which in the Burmese jungle meant moving hills and filling valleys. Thus, most of the work performed by the POWs was making "cuts"—cutting down hills—and "fills"—filling in low spots and valleys with the dirt from the cuts (see figures 6.6 and 6.7). The Japanese used no machinery in the construction of the railway, instead relying on the manpower of the prisoners and Asian conscripts. For the first few months on the railway, the POWs received one day in ten as yasumi, or holiday, during which they performed no work on the railway.[53]

The POWs received crude, primitive hand tools to move the massive amounts of earth required to build the railway bed. They worked in groups of four, one prisoner loosening the dirt with a pick or a heavy Asian grubbing hoe, known as a chunkel. Another prisoner shoveled the dirt into baskets or rice sacks that were carried off by the last two POWs. These men used what were known as "yo-ho poles," or "yo-yo poles," which usually consisted of rice sacks tied at the corners with wire to two six-foot-long bamboo poles.[54] The two men would hold the poles on their shoulders with the sack suspended between them. When the sack was filled, the prisoners transported the dirt to the common dump area, unloaded it, and then returned for another load.[55] Roy Armstrong gave his reaction to this method: "I had no idea what kind of tools we was going to build [the railroad] with. I have never thought about building a railroad with a basket and a shovel."[56]

The engineers allotted a certain amount of work for a kumi to accomplish each working day. Initially, they established a quota for each kumi amounting to 1.0 cubic meter of earth moved per man per day, and they marked out the area to be moved with metersticks. Early in the construction process, the weather was good and the ground was dry, although the health of the prisoners rapidly declined. The kumi usually completed its quota by noon each

THE DEATH RAILWAY AT TAM CHANEE. THAILAND.

Figure 6.6 Typical "cutting" site along the railway at Tam Chanee, Thailand. Courtesy of the USS *Houston* Survivors Association.

day and then spent the rest of the day relaxing in the shade. As the Japanese became aware of this fact, they increased the quota from 1.0 cubic meter to 1.3 cubic meters, then to 1.5 cubic meters, and eventually to 2.0 cubic meters of earth moved per man per day. This prolonged the prisoners' working day and ensured that they would be on the job until sunset each night.[57]

As they had at all camps so far, American officers accompanied the

Figure 6.7 Sketch by John W. Wisecup of prisoners drilling holes in rock for blasting with dynamite. Courtesy of the Oral History Program, University of North Texas.

POWs on all work parties. Officers again took it upon themselves to serve as liaisons between the enlisted men and their guards. On the railway, officers engaged the guards in conversation to divert their attention while men in the kumi moved the quota stakes closer together, thereby lessening their workload. The guards apparently never caught on to this trick, and the Americans never tired of performing it. The guards often treated the prisoners brutally on the railway, beating them for minor infractions or for no apparent reason at all, and the officers did all they could to lessen the severity of a beating.[58]

The construction of the railroad required that a variety of different tasks be accomplished, and the Americans performed a number of various jobs up and down the line. One of the most difficult and dangerous jobs on the railway was bridge construction (see figure 6.8). Being built through the mountainous terrain of Burma and Thailand, the railway necessitated nearly seven hundred bridges, spanning rivers and mountain valleys.[59] POWs cut pilings for the bridges out of native teak trees and narrowed them to a point on one end to facilitate their being driven into riverbeds (see figures 6.9 and 6.10). After the prisoners stood the pilings upright, they constructed a makeshift pile-driving system, fashioned from bamboo and rope, with which they drove the pilings into the bed.

Figure 6.8 Bridge construction at Konkoita, Thailand.
Courtesy of the Australian War Memorial.

The pile driver consisted of a large metal weight, roughly five hundred pounds, that was cut to fit over the top of the piling. A bamboo scaffolding supported the weight, and the prisoners hoisted the weight by a rope-and-pulley system. Prisoners pulled on the ropes in unison, raising the metal weight to the desired height, and then dropped their ropes on the command of the engineers. After the pile driver struck the piling and drove it some distance into the riverbed, the prisoners once again picked up their ropes to repeat the process. Those not hoisting the pile driver stood in water, often waist high, to steady the piling. Since their labor supply was seemingly endless, the Japanese applied no safety measures to ensure the well-being of their workers.[60]

Not all of the Americans labored on the railway, however; some performed auxiliary duties to help keep the camp functioning. The Japanese sent a number of *kumis* into the jungle to cut and gather firewood for the camp's cook shacks and for the fires used to boil drinking water. Prisoners preferred woodcutting details because the work was not as strenuous as on the railway and the guards did not push them as hard since they had no quota to fulfill. Often, the guards on these details enjoyed leaving camp and the watchful eyes of their superior officers and spent the day sleeping while the POWs cut firewood. These details also afforded the prisoners the op-

Figure 6.9 Sketch by John W. Wisecup of prisoners hauling
wooden timbers for bridge construction. Courtesy of
the Oral History Program, University of North Texas.

Figure 6.10 Sketch by John W. Wisecup of prisoners cutting teakwood logs
for bridge construction. Courtesy of the Oral History Program,
University of North Texas.

portunity to slip away from the main group to meet with Burmese natives to trade for food.[61]

Perhaps the choicest jobs in the jungle were in the cook shack. Each nationality prepared its own food, and certain POWs served as the cooks. During a typical day in the cook shack, a prisoner awoke at four or five o'clock in the morning to boil water on the mud-brick oven for the breakfast meal of rice and then tried to devise the best possible way to provide a filling, nutritious meal for his fellow prisoners, which was quite a task given the poor quality and quantity of food available. Those working in the kitchen often slipped out of camp to trade with locals for fresh fruits and vegetables to add to the day's meals. After feeding breakfast to the working parties, the cooks began preparing the midday meal of rice and vegetable stew, which they carried to the work sites. Then it was back to the shack again to prepare rice and vegetable stew for dinner. Certainly, this made for a monotonous day, but the work was not especially taxing, and most important, those in the cook shack had the opportunity to acquire more food than did the rest of the prisoners. American cooks often stole rice and vegetables from the Japanese kitchens either to eat themselves or to add to the dishearteningly scanty rations fed to the POWs (see figure 6.11).[62]

Added to the difficulties of building the railroad was the increasingly harsh treatment the POWs received at the hands of their captors. The Japanese had a strict schedule to build the railway, and they intended to keep to it. Thus, when a prisoner fell behind in his work or appeared to be shirking, he received a bashing from a guard. If a prisoner lost or broke a tool, he could expect a severe beating. Even the sick on the work parties were not immune to brutal treatment, and since they were normally the ones who fell behind, they generally received the worst treatment. The prisoners remembered that the Koreans were again the worst of the guards and doled out the worst punishment. Eddie Fung gave his impression: "The general run of the Korean guards was not humorous at all . . . the Koreans are known as the Bullies of the Orient. There are reasons for it, probably, because they'd been overrun by the Chinese on the one hand, the Japanese on the other hand. I mean, I can understand it, but I can never feel anything but intense hate for these Koreans. He was low man on the totem pole, so he took it out on anyone who was available. But, damn it, he did it with too much pleasure; that was the thing I don't forgive him for."[63]

Lloyd Willey, a marine from the Houston, described the actions of a particular Korean guard: "One Korean guard, 'Liver Lips,' was a mean, ugly, little bastard. He'd walk up to some poor guy he'd picked out, and he'd make him look at the sun with his eyes open. And every time that POW would blink, he'd get whammed over the back of the head with a rifle butt."[64] Max

Figure 6.11 Mess parade in typical jungle camp.
Courtesy of the Australian War Memorial.

Offerle offered his impressions of this guard: "We had some mean Korean guards. We'd nickname them all. We had 'Dillinger'; we had 'Mickey Mouse'; we had 'Liver Lips.' Oh, he was a mean one—great, big, ugly, wore glasses, little eyes, had big lips. He was mean as hell! All he knew was BANG! BANG! BASH! BASH! Some of them, you just tried to stay away from. If you couldn't avoid them, you got beat up."[65]

The beatings, combined with all the other negative factors the prisoners faced on the railroad, rapidly took a toll on the POWs' health. The men were being worked from sunup to sundown nearly every day of the week, and their rations—which were never adequate—did not increase. The lack of any nutritive value in the food left the Americans weak and suffering from malnutrition, rendering their immune systems less able to fight off disease. Pellagra and beriberi became commonplace. Sanitation in the jungle camps was deplorable, and millions of flies spread diseases throughout the camps. Dysentery increasingly took its toll on the POWs—nearly all suffered from it at one time or another. Mosquitoes infected the unprotected prisoners with malaria. The difficult and dangerous jobs on the railroad resulted in dozens of broken bones. Worse yet, prisoners began suffering from tropical ulcers for which there seemed no cure. A small cut or abrasion, usually on the feet or legs, would become infected by tropical microbes, and the wound quickly became a terribly painful ulcer that continued to eat away

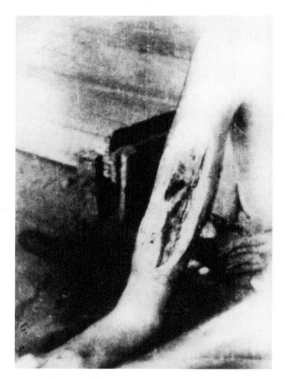

Figure 6.12 Advanced tropical ulcer on lower leg of prisoner. These afflictions proved deadly for many POWs. Courtesy of the Australian War Memorial.

the prisoner's flesh (see figure 6.12). For all the health problems faced by the POWs, the Japanese provided no medical supplies, so the number of sick increased each day.[66]

The Americans found themselves at the mercy of the Japanese and Koreans in the jungle camps, but their captors showed little of it. The Imperial Japanese Army mandated that the railway be built, and the Japanese treated the POWs like expendable pieces of equipment to reach the goal. The Americans learned to depend on themselves and each other to get through each day, and they always maintained the loose military discipline and strict sanitation procedures that had served them well thus far. Life on the Burma-Thailand railway was the most miserable experience the young men had faced in their lives, so they did not think it could get any worse. They were wrong.

Chapter 7

"Speedo!"

THE JAPANESE, THE RAILROAD, AND THE JUNGLE EXACTED A DEVAS-
tating toll on the American prisoners. Work became more difficult as the
railway approached the mountainous terrain of eastern Burma, and the Japanese continued to increase the POWs' working quota. Disease in the camps
became rampant, but the Japanese very rarely provided medicine to treat
it. The prisoners suffered from malnutrition, and their weights dropped
dangerously low. Their guards beat them regularly throughout the working
day and often when they returned to camp at night. The prisoners' ability to
perform work rapidly diminished under these conditions, yet the Japanese
insisted that they maintain a working schedule that even healthy, well-fed,
well-treated laborers could not keep.

Then in May 1943, life on the "Death Railway" suddenly became immeasurably more difficult. From this time until the completion of the railway in
October 1943, the American prisoners faced living and working conditions
in comparison with which the early days in the jungle seemed but a vacation. During these months the POWs experienced deplorable treatment on
a daily basis. Only by maintaining an indomitable will to live and by doing
the things necessary to make it through each day were the survivors able to
come out of the jungle alive.

Faced with wartime realities, in January 1943 Japanese Imperial Head-

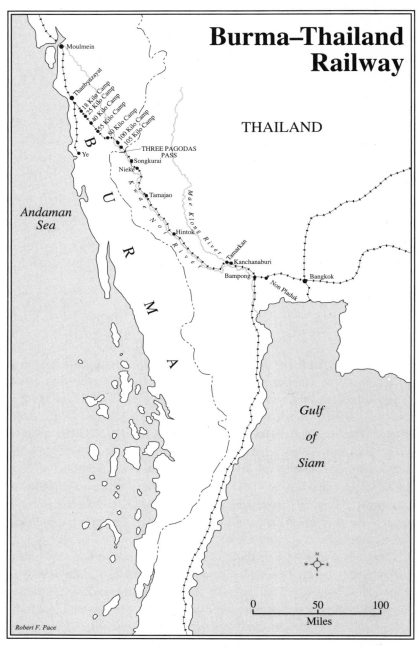

Map 2 The Burma-Thailand "Death Railway."

quarters demanded the rapid completion of the Burma-Thailand railway. By this time, Allied submarines posed a serious threat to Japanese merchant shipping around the port of Rangoon, Burma, and American B-24 bombers—as evidenced by the attack on the convoy including the *Dai Moji Maru*—sank tens of thousands of tons of Japanese shipping each month in the region. Also, the Americans were mining the waters around Rangoon by air, and as each week passed, American bombers increased their range and striking ability. The war had turned against Japan on most fronts by January 1943, so the Imperial Japanese Army in Burma had no other option but to depend on a land route for supplies and reinforcements. American factories were churning out ships and war materiel at a pace the Japanese could not match. The Japanese could not afford to lose any more ships or supplies.[1]

Imperial Headquarters initially stipulated that the railway be completed no later than May 1943. If the railway were operational by this time, the Japanese could resupply their far-flung army in Burma by rail during the monsoon season, which lasted from May to September. The monsoons protected the railway from Allied bombing because of the dangerous flying conditions and poor visibility caused by the rain. When the monsoons ended, the Japanese forces would have ample supplies and reinforcements to capture the rest of Burma and then strike out against India. The opening of the new land route would also hasten the flow of raw materials from Southeast Asia to Japan. It would take more than a redoubling of their effort to meet this deadline, Headquarters claimed, but the sacrifice would be borne out in a Japanese victory.[2]

Despite the attitude in Tokyo and despite the desire to complete the railway by May, the engineers and commanding officers on the line pleaded with their superiors that they could not be finished before November 1943. Work had progressed little farther than the Maeklong River at Tamarkan on the Thailand side of the line, and the steel-and-concrete bridge there—necessary for reliable transport of heavy materials for the remainder of the line—was still weeks short of completion. In Burma, the track progressed little farther than to Thanbyuzayat, and surveyors had still not marked out the route in the mountainous region to the east. They needed more resources for the project, more labor, and more time to complete the railway than Tokyo was willing to allow. Both sides reached a compromise, however, and established the end of August 1943 as the target date for the completion of the railway.[3]

Although the initial orders for the increase in progress on the railway occurred in January, more than three months passed before any such increase could be carried out. During this time the Japanese moved thousands

of tons of railroad cross ties, or "sleepers," steel rails, and bridging canni-
balized from the rail systems in Java, Burma, and Thailand. Most important,
the Japanese moved more native laborers and Allied prisoners to the region
during this time to begin work on the railway, as was the case with Colonel
Tharp's group in Branch Party 5.

In May the Japanese started what became known as the "Speedo" campaign on the railroad. From May to September—which coincided with the
heaviest of the monsoon rains that year—the Japanese drove their captives
like beasts of burden on the railway, with the guards constantly shouting,
"Speedo! Speedo!" to the English-speaking POWs to get them to work faster.
During the Speedo campaign, the American prisoners suffered the most
extreme abuse they encountered while in captivity and lost more men than
at any other time at the hands of the Japanese.[4]

The Japanese moved work parties to different locations along the line,
depending on needs of the engineers, so not all Americans worked as one
unit. A few of the Americans had become too sick to work on the railway
and were transferred back to hospital camps, such as they were, to recuper-
ate. By the beginning of the Speedo campaign, the right-of-way had reached
80 Kilo Camp, and most of the American POWs worked there under Colonel Tharp. Nearly all the Americans suffered from tropical diseases by this
time—some POWs lost nearly one-third of their body weight. Most men
were down to wearing the simple G-string and showed the wearying effects
of bashings given freely by their captors.[5]

Despite the POWs' pitiful physical condition, the Japanese worked them
harder. Japanese engineers increased the quota for each kumi to 2.5 cubic
meters of earth moved per man per day, and the POWs were not allowed to
return to camp until they reached their quota. Ilo Hard remembered that the
guards very clearly explained the new working hours: "No finish, no come
back."[6] On a standard working day, prisoners left camp before dawn and
returned between ten o'clock that night and two o'clock the next morning.
It was a common occurrence for kumis to leave at four o'clock in the morning, returning to camp at two o'clock the next morning, then leave for the
work site again two hours later. Because the Japanese were falling behind the
new deadline, they did away with yasumi, so the prisoners worked seven days
a week. Martin ("Slim") Chambers, a draftee from D Battery, recalled that
during one stretch in the Speedo campaign he worked 133 consecutive days,
often working twenty-four-hour shifts in the jungle.[7] Julius Heinen gave his
perception of Japanese intentions: "[The prisoners were] a very expendable
labor force in that the main purpose is to get the maximum physical effort out of a man, and whether he dies or not is of little concern and of no

importance, other than [the Japanese] need for labor. It was intended that you worked until you could no longer work and were dead."[8]

The Speedo campaign commenced just as the seasonal monsoon rains began in Burma. Although this area receives little rainfall between November and May each year and conditions are hot and dry, from May to October it rains almost constantly. Ilo Hard said that the monsoons "arrive in the form of a real wound-up Texas thunderstorm." Dan Buzzo recalled that "from about mid-May . . . we never saw the sun until October."[9] Small streams became raging rivers when the rains came, and the rivers flooded their banks and washed downstream anything that stood in their path. Despite the rains, the prisoners continued to labor in the jungle. The rains washed out the rickety wooden bridges built along the railway, forcing the workers to rebuild the structures during the monsoons. Those working on cuts and fills in the rain moved mud instead of dirt. They filled "yo-ho" baskets and trudged through knee-deep mud to deliver the load to the common dump site, climbing the muddy hills to deposit the load. By the time they reached the bottom of the hill, the rains had already washed down the soaking earth they dumped at the top.[10]

The Americans were bewildered by the Japanese approach to building the railway under those conditions. According to Service Battery's Garth Slate, "Sometimes it would get so muddy that when you'd pour dirt for fills, there was so much water in it that it just kept washing off." George Burns added, "You'd carry a basket or sack of that mud to put on there, and as you'd come off the dump, it would follow you down. You just couldn't make any headway." The prisoners made thousands of such trips each day, fighting through the rain and the muck, only to see their continuous efforts unpityingly erode in the face of the monsoons. "Sometimes I'd pray for the rain to stop," said Luther Prunty. "That incessant rain! Just rain, rain, rain! It'd almost drive you off the deep end." Thomas Whitehead observed, "It didn't make any difference to the Japs. They had to keep going, and they did keep going. You went out and worked in rain just like the sun was shining."[11]

The monsoons also worsened conditions in the camps. The grounds became choked with mud, and the weary POWs slogged through it to their primitive huts. The atap roofs proved no match for monsoon rains, and water leaked on the prisoners' sleeping platforms. According to Slim Chambers, "You'd get up in the morning, and the side that you had been sleeping on was staying wet until your skin would shrivel."[12] Sidney Matlock said, "I would lie there and shake at night. There is so much dampness in the air that that would penetrate when it got down to forty-some degrees" at night.[13] Water as deep as one foot ran beneath the huts at 100 Kilo Camp, just below the prisoners' sleeping platforms. The Americans recalled capturing and eating lungfish that found their way into the barracks as a result of the flooding.[14] Clothing deteriorated even more quickly during the monsoons, as the jungle rotted the fabric of shirts and shorts and the leather in the few remaining shoes in their possession.[15]

The Japanese officers and engineers on the railway were under great pressure to complete the construction on time, so they in turn pressured the noncommissioned officers and guards to step up daily progress. This naturally resulted in harsher treatment for the prisoners, whom the guards were inclined to mistreat anyway. Mistreatment of prisoners increased during Speedo, as the Japanese and Korean guards sought to increase productivity through threat of beatings. Eddie Fung described this development as "a reign of terror."[16]

To ensure that there were enough prisoners to fill out the kumis each morning, guards strolled through the hospital huts performing the dreaded "blitz" of sick POWs. Guards with absolutely no medical training or knowledge rousted severely ill prisoners, forcing all but the near dead to work on the railroad. Ben Dunn described a typical blitz in a hospital hut: "One of the cruelest tricks of certain guards was to chase sick men from the hospital out in front and hit them in their ulcers with a stick. Other than the intense pain, this would cause the ulcers to grow faster. This was one guard's pet stunt. At the time we were helpless; we lay awake nights after witnessing such an experience, hoping for and planning a day of retribution."[17]

If there were no clearly visible signs of illness, sick prisoners worked a full shift. Malaria victims were forced to work as if they were healthy. According to Garth Slate, "If the Jap guard couldn't see something wrong, he couldn't see why you couldn't go to work. Even with their own troops, a sick man was no good to them. They'd just as soon walk off and leave one of their own lying in a ditch as not. So, if they didn't have enough POWs for the work party, they'd go digging out the sick people and send them."[18] Those assigned to light duty typically sat on the ground and made ballast for the railway by breaking rocks with hammers and sledgehammers. Flying chips of rock commonly caused small cuts on the prisoners' exposed legs, and these cuts almost always evolved into ulcers.[19]

Given the ghastly conditions during this campaign, it is not surprising that the POWs' health continued to deteriorate. All prisoners contracted at least one disease during this period, and most suffered from a variety of diseases at the same time. As was standard in all the camps along the railway, the Japanese provided little, if any, medicine for the ill prisoners, and the rainy conditions precluded resupply of medicine even had the Japanese been inclined to provide it. Very small amounts of quinine were available to treat the ever-present malaria in the camps, but the quantity of pills available never satisfied the demand. The Japanese were apparently deathly afraid of cholera, however, and inoculated the prisoners on occasion to prevent the spread of this contagious disease.[20] Henri Hekking, one of the Dutch doctors, increased the amount of medication available by secretly treating Japanese and Korean guards for venereal diseases in exchange for medicine.[21]

Tropical diseases and vitamin deficiencies laid waste to the prisoners in the jungle. The soggy conditions brought about by the incessant rains provided a haven for malaria-carrying mosquitoes that constantly tortured the POWs in camps. There was no escape from the clouds of mosquitoes that inhabited the camps, and the insects naturally tended to congregate in the relatively dry environs of the prisoners' huts to feast on their blood. Some prisoners suffered from cerebral malaria, which usually drove them insane shortly before they died. Nearly all Americans suffered from malaria at one time while in the jungle.[22] Mosquitoes also transmitted dengue fever, characterized by high fever and severe muscle and joint pain. Hud Wright contracted dengue fever during Speedo, and he referred to it as "break bone" fever because "every time you move, you feel like a bone was breaking."[23]

Beriberi was also prevalent among the prisoners. Caused by a deficiency of thiamine, this malady resulted in the deterioration of the nervous system and caused swelling of the heart. Two types of this disease afflicted the prisoners, both "wet" and "dry" beriberi. Dry beriberi caused extreme pain in the limbs, as well as a loss of muscular control. Thomas Whitehead contracted dry beriberi: "I had loss of control in my right leg. I'd swing my leg, and I had no control over it. My foot would be just limp, and I'd walk with what they called a 'slap foot'" (see figure 7.1).[24]

Wet beriberi affected men in a different, but no less painful, way. Those suffering from this disease saw an accumulation of fluids in different parts of the body. Fluids collected between the skin and muscle, causing intense swelling. Sailor James ("Red") Huffman explained that the skin lost all its elasticity with wet beriberi, and when one pressed a finger into the swollen tissue, the indention would remain for minutes.[25] A man's face and ankles would swell with fluids until he no longer looked like a man, and the testicles were especially vulnerable. Slug Wright developed wet beriberi and claimed that his testicles were swollen to the size of grapefruit. Ben Dunn described the effects of the disease: "Advanced beriberi made those afflicted with it look almost inhuman as it caused them to swell in the ankles, in the face, and heads. We could hear them choking on the fluid that would build up in their lungs as they were dying."[26]

Figure 7.1 Malnourished Dutch prisoners of war, suffering from beriberi.
Courtesy of the Australian War Memorial.

Dysentery was all too common in the jungle and became the second most frequent killer of prisoners. Of the 166 soldiers, sailors, and marines who died in captivity, 48—or 29 percent—perished from dysentery.[27] This ailment stemmed from the lack of sanitation in the camps, especially the open latrines that overflowed in the monsoon rains. Flies swarmed the latrines and laid millions of eggs in the contents, so the latrines boiled with maggots. Men with dysentery had excruciating bowel movements up to thirty times a day in which they discharged mucus and blood. If they were lucky, they managed to reach the latrine to move their bowels; all too often they did not make it and defecated on themselves on the way, further worsening the sanitary conditions. The loss of fluid accompanying dysentery dehydrated the afflicted, and they lost weight and strength. Red Huffman described this condition: "Your body dried completely up, and you turned wrong side out at the rectum. [There was] no fat on your body. You were just a rack of bones. Your body dried right out. All the fluids in your body were gone, and you completely run off at the bowels with sticky mucous. Some days it never stopped. It was always dribbling out."[28]

Slug Wright lost over fifty pounds during Speedo, mostly due to dysentery. He explained how it affected him: "You're so weak. When I got down and couldn't go to the latrine, that's when I got scared! I am pooping on myself, and it's running down my leg. I was begging for something to clean myself up with, because I couldn't live with that. The mental depression that you go through when you have dysentery is as bad on your own mind as it is on your bowels . . . I couldn't control [my anus] or tighten it up to stop the flow. This is depressing and it stinks, and I am a miserable human being, and I'm going to die. But I'm trying to live."[29] There was no medicine available to combat dysentery, and the prisoners continued to eat the burned crusts of rice and charcoal to absorb the microorganisms causing the disease.

Tropical ulcers, the biggest killers, struck fear in the hearts of the American POWs. Starting as small scratches, ulcers grew and ate away the living flesh, leaving only dead, blackened flesh in its place. Left untreated, an ulcer spread throughout the infected area until the leg had to be amputated; yet those who underwent amputations in the primitive camp hospitals stood little chance of survival. If a prisoner unsuccessfully treated his ulcer and refused amputation, death was certain. Oscar Offerle suffered from a severe ulcer and spent weeks in a hospital camp hoping to recover. His brother, Max, visited him as often as he could, and remembered the scene: "My brother died at 80 Kilo Camp . . . This tropical ulcer had spread all up and down his leg, between his knee and his ankle. In fact, it started eating around the bone of his leg. Right before he died, there was two inches of bone showing. Blood, pus, mucous, or whatever it was dripped down on his ankle and the top of his foot, and another large ulcer was there . . . I went over a day or two later, and Oscar was semi-conscious, and he was hot. I put his head in my lap, and he died."[30]

Because they had no medicine, the prisoners were forced to improvise ways to stop ulcers from spreading. The most popular, and least intrusive, method was continually flushing the ulcer with hot water. Upon returning to camp from working in the jungle, ulcer sufferers used boiled water and whatever cloth they could procure to repeatedly bathe the ulcer, loosening the dead flesh and washing it away before it could spread any further. This method did not always prove successful, and when it did, months of such treatment were necessary to achieve results. Others waded in nearby streams in their time off work and allowed small fish to feed off the dead flesh and clean the sore; this remedy was not particularly successful.[31]

Some of the more intrepid prisoners gathered maggots and placed them in their wounds, allowing the maggots to eat the rotten flesh. After the maggots ate the ulcer down to the living, or "proud," flesh, they were removed and the ulcer was covered with reused bandages. Lawrence Brown was convinced of the effectiveness of the maggot treatment: "We used them maggots to eat up all that dead flesh in there. They'd clean it out, eat all that ol' dead flesh out of it. Then you'd scrape them maggots out."[32] Raymond Reed was not convinced of the propriety of this approach. According to Reed, "I tried maggots, but it was so aggravating that I took them out. You could feel them crawling around, and you couldn't sleep. It was extremely tender, and them crawling around in your ulcer would absolutely drive you out of your mind. So I took them out."[33] Others experimented with poultices made of native herbs or covered their ulcers with mud.

The most extreme and most painful treatment for ulcers was "spooning." The Dutch doctors Henri Hekking and Philip Bloemsma acquired a small demitasse spoon that they sharpened on one side, and they scraped an ulcer until they removed all the dead flesh. Marine Marvin Robinson explained the process: "For treating tropical ulcers, it was a matter of what doctors called 'spooning.' That's just literally what it meant. You'd just spoon out the rotten flesh and hope that it didn't spread." Such a drastic approach was unimaginably painful, and since no anesthesia was available, the doctors had to enlist the help of at least four other prisoners to hold down the patient while they dug out the rotten flesh. The wound was then washed as thoroughly as possible with boiled water and bandaged. This treatment proved to be the most successful, if not the most pleasant, but tropical ulcers still killed fifty Americans on the railway—or 30 percent of those who died—more than any other illness.[34]

As scores of prisoners became sick during the Speedo campaign, the numbers of workers on the railway diminished. Initially, ill prisoners reported to the camps' hospital huts to receive the standard rudimentary treatment. Doctors segregated the sick according to malady, with one entire section of the hospitals devoted to those suffering from dysentery. Those too ill from this disease to work in the jungle lay on split bamboo platforms day and night until they regained enough strength to move about the camp. Those too weak to move defecated where they lay and had to be cleaned and fed by the orderlies in the hospital or by their friends when they came in from the jungle. The hospital huts were crowded to overflowing with sick and dying prisoners—the stench of dysentery, decaying flesh, and death was sickening.[35]

Eventually, the sheer numbers of the sick became overwhelming in individual camps, and the Japanese designated the camp at 80 Kilo as the hospital camp. Work on the line had progressed past the 80-kilometer mark, so this camp was no longer of any use to the Japanese. It had been abandoned and deteriorated rapidly. Huts badly needed repair, the water was not safe to drink due to an outbreak of cholera in a nearby camp, and rats and insects infested the grounds. Yet this was where the sick prisoners were sent to "recover" from their medical problems. The Japanese clearly had no interest in the well-being of their prisoners at 80 Kilo Camp, and this camp essentially became a place for prisoners to die. Very few guards accompanied these men to the camp. Charley Pryor explained, "They thought most of us would not recover, so then they'd have us out of the way."[36] The least sick of those at 80 Kilo cared for the rest of the prisoners there, feeding, bathing, and providing whatever comfort they could.[37]

Thus, 80 Kilo Camp became known as a "death camp" among the prisoners, and they understood that if one were sent there, he would most likely not return. In an effort to hold on to life, many Americans refused to go back to 80 Kilo, despite being on the verge of death. Dan Buzzo said it was a "death sentence" to be sent to 80 Kilo Camp, and he held out as long as he could before being taken there.[38] George Burns spent as little time as possible at 80 Kilo Camp; despite his suffering from ulcers, dysentery, and malaria, he forced his way back to work on the railway at 105 Kilo Camp, laying sleepers and rails.[39] Clark Taylor, who was down to ninety pounds at 80 Kilo Camp, also contracted malaria and dysentery, compounded by tropical ulcers, and he lost his sight for weeks due to malnutrition. He knew that if he stayed there, however, he would die; along with Burns, the desperately ill Taylor made his way to work at 105 Kilo Camp.[40]

Quaty Gordon, one of the few Americans who worked on the Thailand end of the railway, described the hospital camps as being "where men went to die—strictly . . . [there was] no medicine, nothing. You got well or you died . . . and mostly you died." Gordon remembered that he eventually reached the point where he would do whatever it took to survive in the hospital. He described one particularly disturbing incident: "There was an Australian bedded [here], and an Englishman, and myself. This Englishman died in between us, so we thought it might be a good idea not to tell anybody for a couple of days so we could draw his rations. So, we split it. Then [the Englishman's corpse] got to stinking so bad that we had to tell the Japs he was dead. They started to haul him away, and he had a pretty good blanket. So, we said, 'Hell, he don't need that blanket where he's going!' So, we took turns using his blanket. God Almighty!"[41]

One of the casualties at 80 Kilo Camp was Capt. Hugh Lumpkin, medical officer of the 2nd Battalion. Lumpkin worked selflessly in the hospitals to treat his patients, and the men held him in high regard. Although he helped save the lives of dozens of prisoners, he could not overcome the dysentery that took his life on August 1, 1943. Clark Taylor was a close friend of Lumpkin, and he described his passing:

I remember Hugh got so sick. He had malaria and dysentery at the same time. He dehydrated so bad. We cut a hole through the floor, so he could put his bottom in it [to defecate] because he was going ten, twelve, fifteen times a day . . . He wanted a Dutch doctor to boil some water and put it through his veins. He felt like the only way to save himself was to get some water in him. That's a treatment for cholera and dysentery. He had been making autopsies, looking for cholera, because a cholera scare had come up the river. This Dutch doctor was afraid to do what Hugh wanted, afraid he would kill him . . . Well, Hugh died. He was a beautiful man. We buried him good, said some prayers over him. I believe Colonel Tharp read the sermon. When a man died his captain read the sermon over him. I'll tell you, it was hard to come to the realization that Hugh wasn't there anymore.[42]

Lumpkin's death was a severe blow to the prisoners' morale. They had witnessed this man work in impossible conditions to help save their lives, and now he was gone. If a man like Lumpkin—who knew medicine and knew how to take care of himself—could die, then death could not be far off for the rest of them.[43]

Although the prisoners lost Lumpkin at 80 Kilo Camp, they found a man whose selflessness and dedication to his comrades stands out. The Japanese sent Charley Pryor back to 80 Kilo Camp because they did not think he would live. Pryor suffered from severe dysentery and from a huge ulcer on his leg, as well as from malaria, when he and forty-five Americans and forty Australians moved to the hospital camp. In spite of his condition, Pryor was the only American who remained ambulatory, and he spent his time administering to those worse off than he. Pryor hauled water and food to the rest of the sick Americans, bathed them, and tended to their ulcers. When one of his countrymen passed away, Pryor dug his grave and helped bury the fallen man. Pryor looked for no accolades; he just believed it was the right thing to do.[44]

If 80 Kilo Camp was a "death camp," the same can be said for the camp at 100 Kilo. Located in a low mountain valley, much of this camp remained under one to two feet of water during the entire monsoon season. Men trudged through mud that came past their knees, and the scratches, bruises, and abrasions that accompanied these conditions resulted in countless tropical ulcers. The standing water throughout the camp provided a perfect medium for the millions of disease-carrying mosquitoes in the jungle, and there was no relief from them or from malaria. Charley Pryor described this as the worst camp he encountered. "It was built almost altogether in a swamp, and there seemed to be no bottom to the mud in this place. You lived in perpetual wetness."[45]

Forty-seven Americans died at 80 Kilo Camp during Speedo, and another fifty-two died in the sick bay established at 100 Kilo. Death visited these camps daily, sometimes taking up to twelve prisoners of various nationalities each day.[46] The sick, but ambulatory, prisoners formed details each day to bury their dead. Participation in these burial details was one of the most difficult tasks the POWs had to perform. That they were ill enough to be in these camps should have disqualified them for the strenuous labor involved in digging graves, but the prisoners knew the importance of burying their fallen comrades. Men on the burial details dug shallow graves for their friends in the saturated ground because the high water table in this part of Burma meant that the bodies would be washed out in graves dug too deeply. The dead men were stripped of any clothing or jewelry they may have had and were wrapped in a thin bamboo mat before being placed in the grave. The survivors shared the dead men's possessions among themselves, rationalizing that an extra blanket or pair of shorts could help those still alive, while serving no purpose for the dead. Another reason was that Burmese natives tended to dig up the corpses and rob them of any possessions (see figures 7.2 and 7.3).[47]

Those who were able attended the burial ceremonies, during which officers gave eulogies and bugler George ("Bandy") Galyean from the Houston played "Taps." The graves were marked with teakwood slabs, and officers kept a record of the date, place, and cause of death, as well as the site of the graves.[48] Every time a man died, the survivors felt a little more helpless. Ben Dunn remembered: "Even though we heard 'Taps' almost daily, we never got used to hearing it for we knew that another of our friends would be left in the jungle—and even today, when I hear it, I always think of all those guys, and tears come to my eyes . . . When 'Bandy' played 'Taps' . . . the entire hut would become deathly quiet, and for several minutes afterwards nobody would say a thing. A tear might be shed by a few, but rarely did anyone break down and actually cry. Death was very real and close to us, and I think that in each mind was the same question: 'Who will be next?'"[49]

It is easy to understand why some men lost hope in such miserable circumstances, and some of the Americans did so. To continue living as a prisoner on the railway meant more misery, more suffering, and watching friends die every day. If one lived, he suffered and worked. If one died, his suffering was over. Some prisoners chose to end their suffering and lost the will to live. According to Kelly Bob Bramlett, "You could usually tell . . . I think a lot of them died just because they gave up. I think maybe if they'd

Figure 7.2 Sketch by John W. Wisecup of burial detail, Hintok, Thailand.
Courtesy of the Oral History Program, University of North Texas.

hung on, they could have made it, but there wasn't much to hang on for them at that time."[50]

There were telltale signs when men had given up and had chosen death. When they were physically and emotionally defeated, they stopped taking care of themselves. They lost interest in personal hygiene, such as it was, and did not concern themselves with sanitation. When a man with dysentery gave up, he would defecate where he lay and not try to clean himself or ask for help. Those without the will to live stopped eating, ensuring the final breakdown of their health. They exhibited no emotion at this point and blankly stared straight ahead, waiting for death to take them.[51] M. L. Rea described the process of a man giving up: "You first noticed it in the personal hygiene of the person. He began to quit taking care of himself in his body cleanliness, in his eating equipment. Dysentery would set in, and he'd begin to dehydrate. Eventually, he lost interest in food. Then they'd get to where they were unconscious, and for a time they'd lie there with no stir in their body. Their mouth would open, and sometimes their eyes wouldn't close. When this happened, it indicated that death was not far away."[52]

The survivors believe that Sgt. Harley Harold Dupler, a marine, was one who lost the will to live. Ilo Hard described Dupler as "a picturesque Marine first sergeant," a tall and well-built man who earned the respect of his men. The Japanese beat Dupler unmercifully in front of his men in Thanbyuzayat

Figure 7.3 Sketch by John W. Wisecup of burial detail, Hintok, Thailand.
Courtesy of the Oral History Program, University of North Texas.

for a minor offense, and he never emotionally recovered from the beating. Dupler contracted dysentery early on in the jungle, and the combination of the disease and the hopelessness of his situation apparently convinced him that he would not make it out alive. Despite his friends' best efforts to share food with him, Dupler refused to eat, so he became very weak. After a few weeks in the hospital hut, where his condition degenerated further, Dupler died.[53]

The prisoners resorted to anything they could think of to keep their comrades alive. If it looked like a man was giving up, his friends tried to persuade him to keep going by talking about his family and his life back in the States. They tried to share food with the dying men and helped them care for themselves by cleaning them and tending to their ulcers. They told them jokes, hoping that if they could raise some laughter, or even a smile, the will to live might return. If kindness would not work, as it often did not, they would try to make the sick prisoner angry by insulting him. If a man could become angry and wanted to argue or fight, they reasoned, then he had enough energy to live.[54] Ray Reed said, "You'd try anything. You'd make fun of them, insult them, tell jokes to try to get them to laugh—anything to get them out of their trance or state of mental deterioration."[55] Julius Heinen added, "If he won't get angry, he won't live; if you can't raise a response to some emotion, he's dead."[56]

Dan Buzzo credited another prisoner, Avon L. ("Blue") Scarbrough, for helping him survive in this way. Buzzo was very sick with ulcers, malaria, pneumonia, beriberi, and dysentery and would not eat his ration of rice. Scarbrough angered him by threatening to eat Buzzo's rice rather than let it go to waste because he wanted to live and Buzzo did not. Buzzo became angry enough at Scarbrough to shout at him, and he ate the rice to spite him. After a few days of this, Buzzo's strength returned, and he survived the hospital.[57]

Some of the prisoners were not so sympathetic to the dying men, however, and became rather calloused to their plight at the time. Dying seemed the easy way out of their predicament, and they resented those who chose this route. Quaty Gordon admitted that at the time he thought they were shirkers for dying: "Hell, he'd wind up and die, and that put more work on somebody else. Sometimes you'd think it was an 'out' for a man to die, because it was no problem to die; and you'd die and you'd be through with it."[58] Eddie Fung observed: "I know it sounds hard-hearted, but my attitude was that if a man didn't want to live, there's no way that I could instill it into him. If he wants to live, I'll help him in every way I could. But if he gave me the impression or showed me the attitude that he didn't care, I just didn't have enough energy to expend on him."[59]

Given the circumstances, it is surprising that anyone wanted to prolong the misery he faced in the jungle. The alternative was death, however, and these young Americans wanted to live to see their homes and loved ones again. The POWs stopped thinking about the end of the war and liberation and focused on the immediate future. To survive the railway, these men had to adjust their mind-set in such a way as to allow them to get through each day. They understood that they had no control over the progress of the war or over the way they were treated by the Japanese, but they could conduct themselves in a way that would bring them safely out of the jungle each night. It was easier for them to focus on daily activities and to make each day pass as smoothly as possible than it was to look longingly forward to liberation, which might never come. In order to make it to tomorrow, each prisoner had to make it through today.

P. J. Smallwood explained his approach: "I can tell you without any reservation whatsoever that I did it one day at a time. I mean just that. I went to bed at night, and tomorrow was a new ballgame. Tomorrow would be the last day we'd be there. I really mean that. I couldn't imagine being there another month. I just couldn't."[60] Wade Webb lived day to day, knowing "that I [would] do whatever is necessary to make it through that day."[61] Ilo Hard said, "Every night I'd make a tally of whether I was ahead or whether the Japs were ahead. If I felt a little better than I did the night before, I'd mark one up for my side; but if I felt a little worse than I had the night before, I'd mark one up for the Japs' side . . . I'd kind of take inventory to see whether I was ahead or behind for that day, and I would think about home momentarily."[62]

Capt. Charles Cates of Headquarters Battery did not expect to be rescued by the Allies, saying that "as a matter of fact, early on I didn't expect to survive. Later, I found myself able to survive for that day only and to worry about nothing. I just lived for today."[63] Living through each day meant they would live to see the next, and the next day was all they allowed themselves to think about.

Once this mind-set was in place, the POWs had to apply it to daily life; so they had to do the daily things that would aid their survival, both on the railway and in the camps at night. Normally, they worked as slowly as they could while on the line, making just enough progress each day to avoid beatings. During Speedo, however, they realized that they would not leave the jungle until the railway was completed, and many determined that the only way out was to finish the job. Marine Jimmie Gee explained that "a lot of people decided, 'Well, let's go to work, get this railroad built, and get out of this damned jungle.' And that's what we did."[64] Eddie Fung added, "[The Japanese are] determined to build this road, so let's get the damned thing built! We didn't think of it in terms of helping their war effort. They wanted this thing done, and the only way out was at the other end. It was as simple as that."[65]

When they came back to camp at the end of the day, the men had to tend to themselves, making sure they were in shape to face the next day. Those with tropical ulcers bathed them with hot water, and those suffering from dysentery found charcoal and burned rice to eat. They constantly kept cauldrons of water boiling to sanitize their mess gear and to wash their rotting clothing, and they cleaned themselves as thoroughly as possible with rainwater, trying to wash off the day's layer of mud. In an effort to keep their teeth from rotting, some improvised toothbrushes out of twigs, the ends of which they chewed until they formed a type of brush. Jungle conditions necessitated that they keep their heads and faces shaved clean, and Paul Leatherwood, the prisoners' barber in the Fitzsimmons group, spent his off-work hours shaving the men in exchange for an extra handful of sugar, salt, or peanuts and occasionally some small amount of the prisoners' pay.[66]

The issue of food became even more critical during the Speedo campaign. The monsoons washed out the dirt road that paralleled the railroad right-of-way through the jungle, making it very difficult for the Japanese to reach the camps with supplies. To help stretch the food supply, the Japanese cut rations for the prisoners, giving them only two and one-half meals of rice each day. Those prisoners too sick to work on the railway had their rations cut even further, receiving only one to one and one-half meals each day. The Burmese natives tended to stay away from the construction site during the heavy rains, thus eliminating opportunities for the POWs to trade for outside food. The rains made eating the midday meal more difficult for the prisoners as they hurried to gulp down the balls of rice before the rain washed them away. Raymond Reed explained: "Everything you had was wet all the time and never dried out. When you were on a working party and ate your noon meal, you had to gulp it down as fast as you could, or your mess gear would fill up with water before you could eat your food."[67]

The Americans resorted to a variety of measures to try to fill their stomachs. Prisoners foraged in the jungle for peppers and edible leaves and grasses to provide them with badly needed vitamins. Some ate snakes and lizards that lived around the camps.[68] George Burns and others killed and ate a dog while at 100 Kilo Camp.[69] Ilo Hard traded his GI barracks bag, which he had managed to keep up to this point, to a Japanese guard for a twenty-five-pound bag of dried fish that crawled with maggots; Hard believed this may have saved his life and the lives of the others with whom he shared the bounty.[70] Quaty Gordon remembered that he and others ate the tripe of a dead carabao. They were so excited by the prospect of eating this "delicacy" that they drooled with hunger. Describing the scene, Gordon said, "Man, it was like a damned bunch of vultures in there."[71]

Of course, acquiring extra food was as important as was anything else to survival. Ben Dunn had managed to keep his boxing gloves with him up to this point in the jungle—they doubled as his and Clay ("Mud") Brumbaugh's pillows—and he traded them to a passing local for a duck egg and some sugar.[72] Eddie Fung resigned himself to eating animals he found in the jungle, but the monkeys were too fast to catch, and the rest of the animals he found were giant poisonous centipedes and scorpions. He was fortunate to be on a kumi that encountered an engorged python one morning, and the POWs killed, cooked, and greedily ate the creature. He went on to explain how he stole food from the Japanese: "The only place you could scrounge anything was from the Japanese. My favorite target was the Japanese kitchen. 'Slug' Wright was one of the American prisoners who worked for the Japanese kitchen, and he told me that they started mining the kitchen because there was so much pilfering from there. So, I decided I had to watch to see which way the Japanese went in, because there had to be a safe way in and out. So, it didn't slow us down too much, except that we had to be careful."[73]

As important as individuals' activities were to daily survival, none of the prisoners could have survived without the help of others. The close-knit cliques that they formed early in captivity became even more important in the jungle. The seriously ill prisoners could not fend for themselves, and they depended more than ever on their friends to help them through each day. According to sailor George Detre: "You had to form a clique to survive. It wasn't a mean thing or a means to cheat anybody or anything like that. You had to have a little clique so that you could take care of each other. If one man got sick, then you would bring his food to him and look out for him, maybe get him back on his feet again. This is the way we all operated. You had to look out for each other."[74]

At the end of a workday, returning prisoners commonly visited their friends in the hospital huts, sharing any extra food or medicine they might have acquired that day. Dan Buzzo recalled that when he was desperately ill and about to give up on life, his friends from Service Battery, Jesse Webb and Lester Fassio, brought him two duck eggs they bought from a local. Duck eggs were priceless at this stage on the railroad, and they were nearly impossible to buy. His friends sneaked out of camp one night to buy the eggs, but when they were discovered by a Korean guard, they were beaten unmercifully. They managed to keep the eggs safe, however, and cooked them "sunny-side up" for Buzzo, who insisted that they take part in the feast with him.[75]

Kyle Thompson lay near death in 80 Kilo Camp in September 1943. He determined he would leave this "hospital," however, and eventually began to overcome the dysentery, malaria, and ulcers on his legs that put him in that camp. When a POW truck driver delivered a load of seriously ill prisoners to the camp, Thompson asked him to tell his battery commander, Maj. Windy Rogers, that he needed help. A few days later the driver returned and gave Thompson ten dollars with which to purchase food. Thompson recalled that "I was able to purchase a few blocks of dark sugar that helped sustain me. I will forever be grateful to 'Windy' Rogers for coming through for me."[76]

Max Offerle's ulcerous leg caused him to spend weeks in the hospital hut at 100 Kilo Camp. He treated his ulcer by standing in a stream and letting the fish eat the rotten flesh, and he received a weak concoction of sulfa powder and ground rice from a Dutch doctor for his leg. Offerle lay on his platform for weeks without moving his injured leg, which resulted in atrophy and in the drawing up of his leg's tendons. He could not straighten his leg at this point, so Dan Buzzo massaged the muscles and knee of Offerle's leg for an entire day until he regained movement. Offerle continued the story: "Then dumb me, I left it straight for several days, and I couldn't bend it. So, he went through the whole procedure again. You found out that you got to know men real well, some of them as well as a brother, and they did help each other a lot—especially in your little groups." [77] Offerle went on to explain how his battery mate Keith ("Zeke") Naylor came to his aid while Offerle was suffering from a severe case of dysentery: "I had dysentery when I had this tropical ulcer, and to go to the latrine I had to crawl backwards on my knees and hands. One day I started out and had dysentery, so I messed in my pants. I was very disgusted and disheartened, and I guess I was feeling sorry for myself. So, I was sitting there crying, and old 'Zeke' Naylor came in from work. He said, 'Junior, what in the world is the matter with you?' I said, 'I just dirtied my pants!' He said, 'Take the damned things off, and I'll wash them for you.' I thought that was one of the finest things a man could do for you, and I've never forgotten it." [78]

Clark Taylor spent time in the hospital at 105 Kilo Camp, suffering from malaria and a near-deadly bout of dysentery. Lester Rasbury and Herschel ("Dude") Cobb, members of his clique from Headquarters Battery, cut a hole in the bamboo sleeping platform for him to use as a toilet so he would not have to walk to the latrine. Lt. Eldon Schmid and his brother, Sgt. Ellis Schmid, gave Taylor a can of sweetened condensed milk to help him get over dysentery; the Schmids had been saving that can of milk since they were captured on Java. Later, Jack ("Doc") Cellum gave him a can of salmon that he had stolen from the Japanese. When the Japanese discovered that Cellum had stolen from them, they stood him at attention in front of the camp's guardhouse and beat him with a bamboo pole for hours. Taylor [weeping during the interview] said, "They kept him there [for] at least twelve hours, and I prayed every time they hit him." [79]

The shared experience of the Speedo campaign brought the men closer together than they had ever been before. Working together in deplorable and dangerous conditions, suffering from unimaginable illnesses, and witnessing the death of their friends and comrades every day strengthened the relationship among the prisoners. When the railroad was finally completed in October 1943, the Japanese allowed the POWs to rest for a few days before sending them to work in other parts of occupied Southeast Asia. When the first train passed over the rail line on October 25, 1943, the Japanese held a number of commemorative ceremonies along the railway, celebrating the completion of the monumental task. In March 1944 at the camp in Tamarkan, Thailand, the Japanese unveiled a twenty-five-foot-tall statue dedicated to those who lost their lives in the undertaking. Lt. Clyde Fillmore wrote: "This stone and concrete structure was the greatest travesty of all. It denied the very date it was dedicated, all the freedoms, liberties, and human dignity that men should accord one another. It was built by slave labor and thus became a symbol of the monstrous perfidy, treachery, and cruelty of a nation. I hoped it would stand forever in condemnation of what the Japanese had done to us."[80] The Japanese were responsible for the deaths of more than one hundred American POWs on the railway during the Speedo campaign, the most men who had died during any time of their captivity.[81]

Chapter 8

Out of the Jungle and Liberation

THE SPEEDO CAMPAIGN WAS A SUCCESS FOR THE JAPANESE. THEIR engineers and laborers accomplished a remarkable engineering feat, constructing over 260 miles of railroad through the hills, river valleys, and jungles of Burma and Thailand—a task too daunting for even the British to attempt. Not only did the Japanese master the hostile terrain but they did so within the time frame originally allotted for the project. Also, they built the railway during the extreme conditions of the monsoon season, when the rains washed away their supply road, as well as bridges and hundreds of yards of track. They were now in a position to reinforce the Imperial Japanese Army in Burma with troops and supplies along the land route, and the railway expedited communications within the region. The Japanese were also able to exploit the region's natural resources more easily by rail, relieving their overworked and exposed merchant marine of the burden. The Burma-Thailand railway had the potential to be a boon for the Japanese war effort, and they were pleased.

The end of Speedo and the completion of the railway meant something different for the American POWs. By November 1, 1943, the Americans had buried ninety-four of their comrades in the jungle since the beginning of the year, and those who managed to survive the hell of the railroad were emaciated and disease-ridden remnants of men.[1] The prisoners were beyond the point of physical exhaustion as a result of the work they performed, and some suffered psychological trauma related to the treatment they received at the hands of their captors. Although the railway was finished, and although they would not again face the extreme conditions they endured during Speedo, the Americans were still prisoners of war and were at the mercy of the Japanese. They could not know what the Japanese had in store for them after the Burma-Thailand railway, but the Americans knew they still had to live one day at a time if they were going to make it home.

With the completion of the railway, the Japanese began to shift groups of POWs to different locations throughout Southeast Asia and the Japanese home islands to continue their work on other projects for the benefit of the empire. Uniformly, the prisoners found their new environs to be much better in every aspect. First, with nearly all POWs moving out of the jungle and therefore closer to civilization, they could more easily acquire food, medicine, and other supplies that they were denied while building the railroad. Second, because the railroad was finished, the Japanese did not drive the prisoners with the same urgency they had while in the jungle, so the harsh treatment of the prisoners eased somewhat. Japanese and Korean guards still resorted to physical punishment but did so much less frequently. The new camps to which they were sent were cleaner, the water and sanitation facilities more nearly adequate, and the prisoners enjoyed better medical care than they had received since leaving Changi.

The Japanese started moving prisoners out of the jungle in November 1943 and sent them to camps in the vicinity of Kanchanaburi, Thailand, near the confluence of the Mae Klong and Kwae Noi rivers. Over the next few months, most of the Americans in Branch Parties 3 and 5 were crowded into the small Asian boxcars and traveled by rail to their destination. As they had on the trip from Singapore to Penang, the Japanese crowded more than thirty prisoners in each car, leaving only enough room to stand for the duration of the trip. Those suffering from dysentery—and there was no shortage of such men—relieved themselves out the open boxcar doors.[2]

Many of the Americans expressed trepidation at the prospect of traveling along the railway they had constructed. Most of them knew of the countless minor efforts of the POWs to sabotage the railway during its construction, and none trusted the crooked and shifting rails or the numerous rickety wooden bridges that lay between them and the camps in Thailand. According to sailor Melford ("Gus") Forsman, "The boxcars swayed an awful lot, and you wondered—especially when you went across a bridge or something like that—whether it would hold or whether you were going to crash in."[3] The railway served its purpose, however, delivering the men to the new camps.

The Japanese intended that the POWs spend a few weeks to a few months resting and recuperating in these camps before sending them to work elsewhere. The most desperately ill prisoners were bound for the large camp at Tamarkan, Thailand, where they would be treated by Australian and British doctors in that camp's hospital facilities. Others were destined for the main camp at Kanchanaburi, where they spent the next months convalescing. The barracks at Tamarkan and Kanchanaburi differed little in structure from the bamboo and atap huts in which the prisoners lived in Burma, but they were newer and cleaner and did not show the effects of the rot and humidity that so quickly deteriorated such structures in the jungle. Ben Dunn, who suffered from both malaria and dysentery when he arrived at Tamarkan, recalled that "Tamarkan seemed like going to heaven after the torments of the jungle for the past year." While recuperating here, Dunn, like the others, received desperately needed medical attention, helping him to regain his strength to face whatever trials lay ahead.[4]

While recovering in Thailand, the Americans also enjoyed greater access to food. During the dry season, supplies moved from Bangkok along the railway with much more regularity, resulting in larger quantities of rice for the prison camps. Since this area of Thailand was heavily agricultural, there was also access to fresh fruits and vegetables to supplement the prisoners' diets, providing much-needed nutrients. The Japanese kept herds of goats and cattle in the vicinity of the camps to feed their troops, and the prisoners occasionally received the scraps of the butchered animals to add to their own meals. In addition to the extra food provided by the Japanese, POWs operated a camp canteen in which they could purchase food, such as duck eggs, peanuts, and fruit, with what few funds they still had or that they had earned while in the jungle.[5]

Moving from the jungle to more heavily populated areas also provided more opportunity to trade with Thai civilians. Prisoners commonly sneaked out of camp to barter with the Thais, trading their few remaining watches and other jewelry for hands of bananas, native gula, or other such fare. The prisoners often stole goods from the Japanese, especially lengths of cloth, and sold them to the Thais for Japanese occupation currency. The POWs then returned to camp to purchase food or tobacco from the camp canteen, thus infusing the camp's economy with more capital.[6] Granville Summerlin once traded for a canteen full of local whiskey, which he brought back to share in a birthday celebration while at Tamarkan. The trade in whiskey quickly came to an end, however, when Japanese guards discovered another prisoner sneaking whiskey into camp. According to Summerlin, the guards forced the prisoner to kneel back on a length of bamboo for hours, cutting off the circulation to his legs and leaving him incapable of walking for more than a day.[7]

Although they intended that the POWs recover from their time on the railway, the Japanese still insisted that the most physically fit prisoners take part in various work parties in and around the camps. There was always work to be done for daily maintenance, such as operating the camps' kitchens, digging water wells, and digging the open-trench latrines. The camps also required a large amount of firewood—both for cooking and for boiling water—so dozens of POWs left camp each day to chop wood. Generally, no more than two disinterested guards accompanied these work parties, and the prisoners often finished their quota early so they could sneak off to trade with Thai locals. Other prisoners worked for the Japanese, hauling supplies from barges on the rivers up to the camps.[8]

Perhaps the most notable of the work details in the Tamarkan-Kanchanaburi area was bridge repair. During the construction of the railway through Thailand, the Japanese built two large bridges that spanned the Mae Klong River a few hundred yards from the camp at Tamarkan. The original bridge was of the standard wooden construction, over which rail traffic moved on through Thailand and into Burma. The second and main bridge was a much larger, more permanent steel-and-concrete structure over the Mae Klong. Allied intelligence reported the construction of the railway in 1943, and as American bombers increased their range over the region, the Allies commenced a bombing campaign against the railway as soon as the line opened for traffic. The steel-and-concrete bridge at Tamarkan naturally became an important target for the bombers, and they repeatedly flew missions over the bridge, destroying large sections of it on a number of occasions.[9]

The prisoners reacted to the bombing raids with guarded enthusiasm. Certainly, they were thrilled to see the American planes so deep over enemy territory and slowly destroying the hated railroad. The raids were a tremendous boost to the POWs' morale because they signaled that the war had turned heavily in the Allies' favor and that the captives might live to see their homes and loved ones again. The prisoners forced themselves to temper their elation, however, because as the raids became more frequent, the Japanese ordered that the prisoners refrain from public displays on penalty of beatings and solitary confinement. Although the end of the war may have been approaching, for the time being these men were still prisoners of the Japanese and subject to severe punishment. If one wished to live long enough to witness the end of the war, he still had to survive each day.[10]

Another, and more prescient, reason the POWs remained rather subdued concerning the Allied bombing raids was the proximity of the camps to the main bridge. Even though the bombers flew over the bridge at a relatively low altitude, they did not have pinpoint accuracy. Dozens of prisoners, mostly Australians and Dutch, were killed and wounded during the bombing raids. The Japanese—again failing to conform to international standards—refused to mark prisoner-of-war barracks so that they could be identified from the air, and they did not provide for the safety of the POWs during air raids.[11] When air-raid sirens sounded, guards and prisoners alike ceased all activities and scurried into the nearby jungle, searching for cover until the planes left the area. When the Japanese placed antiaircraft batteries inside the camp at Tamarkan for defense, they all but ensured heavier POW casualties as the bombers targeted these guns with both their bomb loads and strafing fire.[12]

When the prisoners were not occupied on various work details or busy hiding from Allied bombers, they participated in a number of more pleasant diversions in these camps. British and Australian prisoners constructed stages from bamboo and from discarded—and often stolen—scraps of wood, and the more theatrically inclined prisoners performed stage shows to the delight of the POWs and often to the enjoyment of the Japanese guards. The Americans formed baseball teams and took on all comers, including their Japanese guards on occasion. The prisoners claimed that they did not compete to their full abilities when playing the guards, fearing there would be violent retribution should they defeat their captors. The Japanese even allowed the prisoners to assemble a camp band at Tamarkan, though the quality and number of instruments were as limited as the band members' ability to play them.[13]

The prisoners received their first Red Cross packages while in Thailand. The Japanese had been hoarding the packages of food for months, occasionally pilfering the contents to supplement their own scanty rations. Whether the Japanese experienced an attack of their collective conscience or whether they understood the growing international outrage over their abuses of prisoners of war and sought to improve their reputation is not known, but they began to open up warehouses full of Red Cross parcels and distributed their contents among groups of prisoners. Typically, four to six POWs shared each package of food, making certain that all portions were equal. Rather than ravenously eat the tinned meat, cheese, and hardtack biscuits, the prisoners added small amounts of the food to their daily ration of rice and stew in order to make the bounty last as long as possible. Although a Red Cross package may seem simple and mundane, the Americans—suffering from severe malnutrition for nearly two years—thought it was a feast.[14]

As the prisoners regained some of their strength and recovered somewhat from their illnesses, the Japanese relocated groups of POWs to camps elsewhere in Southeast Asia. Beginning in early 1944, several Americans traveled by rail to Non Pladuk, Thailand, to work at the Hashimoto Works, a complex that contained the marshaling yards for the Burma-Thailand railway.[15] Others were sent to Phet Buri and Rat Buri in southern Thailand to help construct airfields for the Japanese in mid- to late 1944. Although the work was difficult in these camps and the prisoners were still subjected to the discipline of Japanese and Korean guards, the POWs received much better treatment here. Food, though still not adequate, was much more plentiful, and their captors did not drive them as hard as during the railway construction.[16]

One should not draw the conclusion that life in these camps was completely uneventful, however, especially for sailor Red Huffman. While working on an airfield at Phet Buri, Huffman came into contact with Thai natives who communicated to him and his friend, Lanson Harris, that they would lead them through the jungle to meet some "friends." The two Americans, sensing an opportunity, escaped deep into the jungle, following the Thais to an American officer who worked for the Office of Strategic Services (OSS). When plans to evacuate the two former POWs fell through, both stayed with the OSS major and, according to Huffman, "learned to be guerrilla trainers. I learned all this new explosive stuff, and you trained [native] kids that did the job." Both Huffman and Harris remained in the jungle for the next four months until the war ended (see figure 8.1).[17]

While Huffman and Harris worked with the OSS during this period, sailor Gus Forsman underwent a harrowing experience with the Japanese secret police, the infamous *Kempei Tai*. While herding goats for the Japanese in French Indochina, Forsman was contacted by a Portuguese doctor who worked with the Vietnamese underground. They exchanged information, Forsman giving details about the prison camp and the doctor providing information on the conduct of the war, and Forsman secretly purchased medicine and newspapers that he smuggled back into camp. The *Kempei Tai* finally caught Forsman and sent him, Windy Rogers, and Capt. William ("Ike") Parker—both of whom helped disseminate the information throughout the camp—to Singapore for interrogation. The *Kempei Tai* tied Forsman to a table and beat him unmercifully with a bamboo pole and with electrical wire, trying to gain information.

Figure 8.1 Liberated American prisoners at OSS Mountain Camp, near Phet Buri, Thailand, August 1945. From right to left: Jack T. Cellum, Arthur B. Clark, Wade Webb (behind officer), John Lee (back to camera), unknown OSS sergeant, Henry Drake, unknown OSS captain, Charley L. Pryor (behind OSS captain), Vincent ("Zip") Zummo (in white pith hat). Courtesy of Ronald E. Marcello.

Satisfied that the Americans were guilty of spying, the Japanese sentenced the trio to six years in military prison. According to Forsman, "That's when Rogers told them, 'Six years, hell! We'll be lucky if we serve six months!' Of course, immediately, the Japs knocked him to the floor." The three men spent the next six months in solitary confinement in Outram Road Gaol in Singapore. Their concrete cells had large wooden doors through which a guard served food twice a day, and no windows. The prisoners were stripped of all clothing and were not allowed to bathe or communicate with others for their entire sentence. Forsman described how he coped with the situation:

> I talked to myself all day long. Asked myself questions, counted the bricks and counted the cracks in the bricks, got a fly and pulled his wings off so he couldn't fly away, and talked to him and played with him. I had an odd cell. It had 437 bricks on one wall and 435 on the opposite wall. I could never understand that, but I counted them and counted them. I lost track of days. You had no way of keeping track, so

you didn't know what day it was. You had no way of knowing what was happening . . . As bad as the jungle was, I'd have to say this was worse. I think the six months in solitary was as hard as the other three years . . . Maybe if, just if, the routine would have been broken here and there, that would have made a lot of difference, but it never was—it was the same, day in, day out.

Because he was not allowed to bathe for six months, Forsman's hygiene suffered incredibly. He was covered from his head to his feet with dead skin, dirt, and grime and had to live in his own filth. Forsman described his condition: "Now, in here, I used my fingers to eat with, and they were filthy. At times they would almost nauseate you, knowing they were so filthy. I'd have given a thousand dollars for a Dixie cup of water or something to wash my hands. I felt like an alligator probably feels with scales, because I could actually peel off the dirt. I didn't know a human being could get so filthy, but, then, there wasn't anything I could do about it. I had a low opinion of myself, but at the same time, I realized, hell, there wasn't anything I could do about it."[18]

When the war ended, the Japanese released Forsman, Parker, and Rogers, without telling them they were free. The confused men were allowed to wash themselves briefly, and the Japanese gave them clean uniforms. The guards opened the main gate to the jail and told them to go.[19] Believing that they would be shot in the back as they left, they ran in a zigzag course as hard and as far as they could. Forsman recalled that he was so weak that he could not run in anything but a zigzag course. Running down the hill from the Japanese, the men expected to be shot at any time. When the trio reached the bottom of the hill, a Chinese boy on a bicycle stopped them and told them the war was over. Forsman explained, "We still didn't believe him, but he did get across to us that the best thing for us to do was to go to Changi, so we did. That's where we went." On seeing the others at the camp, Forsman said, "My God, it felt like a hero's welcome."[20]

In mid-1944, the Japanese separated various groups of prisoners for shipment to the Japanese home islands. Due to American submarine activity along the eastern coast of Southeast Asia, however, very few of the prisoners were transported to Japan and instead spent the remainder of the war in and around Saigon, French Indochina.[21] The Japanese housed the prisoners in abandoned French military barracks that proved to be the most comfortable they encountered during the war. Food was much more plentiful in Saigon than it had been to this point, and the quality of the rations improved markedly. The Japanese and Korean guards largely left the prisoners alone in their off hours. The POWs took advantage of ready access to clean, running water to bathe as regularly as they liked; they remembered that this was an unknown luxury only a year earlier.[22]

Most of these POWs worked on the docks of Saigon, unloading food, fuel, and other supplies for the Japanese army. Once again, it proved to be hard physical work, especially for those still recovering from the railway, but their guards did not drive them too hard, and they enjoyed one day in seven as *yasumi*. Sailor Otto Schwarz liked working on the docks because it provided him ample opportunity to steal from the Japanese.[23] Others labored in a nearby oil refinery, rolling and stacking barrels of oil and fuel in warehouses. Other work parties repaired the airfields near the city after each Allied bombing run; this quickly became a daily routine as American bombers regularly hit Japanese bases in the area.[24]

As the war continued to turn in the Allies' favor, the Japanese concern about a possible invasion of French Indochina increased. Toward this end, they reinforced their defenses around Saigon, especially around the small mountain resort town of Da Lat, north of Saigon. American POWs were shipped by rail to Da Lat and went to work digging an elaborate system of tunnels throughout the hilly countryside. Once again using picks and shovels, the prisoners labored for months, tunneling into the hillsides to provide the Japanese with defensive positions from which they would try to repel the Allies should the invasion come.[25] According to Marvin Tilghman, "Those mountains are just honeycombed where we dug holes [in them]."[26] When the prisoners finished the tunnel network to Japanese satisfaction, they boarded a train southbound for Saigon and remained in the city throughout the summer.

By August 1945, American POWs were scattered throughout Southeast Asia. Those who did not remain in the Tamarkan-Kanchanaburi area, work at Non Pladuk or at Rat Buri, or remain in French Indochina spent the balance of the war laboring for the Japanese in various camps. Some, like Quaty Gordon and Paul Papish, returned to Changi after their work on the railway was complete.[27] Hud Wright, Charles Cates, and others found themselves in the vicinity of Bangkok when the war ended.[28] In early 1945, the Japanese established separate camps for POW officers in Kanchanaburi and in Nakhon Nayok, Thailand, and gathered Allied POW officers there. Ilo Hard, George Detre, and Slug Wright, among others, spent additional months in Burma, cutting firewood for the locomotives on the railway and repairing the line until the Japanese shipped them to other locations under their control.[29]

The Japanese grew increasingly desperate as the war dragged on in 1945 and continued to make preparations for the anticipated Allied invasion of

Southeast Asia. In the various camps in the region, the Japanese put their prisoners to work building defensive fortifications to help slow the Allies' advance, should that day come. Prisoners dug underground tunnels in the hills surrounding the camps and worked on antiaircraft gun emplacements within the camps to discourage the bombing raids of American B-24s and B-29s.[30] At some camps prisoners dug deep moats with high embankments and built tall bamboo fences around the camps, complete with towers where guards could closely monitor the prisoners' activities.[31] The prisoners were well aware that the Japanese were losing the war, as evidenced by the increasing number of air raids they witnessed, and they knew that their captors were preparing for a drawn-out struggle against the Allies.

The POWs then began to question their place in this struggle. Although it would be a significant morale boost for the Allies to take the fight to the Japanese in Southeast Asia, it would also mean that the POWs would be caught between the two enemies. The Japanese had clearly proven that prisoners' lives meant little to them; if the Allies launched an invasion, there could be no guarantee of the prisoners' safety. The Americans had correctly surmised that the Japanese might gather all POWs in the region and massacre them outright. The Japanese would thus be relieved of the obligation to care for the prisoners, and by killing all POWs, they would be destroying the living evidence of their brutal treatment of them.[32] According to Marvin Tilghman, "They made us build pillboxes around the camp. Instead of having the opening for the gun turrets pointed out away from camp, they had them pointing in toward the camp. That made us think that if they ever had a landing around there, the Japs just might machine-gun the whole camp. We didn't know."[33]

Ilo Hard formed a contingency plan while in the camp at Kanchanaburi. On Japanese orders, he and other prisoners dug two large ditches in the camp, each estimated to be capable of holding up to four thousand people. Should fighting erupt near the camp, Hard planned to hide in one of the ditches until the fighting ceased. A nervous Japanese guard in the camp told him to avoid these large ditches, however, because the other camp guards "would take the machine gun to [them]." This guard offered to share his private foxhole with Hard in exchange for a favor. He told Hard that if the Americans came into the camp, he would give his rifle to the prisoner and surrender to him, and according to Hard, "I was supposed to tell the Americans that he was a good Jap." This chain of events did not take place, however, and Hard was sent up to the camp at Nakhon Nayok shortly thereafter.[34]

In fact, none of the prisoners had to face the grisly end of the war they predicted and feared. Despite the efforts of the Japanese to stave off defeat in the Pacific war, the end came in August 1945. The Japanese chose to surrender shortly after the United States obliterated the Japanese cities of Hiroshima and Nagasaki with atomic bombs and after the Soviet Union entered the war against Japan. After more than three and one-half years, the war between the United States and Japan was over. The time came to bring about peace between the two nations and to bring home American servicemen in the Pacific theater. Foremost among these servicemen were the soldiers of the 2nd Battalion and the marines and sailors of the USS *Houston*.

Predictably, liberation of the American POWs came in a variety of ways, and the prisoners greeted it according to their own particular frame of mind and circumstances. Rumors about the war's end had been circulating for weeks. Of course, there were the obligatory "bore-hole" rumors—those circulated in and around the bore-hole latrines—that the Americans were preparing to launch an all-out invasion of Japanese territory or the Japanese home islands. Some of those spreading rumors told the seemingly fantastic tale that the Americans ended the war by dropping a new type of bomb that destroyed entire cities and killed hundreds of thousands of people. Ben Dunn had heard these kinds of far-fetched rumors since being captured on Java but did not believe that this particular one had any credence. It was clear, however, that the war would be over for him soon. All he had to do was wait and make sure he survived to witness it.[35]

There were other telltale signs that hostilities might be coming to an end. The daily work routine became less strenuous, and the guards did not push prisoners to work as hard as they had previously. Punishment of the POWs stopped almost entirely in early August 1945. Eventually, the Japanese stopped sending out work parties and allowed the prisoners to spend the entire day in camp. Food became more plentiful for the prisoners, and the Japanese distributed Red Cross parcels among the men. Some prisoners received better clothing from the Red Cross, and American cigarettes appeared in the camps. Locals around the camps began talking about the end of the war; though still limited, prisoner contact with OSS operatives became more common.[36]

Eventually, the rumors of the war's end and the behavior of the Japanese proved prophetic. Word spread throughout Southeast Asia that the Japanese had capitulated and that the war was over. One group of prisoners, including Clark Taylor, was headed south to Bangkok by train when they received word of the surrender. The train stopped, the prisoners were off-loaded, and a Japanese officer stood on a platform and announced that hostilities had ended and the Americans had won.[37] American planes dropped thousands of pamphlets over Saigon, informing the prisoners of the war's end. The pamphlets also urged the prisoners to remain in their respective camps until they could be taken care of by American troops.[38]

On August 17, 1945, the prisoners at Nakhon Nayok received the news. They were gathered on the camp's parade ground and "Mother" Stimson, the British warrant officer in charge of the POWs, made the announcement. According to Ben Dunn, Stimson said, "The rumors you men have been hearing for the past few days—and which we wanted to believe but were afraid to—are true. The war is over." Camp humorist Slim Chambers, who still suffered from malaria and malnutrition, stood beside Dunn on the parade ground. "Well," Chambers drawled in his heavy East Texas accent, "I'll be damned!" Dunn asked Chambers what the matter was, and Chambers replied, "Well, I'm going to get back to East Texas just in time to start picking cotton!" Dunn then threatened to punch his friend in the nose for his sarcastic reaction to the wonderful news.[39]

The prisoners received the announcement with a stunned silence. They looked at each other, trying to decide whether to believe what they just heard. They knew the end was coming, but after having been in captivity for three and one-half years, it did not seem real. "Well, I couldn't believe it," said Clark Taylor, "I couldn't believe how it could end so fast."[40] Eddie Fung recalled: "Now to an outsider, you probably picture, you know, hats thrown in the air and screams of joy. Everyone was just silent for about . . . I would guess about two minutes, because I think everyone was figuring, 'This is almost too much to take in. It's really over? Okay, what does it mean?' You know, we haven't seen any [Allied troops]. Just like when we capitulated to the Nips, we never saw any Japanese. [We thought,] 'Now you're telling that it's all over. We don't know anything yet.'"[41] Otto Schwarz described a similar scene in Saigon. "[It was a] very strange reaction," said Schwarz, "very quiet acceptance. No jumping around, running, screaming, hollering . . . Nobody jumped all over the place, and nobody was celebrating. It just was, oh, great! It just seemed like a great relief. It was all over, and we were pooped."[42]

Once the prisoners fully absorbed the information, however, the celebrations began. Those with hats threw them into the air and began screaming at the top of their lungs. Max Offerle said that everyone "went 'ape!' There's no news in the world that anybody could get that could cheer you up more."[43] Men of the various nationalities sang their respective national anthems, but the Americans sang "God Bless America." According to Ben Dunn, "It seemed to express our feelings of victory and freedom and gratitude to our great country."[44] POWs raided Japanese warehouses, "liberating" any food, clothing, and Red Cross parcels they could find, distributing their bounty to those most in need. In both Bangkok and Saigon, American prisoners sneaked out of their camps and stole ceramic crocks full of sake from the Japanese. They sneaked the wine back into the camps and shared it with their comrades until most of them were quite drunk.[45]

During the celebrations all nationalities in the camps produced their national flags and vied with each other to raise their banners on the highest flagpoles.[46] In Nakhon Nayok, the British, Australian, and Dutch prisoners raised flags that they had kept hidden from the Japanese for the entire war. The Americans, feeling somewhat ashamed because they had no flag to raise, quickly went to work sewing one out of whatever materials they had at hand. Piecing together numerous scraps of cloth and coloring them with improvised dyes, the Americans produced their flag, and within two days it was flying over the camp. According to Ben Dunn, "To see that flag slowly raised to eminence over this camp of the enemy at whose hands we had suffered for so long was an experience the memory of which will remain with me forever. Francis Scott Key could never have been prouder of 'Old Glory.'"[47]

Although the men were no longer prisoners of the Japanese, their officers encouraged them to remain in the camps for their own safety. The Japanese remained in charge of the compounds and were still responsible for the well-being and security of the former POWs. Toward this end, the Japanese kept their weapons and patrolled the camps' perimeters, trying to limit contact with the native populations and to maintain order. Frontline Japanese troops replaced many of the camp guards and were better able to manage the camps. The Korean guards, who served in the camps prior to the surrender, abandoned their posts and deserted from the Imperial Japanese Army. The Koreans had been pressed into service by the Japanese, who treated them very badly during the war, so they wanted to return to their normal lives as soon as possible. Another probable reason for the rapid disappearance of the Koreans was that had they stayed in the camps, they may have faced the violent retribution of the prisoners, whom they had abused for over three years. There was also the possibility that the former Allied POWs would testify against these guards, should there be war crimes trials in the aftermath of the conflict.[48]

Most of the former prisoners, however, had little intention of exacting revenge upon their guards once the surrender had been announced. Certainly, the prisoners dreamed that some day they might be able to get even for the appalling treatment they received on the railroad, on the "hell ships," and in the prison camps. This hope of revenge and intense hatred they felt toward their captors possibly helped them survive each day on the railway. Despite being starved, beaten, and humiliated by their guards for the entire war, the American POWs expressed no strong urge to behave violently toward their guards. Max Offerle explained this as a practical matter: "With the situation that we were in, there were several thousand Japanese troops in this area that had come out of China. They were combat troops, and they had arms. Any uprising that we could have started there could have been easily put out by them. They could have killed all of us."[49] Luther Prunty admitted that although he would have liked to find one particularly rough guard, "I wasn't in shape to really hunt him."[50]

Rather than dwell on thoughts of revenge, the Americans spent their remaining days in these camps engaged in various pursuits. The American officers gathered together the men in their particular units to better account for them when the time came to leave the camps. Enlisted men spent their days playing poker, bridge, and dominoes and carrying on the standard bull sessions. Now their conversations turned to peacetime life and what they would do when they returned to their homes. Some continued to trade with the locals outside the camps.[51] American planes dropped food in fifty-five-gallon barrels around the camps, and most ambulatory men gathered the food, as well as all the medicine they could scrounge to treat their sick friends. The most painful and frustrating thing these men had to endure was waiting for the day when they would be taken out of camp, but this fantastic and grueling process kept its own pace.[52]

The Americans waiting in camps around Saigon experienced something quite different. After being apprised of the war's end, and after the accompanying celebrations inside the camps, many Americans ignored the pamphlets requesting them to stay in camp; the temptations of Saigon proved to be too alluring. Dozens of men left their camps and ventured into the city, looking for food, liquor, and entertainment. These former prisoners wanted to make up for the time they had lost to the Japanese. They swarmed local restaurants, eating until they were near bursting, and moved on to see other parts of the city. They found liquor readily available, and they drank all they wanted; what they could not finish, they brought back to camp.[53] John Owen and a camp's doctor got drunk on a barrel of rum at the camp's hospital. Owen recalled that he was showing off, walking a wrought-iron balcony on the hospital's second floor. He added, "It's a wonder I hadn't fell and broke my neck after going through what all I'd been through."[54]

The parties in Saigon were short-lived, however, as the stark realities of French Indochina politics became apparent. The end of Japanese rule in French Indochina accompanied the end of hostilities, and the native

Vietnamese demanded complete independence from both Japan and France. The streets of Saigon were alive with revolution in September 1945, and no Caucasian, regardless of nationality, was safe from the angry mobs. French nationals were rounded up and beaten; some were killed by the Vietnamese.[55] Otto Schwarz, who escaped into Saigon from camp just prior to the end of the war, fled from a mob and found temporary sanctuary in an abandoned government building. Schwarz described the scene: "We ran in and they surrounded us, and they're throwing rocks at us, and they're shooting in the windows. Finally, we retreat up to the second floor, and we can't go any farther now. Then they swarmed up, and I'm underneath a desk. They had spears, sharpened bamboo poles, all kinds of makeshift weapons. This guy's lunging at me with a spear, and he just stopped when he reached my chest, and he captured me. They captured all three of us, and they dragged us downstairs, and they started dragging us through the streets. There's truckloads of bodies going by—wounded French people, and dead ones—and blood all over the place. People from both sides are taking 'shots' at us, coming out and hitting us." Schwarz and his companions were taken to a crowded jail, where they finally convinced the revolutionaries they were Americans, and they were set free.[56]

In Singapore, the American situation was much less volatile and more subdued. The few Americans there remember that there were no huge celebrations at Changi, just a monumental feeling of relief. Quaty Gordon experienced "jubilation" when he heard of the war's end.[57] The men in Changi wanted little more than a big meal, which they received courtesy of the barrels of food dropped by American planes, as well as the Red Cross parcels they acquired from the Japanese. For the first time since becoming prisoners of war, these Americans received mail from their families and friends in the United States. The Japanese had been receiving mail for the POWs for quite some time but chose to store it in a warehouse rather than distribute it to the prisoners.[58] Herbert Morris offered his point of view: "Some of them went sort of off their rocker and went through the wire and walked to town and probably got all drunked up and everything else. I looked at it this way. I had spent three-and-a-half years there, and I wasn't about to get out and try to do something foolish and jeopardize my getting home after sweating it out all those years. So, I just stayed in camp until they came and told me it was time to go."[59] Morris and his comrades did not have to wait long. American cargo planes carried them out of Singapore and into freedom on September 7, 1945.

The Americans in Thailand and French Indochina also made their way out of the Japanese camps in late August and early September. Japanese troops trucked some of the former prisoners to nearby airports in Bangkok and Saigon, while others had the privilege of being taken by the first American soldiers they had seen since they left the United States in November 1941.[60] The men boarded the planes—for some it was their first time in an airplane—and started out for their first destination, the 142nd General Hospital in Calcutta, India. The flight crews of the planes treated the hungry men to whatever food they had on board and all the K rations they could eat. Clark Taylor recalled that the pilot of his plane asked him to visit the cockpit. When the pilot asked him where he was from, Taylor proudly replied, "Hell, I'm from Texas!"[61]

Having spent so much time in Japanese camps, some of the men admitted that they were still in the POW mind-set. On the C-46 Curtiss Commando cargo plane that took Arthur Clark out of Bangkok, the crew opened up boxes of uniforms, food, and cigarettes and told him to help himself. Clark said, "We were afraid that we wouldn't get any more, and so we put a carton of cigarettes [here, here, and there in his dungarees pockets] and under our belts. That was our business! We thought we wouldn't get any more."[62] Sailor John Wisecup recalled that the crew of his plane opened the plane's galley to him and Willie Robinson. According to Wisecup, "We get up there, and we look in there, and, Christ, they got all kind of goodies. And they had a couple boxes of Butterfingers [candy bars]. I never will forget this. We got into them, and, Jesus Christ, I must have ate fifteen of them son-of-a-bitches! Finally, we go in the back and sit down. We figure we're going to get in trouble."[63]

Albert Kennedy had another kind of difficulty on his flight out of Saigon. The night before he was to leave for Bangkok, the Americans threw a big party, complete with plenty of liquor. Apparently, the pilot of his plane attended the celebration and overindulged in the free-flowing spirits. When they left for Bangkok the next morning, according to Kennedy, the pilot was still quite drunk and made a low-altitude pass over some Japanese barracks. Kennedy explained: "The pilot decided he was going to buzz the Japanese barracks, so he turned that thing over on its side, and we must have missed that barracks [by a few dozen feet] . . . people laid down on top of the barracks because we were that close. Here again, I thought, 'We've gone through all this shit, and here this idiot is going to crash us.'"[64] Kennedy and the rest of the former POWs made it safely to their destination, however, and began the long process of becoming acclimated to civilization.

As the men came into Calcutta, they were sent to the 142nd General Hospital to be treated for their various illnesses and other medical problems. Each man received a standard physical examination, but the medical staff performed little in-depth investigation of each prisoner's physical health. Everyone was deloused and thoroughly washed, and the remaining tropical ulcers were cleaned and bandaged, for the first time with clean cloth and gauze. Those suffering from malaria received regular doses of Atabrine or quinine, and the men with stomach and intestinal parasites were put on special diets. Doctors reset the numerous broken limbs, and the hospital's dentists pulled dozens of rotten teeth from the mouths of the abused men.[65] Although the medical staff in Calcutta treated them for their general physical problems, none of the former prisoners received anything but the most rudimentary psychological examination to determine their mental state after years of brutality and imprisonment.[66]

In all fairness to the medical staff at the 142nd General Hospital, the Americans returning from Southeast Asia had little interest in being psychologically evaluated. Once they reached Calcutta, they immediately turned to the topic that had dominated their thoughts for over three years: food. While they labored in the jungle, thoughts of food were both their sanctuary and their torment. When they thought of food, they did not focus on the hell they were forced to endure. These thoughts also drove them beyond the point of frustration, however, because there was no relief for their longing. All the former prisoners claimed to have had strong cravings for particular foods. Some wanted steak and potato dinners; others desired fresh vegetables. Nearly all agreed that they would go to great lengths to have ice cream, milk, and other dairy products. Now that the war was over, they had their opportunity.

Because these men suffered from severe and prolonged malnutrition, and because their digestive systems might not have been able to handle rich American food, many of the doctors warned them not to overindulge. They offered the advice to eat small meals of rather bland food and gradually build up tolerance to their normal, prewar diets. Some of the men paid heed to this advice, and it worked well for them.[67] Others chose to indulge their culinary desires and piled their plates high, only to find that they could eat only a few bites; many of these men became ill.[68] Luther Prunty ordered a sirloin steak and baked potato at the commissary, only to find that he could eat only three bites. Prunty said, "It was terrible—a terrible waste of food. There was enough food on my plate to have fed ten or fifteen men for a day's ration [in the jungle]."[69] Not all of the men encountered this problem, however, and many ate as much as they could get their hands on. Said Otto Schwarz, "We ate our brains out!"[70]

Once their hunger for American food was satiated, the young men set out to see the world around them. Calcutta was a very crowded and bustling

Figure 8.2 Photo of American former prisoners returning home from Calcutta, India. From left to right: Luke D. Calliton, Charles T. Atterberry, and Leonard W. Kooper. Notice the men enjoying their Red Cross parcels. Courtesy of the USS *Houston* Survivors Association.

city in the late summer of 1945, and the returning prisoners wanted to take it all in. As liberated prisoners of war, they received somewhat special treatment from the military authorities in Calcutta, and they took advantage of it to the fullest. The army paid the former prisoners three hundred dollars as partial payment for their back pay; according to Ben Dunn, "The money was burning holes in our pockets."[71] The men roamed the streets of Calcutta, eating and drinking to excess and taking in all the sights. They often missed bed check at the hospital, but when they were in their ward, they were unruly patients. In the eyes of the liberated prisoners, they had been taking orders from the Japanese and from the Koreans for far too long. They did not intend to start following anyone else's orders until they had had their fun. According to Slim Chambers, they were trying to make up for lost time, "and we were in a hurry to live it up."[72]

Although they were living it up in Calcutta, all of the men wished to be back in the United States, reunited with their loved ones. They soon got their wish—over the next two months the liberated prisoners began the journey home (see figure 8.2). After stops in Egypt, Morocco, the Azores,

and Newfoundland, the soldiers of the 2nd Battalion and the marines and
sailors of the *Houston* made it back safely to the East Coast of the United
States. They left their country as young men—boys, many of them—but
they returned having experienced some of the basest horrors of the war.
After spending three and one-half years under the yoke of the Japanese,
these men came to know each other and themselves—as prisoners and as
survivors—more thoroughly than they could have imagined. Now that they
were home, it remained to be seen how they would adjust to freedom.

Chapter 9

Becoming Whole

WHEN THE AMERICAN POWS RETURNED HOME, THEY ENCOUN-
tered a world vastly different from the one they had left. The nationwide economic problems of the Great Depression were over, and the United States
stood as the most powerful and stable nation in the world. A grateful public
greeted the returning veterans as heroes, showering them with attention,
affection, and ticker tape. The parades soon ended, however, and Americans
sought to return to the lives they enjoyed before the war. The men of the
2nd Battalion and the sailors and marines from the *Houston* had spent the last
three and one-half years adjusting to life as captives of the Japanese. It remained to be seen how they would adjust to freedom in a country that had,
at least from their perspective, changed dramatically since 1941.

  · The former prisoners, anxious to get home, began trickling back into
the United States in the fall of 1945. Most of them spent a short stint in various military hospitals, where physicians briefly observed them and made
records of their conditions. Upon receiving ninety days' leave from the
army, they went back to the homes of which they had dreamed since March
1942. Over the next several weeks, most of the Texans boarded trains bound
for the Lone Star State, while the survivors of the *Houston* set out via car or
airplane to meet their families around the country. Frank Fujita, who arrived
at the bus station in Abilene, Texas, in October, described the reunion with

his mother and sister: "I walked past my mother and baby sister without recognizing them. My mom must have been drowsy, or the sight of me froze her into immobility, for I was two or three people past her before she came into action. She let out a whoop that could be heard for blocks and grabbed me from the rear. It still took a few seconds for me to realize that this was my mom. I didn't know my little sister at all." After hugging each other, and laughing and crying together, Mrs. Fujita led her son out to meet dozens of their friends. According to Fujita, "It seemed that everyone in the station had joined in on the homecoming. It was a happy moment, and it sure was good to be back home."[1]

This scene was replayed dozens of times with dozens of families in the small towns of North and West Texas that autumn. Hometown newspapers followed the progress of their returning veterans, trumpeting the American victory in the war and rejoicing that their young men were coming home. Amarillo held a citywide homecoming for the returning prisoners, especially for Col. Blucher Tharp, an Amarillo resident.[2] The people who watched the men of the 2nd Battalion march off to war more than four years earlier met them with enthusiasm, gratitude, and genuine sympathy. These communities also mourned the losses they suffered during the war.[3]

During the war, the mothers of these Texans formed a support group to help each other deal with the stress of having their sons disappear from their lives. Because the 2nd Battalion was taken prisoner essentially intact in 1942, because there were no other American units on Java at the time, and because there were no records and only the most basic announcements made concerning their fate, these women's sons were truly lost. Appropriately, then, they named their group "The Lost Battalion Club."[4] In October 1945, the organization held a reunion in Wichita Falls, Texas, complete with a barbecue dinner, and Gov. Coke Stevenson proclaimed October 29, 1945, "Lost Battalion Day."[5]

As one might expect, when the former prisoners came home, they wanted to make up for lost time. In spite of everything they endured at the hands of the Japanese, these were still young men, and they wanted to enjoy their freedom. Many drank alcohol in excess, going on benders for days at a time. Others sought the affection of young women and attended dances and various social functions to court the Lone Star lovelies. Marvin Tilghman called on the girlfriend he left so many years ago, only to find that she had gotten married during his absence.[6] Clyde Shelton purchased a new hotrod with his back pay and took extended high-speed tours along the back roads around Abilene. As Shelton put it, "[We] whooped it up!"[7]

Eventually, the euphoria of being home began to wane, and their thoughts turned toward the future. Dan Buzzo married his longtime girl-friend on October 4, 1945, resumed his collegiate studies, and earned his bachelor's degree in geology at the University of Texas.[8] Huddleston Wright and Ilo Hard chose to stay in the army after returning, and Cleon Stewart joined the air force.[9] Stewart explained his decision: "I decided to join the Air Force shortly after I was liberated. Why? The Navy carried me over there. The Army left me there. And the Air Force brought me back."[10]

Of course, all of the survivors had little other choice than to go on with their lives, coping with their past while trying to make sense of the present, all the while working toward the future. Adjusting to life after the harrowing experiences of Japanese prisoner-of-war camps was a highly personalized process for the members of the Lost Battalion. No one survivor dealt with his personal circumstances in exactly the same manner as did any other, and one can never know with certainty how each has healed emotionally. A historian can examine the former prisoners' statements and writings to determine what happened, how it happened, and even why it happened. But immeasurably more difficult—if not impossible—is to understand the depth of the damage inflicted upon these men and how it affected each individual's life after liberation.

There are a number of conditions that one must take into consideration as one examines these men's lives following the war. First, as alluded to earlier, the experiences faced by these men were as varied as the men themselves. Time, place, family background, physical condition, and myriad other variables influenced these men after the war. Second, one cannot declare one man's efforts to deal with the legacy of captivity as a success, while claiming another's are a failure. Taking into account each man's personal circumstances, one has to understand that success and failure in each context are entirely relative. Next, although most of the survivors were certainly honest, candid, and forthcoming about their experiences as prisoners, the same is not necessarily true concerning their thoughts and emotions and how they have conducted themselves after liberation. Rather than risk being seen as weak or unmanly, they may have convinced the world—and themselves—that they had no problems adjusting to life after liberation. One human rights observer called this the "process of normalizing life through denial," which can help survivors make the transition from captivity to freedom.[11]

The POW experience may have provided the motivation and confidence necessary to excel in the postwar world. Many of the survivors worked hard and led successful lives after the war. Slug Wright entered the political scene in Oceanside, California, becoming mayor and then serving as city councilman for fourteen years. Commenting on his readjustment, Wright said that when he got back home, "I did things I never thought were possible. But when you represent your city and people re-elect you for office time and again, you must be doing something right. I can look back [at the prisoner-of-war experiences] and say, 'Through adversity, I learned something. I learned some honest values. I think I did some good.'"[12] Luther Prunty also entered local politics, holding the office of county auditor for Jack County, Texas, for fourteen years.[13] Many went on to earn college degrees, while others became successful businessmen.[14]

Charley Pryor, the man so instrumental to the survival of those left by the Japanese to die at 80 Kilo Camp, offered his opinion concerning POW adjustment. Pryor believed that too much attention has been given to returning POWs and that this attention and examination have hindered prisoner adjustment. "I said all along," claimed Pryor, "bring them back and turn them loose and let them go their own way. Let them do what they want to do, and they will do it." It will be difficult for former prisoners to come to grips with the realities of freedom, but society must allow them to do it on their own and at their own pace. Pryor added, "You cannot just remain outside the mainstream of all of one's society and the things that go on in society, and the very subtle changes to these people would be pronounced changes [for the returning prisoners]. We observe them day by day, week by week, month by month, year by year, but, by thunder, it's been years for us. So there is a period of adjustment, but it is not a traumatic thing, not in any sense, and I think that just give these people the opportunity to go at their own pace and in their own manner and do what they choose to do."[15]

For Arthur Clark, the key to adjustment was not forgetting or denying what happened but realizing that it was over and that he had entered into a new phase of his life. Clark's approach was simple: "Really, one thing that doesn't bother me is what's left over there. I left it over there, and it doesn't bother me whatsoever. I think about it, but it doesn't bother me."[16] Quaty Gordon claimed that he had to have a sense of humor when coping with freedom. According to Gordon, "I think if we dwelled on the horrors of this thing, we would have [gone] mad long ago. So, you see, the comedy of all of it, why, it's the only way you can live."[17]

Predictably, others encountered more difficulty adjusting. Aside from the physical problems that continued to afflict many of the survivors, there were emotional blocks prohibiting discussion of their time as POWs. Some of the survivors expressed their discomfort about speaking of their experiences in the POW camps, while others stated that they did not speak extensively about their captivity until thirty, forty, or even fifty years later. Many of the men expressed no hatred for the Japanese, claiming that, like themselves, Japanese soldiers were simply men caught in extraordinary circumstances who performed to the best of their limited abilities. Many others, understandably, maintained an intense hatred for the Japanese and Korean guards.[18]

When examining the statements of those survivors who claim to have had difficulty adjusting to freedom, certain patterns become apparent. Largely, these men experienced unusual restlessness and had to stay active and moving to feel comfortable. According to Max Offerle, "We were like a cat on a hot tin roof; you couldn't keep your feet down long. I couldn't sit through a movie. I would go into a room with people, and we would get to talking, and I would have to get up and leave. No reason—you just felt the urge."[19] Cecil Minshew said that he had to keep busy doing something, "or it would ruin me."[20] Lester Rasbury claimed to be very nervous as a result of his imprisonment and could not stay in the same place or talk to the same people for very long.[21]

For some, the postwar reality was too much to face, and they turned to alcohol. Many of the former prisoners drank to excess upon returning home, but this was more celebratory in nature than what came later. Frank Fujita remembered that when he came home to Abilene, he "went on a year-long drunk."[22] Paul Stein believed his alcoholism was brought on by his POW experience: "I had a severe bout with alcoholism when I came back. I thought that I had to stay drunk all the time to drown my thoughts. I made up my mind one day that I was losing my wife, and I was losing my job. I made good wages, and I was losing my job, and I was losing my wife. I was losing everything."[23] Stein eventually overcame his addiction, but he regretted losing that time to alcohol in addition to the time he lost to the Japanese. Altogether, fourteen of the former POWs died of liver diseases associated with alcoholism.[24]

Almost all of the survivors expressed other emotional problems as a result of their experiences. Many did not like to be in crowds, preferring to keep to themselves. Charles Cates, who stopped in the nation's capital for medical care before returning to Texas, recalled that he "was terrified in Washington, D.C.," because he was not used to the activity in the city.[25] William Visage was terrorized by nightmares for years after he returned home.[26] Eddie Fung said that he became acclimated to postwar life pretty quickly but that he could never completely escape the feeling of guilt about not doing enough for the war effort, or that he came home while others did not.[27] Robert Charles suffered for years, experiencing recurring nightmares about the Japanese, losing sleep, and having great difficulty cultivating relations within his family. Finally, Charles was convinced to speak about his problems, and his book, *Last Man Out*, is a compelling example of one man's fight with his past.[28]

Mental health professionals who examine the effects of post-traumatic stress disorder (PTSD) on prisoners of war explain that the trauma suffered in these cases often leads to great bouts of depression and eventually, premature death. One study conducted in 1954 found that prisoners of the Japanese experienced "excess mortality," primarily due to accidents, but also due to alcoholism.[29] To deal with this depression, as noted earlier, many POWs turned to alcohol and in many cases drank themselves to death. Also, many sufferers of PTSD commit suicide rather than live one more day with their crippling depression. A total of nine members of the Lost Battalion died of gunshot wounds after the war, and twenty-five others died of various types of nonmedically related accidents. Although no one can be certain if these were suicides or tragic accidents, the fact still remains that these men put themselves in dangerous situations for some reason.[30]

In his groundbreaking study conducted in 1975 comparing the effects of captivity on POWs of the Japanese with those of the North Koreans during the Korean conflict, G. W. Beebe found that prisoners of the Japanese underwent more hospitalization for anxiety, alcoholism, and schizophrenic disorders. Beebe argued that these prisoners, who witnessed brutal executions and experienced beatings, torture, and starvation, suffered significantly more trauma than other POWs.[31] Clearly, the experiences of the members of the Lost Battalion bear this out.

The most difficult aspect of returning to normal life after their years in prison camps seems to have been dealing with the changes in American society. Although the day-to-day changes in their country occurred almost imperceptibly to most Americans between 1941 and 1945, these nuances loomed large for the returning prisoners, who had not been exposed to the gradual processes of this change. They remembered America as it was when they left, and then they romanticized it in their minds while being held captive, hoping to one day return to this idealized, but nonexistent, place. An American who was taken prisoner by the Japanese on Wake Island explained: "To sustain us in those dark days of imprisonment, we made the error of glamorizing our past lives, sanitizing our memories, and glorifying the mundane aspects of life in freedom. We struggled desperately to survive in order to return to that life, only to find that it didn't exist. We had set ourselves up for disillusionment and we found it: the realities of personal relations and living conditions could never match our unreal expectations of life after liberation."[32]

Members of the Lost Battalion echoed this sentiment. According to William Visage, "The hardest part about coming back home is that we were thinking of America as it was in 1941 and 1942 rather than 1946. We were behind on everything."[33] The former prisoners were often shocked by the way Americans wasted food and by their carefree attitude in general. They were taken aback by the changed role of women in society, especially their style of dress and their presence in the workplace. George Burns lamented that "it even seemed like the hills wasn't near as high."[34] Pete Evans of E Battery described the effects of POW life: "I know that everybody that came back didn't come back [the same] regardless of where they served. You see men go forth, and they never come back the same. They don't come back. A part of them is left somewhere, and they never get it back. It's lost."[35]

Although their experiences undoubtedly influenced their lives in a number of ways, both positive and negative, the fact remains that these men survived. They left the United States as raw, naïve young soldiers, and they endured the unimaginable horrors of being prisoners of the Japanese. In order to survive this ordeal, these men dedicated themselves to living through each day, taking the necessary measures to provide for their well-being and the well-being of those around them. There is no single key as to why these men came home, but there are a number of important elements that led to their survival. No one element is more important than any of the others, and they are all inextricably linked.

First, these men maintained a loose military discipline during captivity. Although they did not salute their officers or address them in proper military fashion, they did obey the orders and requests of their officers. For their part, the American officers, many of whom had grown up in the same towns with the enlisted men, worked in the best interests of their men. On work parties, officers acted as liaisons between the Japanese and the prisoners, helping to minimize the misunderstandings that would lead to beatings and extra work. When they had the opportunity, officers secured extra food for their men with unit funds, even when this could have resulted—as it often did—in their being beaten by Japanese and Korean guards. Officers lodged protests to the Japanese concerning their treatment of prisoners, and the officers kept what records they could regarding prisoner location and disposition. The officers were flexible enough to understand that by-the-book discipline would have resulted in hard feelings with the enlisted men, and instead of demanding their respect, they earned it. According to Quaty Gordon, "When you have a rabble, you have nothing."[36]

Promoting the welfare of the entire group proved essential for American prisoners. Individuals could not have survived the experience on their own. At a more basic level, however, these prisoners formed subgroups, or cliques, in which they looked after the welfare of their closest comrades. When one man became too ill to successfully fend for himself, others around him brought him food and medicine, cleaned his wounds, and kept his spirits from sinking. When Clark Taylor was down and needed food, Jack Cellum stole a can of salmon from the Japanese to feed him, even though it cost him a severe beating. The Schmid brothers gave Taylor a can of sweetened condensed milk they had saved for over three years to help him survive.[37] When Max Offerle could not walk because of his ulcers, Dan Buzzo massaged his legs to get him on his feet.[38]

One facet of the POWs' experience peculiar to the Texans, which aided in the formation of cliques, was the fact that most of the artillerymen hailed from the same small towns of North and West Texas. These men had known one another for years; and many, since childhood. This familiarity helped breed a group cohesion that other prisoners of war of the Japanese lacked. These men were not strangers who were out to serve their own interests but were lifelong acquaintances and friends who had formed bonds over the years before captivity. It is only natural that they would look after one another more carefully than would a group of self-interested strangers. Ilo Hard illustrated this point: "It's rough in a way, like the time when we went through Lubbock [en route to Camp Bowie in 1941], and these mothers and so forth would say: 'Oh, Lieutenant Hard'll take care of my boy for me.' But I'll guarantee I made every effort possible to do it, where if I hadn't known them and their mothers and everybody, I might not have made the effort."[39] According to Raymond Reed, one had to have faith in his fellow man, knowing "that they will be there when you need them most."[40] So, in part, a support system for the Texans was already in place by the time they were captured.

The experiences of F Battery support this point. Based out of Jacksboro, Texas, F Battery was a tightly knit unit—most of whose members had known each other for their entire lives—and the battery contained seven sets of brothers, all from Jacksboro.[41] The "Jacksboro Boys" maintained a cohesion admired by others in the 2nd Battalion. Slug Wright joined the unit at Camp Bowie, and he recalled that the others in the battery did not accept him as a true member right away. "I had to prove myself," said Wright, and when the Jacksboro Boys finally accepted him, he felt right at home.[42] Ilo Hard, who transferred to F Battery in October 1941, commented: "That Jacksboro crowd, they really stayed together."[43]

Speaking of the importance of these hometown ties, Roy Armstrong of F Battery added: "That was a main key to [survival]—a lot of it—because we helped one another. Without that, when a man's sick, he's not able to get out and get anything. You take those where they weren't bonded as close as we were, they didn't take care of one another, and they didn't make it."[44] Statistics bear this out for F Battery: of the 108 men taken prisoner, only 11 died in captivity. F Battery suffered the lowest percentage of deaths of any American unit that worked on the railway.[45]

Working together to help ensure the survival of the group was absolutely vital to the survival of these men, but it also took daily individual efforts to keep men alive. Prisoners had to be willing and able to adapt to the uncertain environment of a Japanese prison camp. They discovered that they could maintain some small measure of control over their lives in this alien system by performing the daily activities necessary to survival. They followed Japanese orders explicitly and obeyed their customs.[46] They ate spoiled rice, snakes, cats, and dogs, as well as strange jungle plants to keep themselves alive. They ate charcoal to combat dysentery, and they fashioned toothbrushes from twigs. Individuals were forced to maintain a high standard of hygiene—considering the circumstances—to stave off disease. These men kept water boiling day and night to ensure there was enough safe water to drink and to bathe their ulcers. They were resourceful in that they scrounged any and all material that they might be able to use later: a hubcap became a mess kit, and bits of wire and a broken receiver became a radio. Individuals were also daring. They took risks stealing food and medicine from their captors, knowing that if caught, they would be severely punished.

Another important factor in their survival helped make them more adaptable to the harsh environment: for the most part, these men were raised in North and West Texas during the Great Depression. They grew up being used to physical hardship, intense labor, and a very hot climate. Many of their homes were not wired for electricity and did not have indoor plumbing. They were accustomed to working in the dirt for long hours, while receiving limited amounts of food. The farms, ranches, and oil fields of West Texas toughened them for what lay ahead in the jungles of Burma and Thailand. Slim Chambers, a draftee who grew up in the eastern part of the state, commented, "When I came back, my granddaddy asked me: 'How was it [being a prisoner of the Japanese]?' And I told him, 'Papa, other than not seeing your folks, it was just like East Texas. The Japs worked the hell out of you and starved you to death.'"[47]

The most important individual trait shared by the survivors is that they all possessed an uncommon will to live. There is no doubt that all POWs wanted to live through their experience and return home, but those who survived were willing to do whatever it took under the circumstances to survive. Evidence of this trait has been presented throughout this study. For example, these men were willing to have their ulcers scraped without anesthesia. Even though they were exhausted at the end of the workday, they were willing to stay awake late at night boiling water for drinking and cleaning. When they were down in the hospital at 80 Kilo Camp, afflicted with numerous diseases and near death, they were willing to eat their rations and to crawl to the latrine. Wade Webb said that they had to have "that will to do whatever is necessary to make it that day."[48] Eldridge Rayburn echoed this sentiment: "It was hard to take, but you'll take it if you want to survive."[49]

Slug Wright witnessed many men fighting to live in the jungle. Wright served as an orderly for Henri Hekking in the various camps in Burma, tending to the most critically sick prisoners. Each day he helped feed dying men, cleaning their wounds and trying to keep their spirits high. He saw dozens of prisoners die, and he watched those with the will to live fight to survive. According to Wright, the dying POWs simply had no fight left in them. They would not respond to kindness or to insults. They would not eat their rice but would stare straight ahead, seemingly waiting for the end to come. Wright explained, "You know, it's easy as hell to die, but it's hard to live. A man can give up and go very quickly. Without the will to live, without that spark, you lost it."[50]

Wanting to live meant that these men took extraordinary measures to deal with their suffering. While at 55 Kilo Camp, Eddie Fung was afflicted with tropical ulcers, malaria, and dysentery. Ordinarily, men in this condition died. Fung refused to give up, however, and he refused to go to the hospital camp at 80 Kilo. Although stricken with these diseases, he would not make sick call. Fung would not admit to himself that he was sick because to do so would be the first step toward death. Fung was determined to stay on the railroad. He would receive no treatment at the hospital at any rate, he reasoned, and he would draw a full day's ration of rice if he reported to work. At any other time in his life, a ration of rice would have meant very little. In the jungle, however, that rice could make the difference between living and dying that day.[51]

Like Eddie Fung, these men always believed that if they lived through one day, then they would be ready to take on the next. If they lived day by day long enough, eventually the American military would liberate them. They had no doubt that the United States and its allies would prevail in the conflict—it was just a matter of time. If they hoped to live to see that day, they had to survive every day before liberation. According to Roy Armstrong, "I always had a feeling that I was going to make it. You know, you have hunches and things. I guess it was being close to your family, more than anything, which gave you some reason to want to live. That was the way most of them made it; they had a reason for living."[52] Perhaps Jimmie Gee said it best: "I never lost hope, and I never believed that I didn't have a round trip ticket home. But there were many times in the jungle when, boy, you wondered if you had misplaced it."[53]

Finally, those who made it out of the jungle attribute part of their success to luck. Some developed diseases that could not be cured despite their best efforts, while others were able to deal with them successfully. Prisoners who labored on a certain work party may have suffered more physical abuse than those on another work party, resulting in beatings and a further erosion of the POWs' ability to survive each day. Some jobs were more strenuous than others, and some were more dangerous. Prisoners did not know from day to day which job they would be performing or which guards would be watching them because the Japanese made these decisions. Those working for guards who did not beat them stood a better chance of surviving than did those working for brutal overseers. The eighteen American POWs killed in submarine attacks were randomly picked by the Japanese for shipment to Japan.

Charles Cates tried to keep his experiences and his luck in perspective. People often asked him about his bad luck of being sent to Java and then being taken prisoner. When the 2nd Battalion split from the 36th Division in November 1941, he left many friends at Camp Bowie. The 36th Division saw extensive, bloody combat in the European theater, especially during the invasion of southern Italy, particularly at the Rapido River, in 1943.[54] Cates said, "I couldn't question my luck, either, because some of the fellows that we left back at Camp Bowie hit Salerno and didn't get out. Okay, who had the good luck, and who had the bad luck?"[55]

Although the survivors did a great many things to help themselves while being held by the Japanese, there simply is no overarching answer as to why some made it home and others did not. Commenting on why he survived, Eddie Fung said, "I can't give you an answer to that, because I know there are a lot of men who wanted to live that didn't make it. I mean, the survivors are not all good; we're not all bad."[56] George Detre replied, "Why I made it and some other guy didn't, I don't know."[57] Charley Pryor claimed there was no key to his surviving: "I guess all one can say is that it was just not yet my time. I saw weaker people survive; I saw stronger people die. I saw people who lived a good life, an exemplary life. Many of them died, and some of the orneriest that you ever run onto lived. So there is no way that one could say that I was better or that I was stronger or any other such thing. I should have died. There is just no explanation for why I didn't. But I did not die, and I don't know why I didn't die. I beat that ulcer. It took eleven months to heal, but I stopped it. Why didn't it go ahead and consume my whole leg before I could stop it? So I don't think there's any key to my survival other than the fact that it was just whatever fate there is that is set for man, and it was just not yet my time."[58] Despite all the survivors experienced, it was not the time for any of them to die.

While they were held by the Japanese, the men of the 2nd Battalion and the sailors and marines of the *Houston* witnessed the most admirable traits human beings possess, as well as the most deplorable. Bravery and selflessness were seriously challenged by brutality and self-interest, and the latter all too often triumphed over the former. In the final tally, 89 of the 534—or 16 percent—of the soldiers taken prisoner died while working for the Japanese; 77 of the 368—or 20.9 percent—of the sailors and marines died. Of all the Americans taken prisoner on Java, 18 percent perished as POWs. More important, however, 445 members of the 2nd Battalion, 131st Field Artillery Regiment, of the Texas National Guard, and 292 sailors and marines from the USS *Houston* survived.[59]

Appendix

Prisoners Held by the Japanese

2nd Battalion, 131st Field Artillery Regiment

D Battery

Armistead, Jack D.
Arroyo, Salome G.
Ashworth, Hix C.
Bailey, Jack W.
Betancud, Santos L.
Bird, Hilton B.
Blackwelder, Alton J.
Boatman, Harvey W.
Boren, Lemuel M.*
Bowers, Walter A.
Bowley, R. J.*
Boyle, A. C.*
Branum, Delton D.
Brinker, Harold A.
Bruner, Edgar C.

Butler, Jessie W.
Carpenter, Albert L.
Chambers, Martin J.
Clark, Braxton
Coffee, Robert C.
Combs, Dale W.
Cox, C. A.*
Curley, Lavern A.
Daley, Michael J.
Delasio, F.*
Derrick, Cecil L.
Dickens, W. H.*
Dickenson, Wilburn D.
Dove, Deton R.
Dove, Miley D.

Drake, Leonard H.
Eastham, Ramon G.
Eichorst, William D.
Ewing, John A.
Falk, George A.
Fenrick, Harlin F.
Galbraith, Stanley J.
Garcia, Alfredo G.
Gillen, Earl W.
Gilliam, R. E.*
Gnat, Frank J.
Godfrey, Millard E.
Griffin, C. R.*
Griffith, Hubert W.
Guzzy, Walter K.

* Prisoner who died in Japanese captivity.
** Sailor or marine from the USS *Houston* who survived the ship's sinking to be taken prisoner by the Japanese.
*** Soldier killed in action on Java, February 3, 1942.

Hallendy, Mathews J.
Hammack, Zack A.
Hammons, Roy H.
Hampton, R. W.*
Hanser, Charles D.
Harris, DeWitt D.
Harrison, J. W.*
Higginbotham, Howard
Hiner, David A.
Hooper, Chris
Hooper, Marlin W.
Hovis, Howard C.
Hufstetler, Other D.
Huggins, George L.
Johnson, Donald F.
Karney, Jack M.
Karr, Nick P.
Kelley, Ben K.
Kenny, Robert W.
Kershner, Horace V.
Ladwig, Lawrence E.

Lamb, Floyd R.
Landin, Mario E.
Lewis, Dale A.
May, Richard R.
McElreath, Jesse A.
Messer, George E.
Morgan, Isaac A.
Morrison, C. D.*
Morrow, Adolphus C.
Naylor, Keith F.
Offerle, I. O.*
Offerle, Roy M.
Pfeil, S. A.*
Pitts, G. E.*
Ramzy, Avery P.
Rea, Maston L.
Richardson, Elmer S.
Rogers, William C.
Rumbeck, James V.
Russell, C. E.*
Salazman, M. F.*

Scroggins, Herman W.
Sewell, H. T.*
Shaver, H. D.*
Sickels, Melvin I.
Sisk, Jewel L.
Skillern, Paul W.
Skinner, Walter S.
Smith, Travis J.
Spann, Buster H.
Stambraugh, Clyde M.
Stewart, Cleon
Thompson, Lloyd D.
Tims, Roy E.
Tople, Emil F.
Walling, Hal C.
Weiss, Earl C.
Wilson, E. P.*
Wilson, T. A.*
Yarbrough, William E.
Zeigler, Lundy L.

E Battery

Adams, Earl D.
Aleman, Juan
Allen, Hollis G.
Barker, Cophus E.
Campbell, John P.
Campbell, Odell
Carter, Uell M.
Choate, Rufus R.
Ciplinski, Frank P.
Clements, Carl C.
Cook, Robert G.
Costlow, Eldred L.
Croft, J. B.
Cuellar, Francisco
Cumberledge, Allen B.
Davis, John S.
Dodson, Thomas A.
Donoho, Eddie L.
Drake, Theodore N.
Eaton, C. J.
Evans, Peter

Farmer, Walter L.
Farrar, James W.
Fender, Joseph G.
Fujita, Frank
Garcia, Calixtro C.
Garland, Hugh A.
Gilbreth, Troy C.
Gilliam, Farris F.
Gonos, George
Gosler, Paschal G.
Hanks, Horace E.
Hargett, Leo
Heleman, D. N.*
Hernandez, A.*
Hinton, Roy
Holder, Harold L.
Holder, Joseph N.
Kalich, N. O. F.*
Keith, Ben C.
Killian, George B.
Lawson, T. E.*

Lofley, Cecil
Lynn, George W.
McMahan, R. W.*
Martin, Arnold W.
Martinez, James G.
Martinez, Ramon P.
Matthews, W. F.
Mayo, Dayton G.
Miller, Everett W.
Minshew, Cecil T.
Morrison, Vere E.
Moses, Ronald N.
Mygland, Oris D.
Noddin, Carl O.
Norris, Lawrence O.
Ortiz, Luz H.
Perez, Frederick T.
Plant, Howard B.
Powers, Cecil F.
Preslar, Coy J.
Robertson, B. W.

Robinson, William J.
Rogers, Novle W.
Rosas, Rudolfo R.
Salinas, Alex
Savell, Robert D.
Sharp, Henry T.
Shelton, Clyde J.
Shelton, Archie E.
Shields, Richard E.
Slone, W. R.
Snelling, Marvin M.
Spalding, Henry R.

Starnader, Walter A.
Staver. L. P.*
Stein, Paul D.
Straughan, Millet A.
Stubbs, Robert L.
Thomas, B.*
Tucker, Cletus L.
Turner, Jack E.
Van Cleave, Curtis L.
Visage, William A.
Watson, Thomas P.
Wetsel, Arlee

White, Roger H.
Williams, David A.
Williams, O. B.
Winn, Angus N.
Wismann, E.*
Woodall, Monroe D.
Woodward, Carl R.
Woody, Thomas B.
Wuest, Raymond A.
Zimmerle, Milton

F Battery

Anderson, Luther L.
Anthony, Nolan D.
Argabright, Joseph W.
Armstrong, Roy G.
Baker, John T.
Baker, Millard L.
Bankhead, C. L.
Barnes, Dan F.***
Barnes, Don H.*
Bowen, G. M.*
Brandenburg, J. B.
Bray, Clifford O.
Brimhall, Clifford O.
Brimhall, Onis L.
Bryant, James H.
Bumpass, Jesse F.
Campbell, Charles
Carpenter, Lonnie J.
Cellum, Jack T.
Chapman, Henry E.
Chapman, William J.
Clark, John D.
Clay, Joseph F.
Clay, Melvin L.
Clendenen, J. G.
Cobb, Robert J.
Cooper, James M.
Crain, Drew W.
Duckworth, James H.
Eastwood, H. W.*

Ecklund, R. L.*
Elliott, Edward L.
England, Clifford J.
Feagle, Willie K.
Fillmore, B. D.
Forgey, J. C.*
Frazior, Harold R.
Frie, James W.
Frie, Marion L.
Fung, Edward
Garcia, Alfredo G.
Garcia, Jose, D.
Garner, Edward L.
Gilmore, James W.
Glazner, T. H.
Gregg, Robert N.
Gregg, Roy L.
Hard, Ilo B.
Heinen, Julius B.
Hensley, James E.
Hensley, John C.
Hicks, J. M.
Holton, Melvin G.
Hoover, J. W.
Johnson, Clifford R.
Jones, Glen W.
Jordan, Roy E.
Jordan, William V.
Kenner, Jack W.
King, Ray

Laird, John M.
Lattimore, James P.
Lawley, George P.
Leatherwood, Paul
Ledbetter, James J.
Lee, John W.
Long, Luther J.
Lucas, Herbert A.
Luna, E.*
Maher, Boyd E.
Matlock, Sidney C.
Mattfield, W. F.*
Medina, Refugio S.
Miller, G. R.*
Morris, James R.
Ogle, Ray
Oliver, Garth
Oosting, Charles G.
Owen, John H.
Pitts, Jennings B.
Prunty, Luther G.
Ray, George F.
Ray, James E.
Rayburn, Eldridge L.
Reichle, Grover
Robertson, William F.
Rogers, J. W.*
Ross, George E.
Self, Glenn
Sewell, D. H.*

Sherrill, Cleo N.
Sherrill, Cosby R.
Simpson, Ward H.*
Slate, Garth W.
Smith, J. W.
Smoke, Albert F.
Sparkman, L. S.*

Solomon, Wayne
Spencer, Thomas J.
Stone, Preston E.
Teel, Horace G.
Thomas, Claude A.
Tidwell, Walter L.
Tilghman, Marvin

Torp, Franklin B.
Wade, Arnold W.
Wehring, Theodore B.
Wood, Chester L.
Worthington, Charles E.
Wright, Houston T.
Wright, Huddleston W.

Headquarters Battery

Alexander, J. G.*
Anderson, J. A.*
Badger, Marvin W.
Badgwell, Lloyd T.
Bailey, J. W.
Bailey, Walter L.
Baldock, Earl F.
Barnett, George W.
Biffle, William M.
Bingham, J. E.***
Bowman, William A.
Bramlett, Kelly B.
Brandon, Henry A.
Brown, Alf
Brown, J. R.*
Brown, Lawrence M.
Buck, Johnnie W.
Burns, George M.
Bussey, S. M.*
Buzzo, Dan C.
Campbell, Leonard
Capps, Thurman L.
Cates, Charles A.
Chumley, Horace E.
Clark, Arthur B.
Cobb, Herschel R.
Collins, C. M.*
Curtis, Frank E.
Darden O. L.
Davis, Ozro O.
De La Fuente, Willie
Deats, L. F.*
Dunn, E. Benjamin
Elkin, Harold G.
Eves, J. O.

Faulkner, A. O.*
Ficklin, Frank W.
Fillmore, Clyde C.
Fitzsimmons, Arch L.
Fowler, Ira H.
Gibbens, Merrell R.
Glatzert, P. A.*
Goodwin, George E.
Grass, Fred C.
Green, Charles W.
Guthrie, W. L.*
Gutierrez, Victor P.
Hall, H. L.*
Holzkamper, Philip E.
Hammer, H. B.*
Herrera, L. M.*
Hudson, Edgbert T.
Ivey, D. B.*
Jaster, A. H.*
Jeter, Lewis W.
Jones, Bert F.
Jones, Bruce M.
Jones, Clyde E.
Jones, S. A.*
Kalous, E. B.*
Key, Jack D.
Kitchings, H. A.*
Kirk, John C.
Kuykendall, E. L.
Lasiter, A. W.
Lewis, Marlin B.
Lumsden, Thomas B.
Mabe, Ardie M.
Malavear, Joseph
Martin, Elton L.

Martin, John W.
Martinez, Martin
Mason, Noel T.
Mendoza, Peter C.
Miles, Fred H.
Moore, G. E.*
Morrow, Roy L.
Parker, William O.
Patterson, J. T.
Patterson, Paul L.
Railford, Herbert M.
Rasbury, Lester C.
Reed, Wilson G.
Reis, George H.
Rhine, Thurman C.
Rhine, Wayne M.
Rhodes, B. E.*
Rich, John E.
Rich, R. L.*
Rios, Felepe
Robbins, Howard H.
Robinson, Ray F.
Rockett, Wilburn W.
Rodriquez, Cristoval H.
Rogers, Winthrop H.
Saldana, Reynaldo
Scarbrough, Avon L.
Schandua, J. E.*
Searle, Albert C.
Shaw, E. E.*
Shores, Denzil O.
Silva, E. J.*
Singleton, Ray O.
Slavens, Charles O.
Smith, Arthur E.

Smith, Walter O.
Speece, Jack R.
Stanbrough, Jess H.
Starnes, Woodrow L.
Stensland, Roy E.
Stout, G. W.*
Summerlin, Granville T.
Summers, J. L.

Summers, L. M.
Tharp, Blucher S.
Thompson, Kyle O.
Thornton, H. C.
Upperman, M.*
Vallejo, Jose F.
Vinje, Harold M.
Whitaker, Charles W.

Williams, Warren A.
Williamson, B. R.*
Wisdom, Wiley W.
Woltz, D. G.*
Woodall, Carol K.
Wootan, Thomas C.
Zerbis, George

Service Battery

Anderson, Frank S.
Anderson, Walter R.
Atkinson, Warren T.
Barash, William H.
Baxter, B. R.*
Biggs, Thomas L.
Bray, C. B.*
Brown, Donald N.
Brumbaugh, Clay L.
Callender, Horace W.
Casey, Otho C.
Costabile, Harold G.
Crum, James E.
Daniels, Homer B.
Dempsey, A. E.*
Dinkins, Broadus C.
Doiron, L. W.*
Drake, Henry C.
Embrook, George
Fair, Cecil G.
Fassio, Lester T.
Gordon, Crayton
Harrelson, M. T.
Hendrick, Odos

Hicks, J. W.*
Humble, Maxwell F.
Jordan, Daniel J.
Joyner, Charles W.
Kelm, A. M.*
Kilpatrick, Roy F.
Krizan, Dan L.
Krol, Joseph A.
LaBonte, Robert J.
LaBove, John R.
Lee, Robert E.
Looney, F.A.*
Mallard, William J.
Martinez, Homero L.
McKelvey, Robert O.
Miller, John P.
Mireles, Fred R.
Morris, Herbert R.
Moss, Jack D.
Mundy, Laffie H.
Ochoa, Daniel J.
Redwine, A. L.*
Richey, Raymond A.
Rickel, Audie B.

Rivero, Louis J.
Samples, Emil R.
Schmid, Eldon W.
Schmid, Ellis B.
Schultz, L. D.*
Smallwood, Peter J.
Snake, Lawrence L.
Sokolowski, J. R.*
Stephenson, William H.
Tieman, E. W.*
Toalson, Elmer C.
Tremonte, T. J.*
Valasez, Efraim G.
Voge, Warren H.
Waters, N. H.*
Webb, Jesse E.
Webb, Wade H.
Western, Weldon O.
Whatley, S. J.*
Williamson, Donald T.
Wilson, Fred O.
Winchester, Charles H.
Yell, A. B.*
Zummo, Vincent

Medical Corps

Carney, W. D.*
Drake, J. P.*
Gray, H.*
Harris, Claude R.
Jones, Paul C.
Jowell, J. D.*

Knight, Douglas F.
Lumpkin, Samuel H.*
Parker, A. T.*
Redwine, James D.
Reed, Raymond D.
Rochford, Eugene D.

Rogers, John E.
Webster, Oscar C.
Wilhite, Herman L.
York, William
York, Coy D.

USS Houston Personnel**

Abrams, R. E.*
Agin, Gerald L.
Albers, Aaron M.
Alderman, H. P.*
Aleva, J. C.*
Allen, Henry A.
Armour, F.*
Arnold, Floyd V.
Atterberry, Charles T.
Autrey, James G.
Axelson, Walter C.
Back, Col A.
Baerman, D.*
Ballew, James L.
Ballinger, James M.
Barbatti, Henry T.
Barnes, Stanley D.
Bartz, John E.
Batchelor, W. C.*
Beardsley, Marvin M.
Beatty, Paul E.
Bedford, Wendell J.
Beeson, Walter L.
Bender, G. F.
Benner, C. W.*
Bergam, Samuel J.
Bergen, James T.
Bevel, Virgil B.
Biechlin, Louis E.
Biggers, Delwone B.
Bingham, Joseph L.
Bird, Leo C.
Black, Arthur R.
Blair, K. S.*
Bolt, Clarence L.
Boz, Wallace S.
Brain, Donald C.
Branham, L. R.
Brooks, Harold R.
Brooks, Howard E.
Brothers, F. W.
Buckner, LeRoy A.
Buhlman, C. W.*

Bunch, Jerry J.
Bunyard, Basil C.
Burgard, Carl N.
Burge, Jack
Burge, Jack O.
Burroughs, Clement D.
Bush, Elmo A.
Bushnell, E. W.*
Butler, Jesse
Callahan, Leo
Callahan, M. C.*
Callahan, Myron J.
Campbell, John F.
Campbell, Rollin L.
Cantrell, J. A.
Carroll, Charles E.
Carter, F. L.*
Case, Alexander
Castro, Manuel P.
Cerruti, Julius E.
Chambliss, J. Cecil
Chapman, George T.
Chie, Ah
Childers, Mitchell K.
Clark, Dallas R.
Clark, Preston R.
Coderre, Ernest J.
Collins, Charles M.
Colliton, Luke D.
Conner, Marion E.
Cooper, D. R.*
Crispi, Eugene C.
Dalton, Joseph F.
Daniels, Warren W.
Davis, Charles B.
Davis, Homer E.
Day, Clarence N.
Day, Raymond
De Moss, Donald D.
Demoen, A. R.*
Dethloff, Robert L.
Detre, George
Donohou, George W.

Douglas, Griff L.
Du Haime, Arthur R.
Early, James D.
Ebaugh, F. V.*
Eddy, Merritt V.
Egelston, Douglas W.
Elam, Richard W.
Ellis, F. D.*
Epstein, William A.
Ewing, James C.
Fanchor, G.*
Fannon, Buel R.
Fay, Henry L.
Feeley, J. J.*
Feldscher, Johann P.
Felix, I. A.*
Feliz, Jack M.
Ferguson, John A.
Feuchack, Stephen
Fitzgerald, James R.
Flanigan, George P.
Flynn, David C.
Forrester, John E.
Forsman, Melford L.
Fowler, Charles P.
Fulton, Robert B.
Galbraith, William L.
Galski, Leon H.
Galyean, George L.
Gans, Joe
Garrett, Jordan J.
Garwood, E. D.*
George, Perlie M.
Gilleland, Jesse
Gilliam, Leonard O.
Glover, Ross M.
Godfrey, D. F.*
Goodson, Ray
Gore, James P.
Graham, R. G.*
Grant, Larry
Gunnerson, Carl F.
Guy, H. A.*

Hainline, John W.
Hall, E. L.*
Hamil, John M.
Hamlin, Harold S.
Hanley, R. L.
Hansen, R. R.*
Harnden, Robert D.
Harrell, John A.
Harris, Lanson H.
Hatlen, E. A.*
Hawkins, Depoix W.
Heavey, Thomas V.
Hedrick, George R.
Heitt, Herman V.
Hendricks, R. H.*
Herman, Richard J.
Hirschberg, L.*
Hittle, R. G.*
Hobbs, Merle H.
Hood, John E.
Howard, Reese
Huebler, Eugene A.
Huffman, James W.
Humphrey, Earl C.
Hurd, Maurice C.
Hutchingson, B. M.*
Ingram, William
James, E. R.*
Jenkins, Frederick C.
Johnson, E. I.*
Johnson, H. M.*
Johnson, Warren L.
Johnson, Wayne
Jordan, Raymond G.
Justice, Harold M.
Kalinowsky, Robert J.
Keast, William
Kei, Shun Ching
Kelley, Albert M.
Kelley, Harry T.
Kennedy, Albert E.
Kenney, James
Ketman, R. E.*
Kirkpatrick, Harlan G.
Kocher, Bernard F.

Koelling, V. L.*
Kondzelal, F.*
Kooper, Leonard W.
Kopp, Alois
Kramer, Tony Q.
Krass, Raymond G.
Krekan, Albert F.
Kulibert, Chester L.
Kun, Yu
Kunke, C. J.*
Lamb, Robert V.
Lawson, Gains W.
Lee, E. H.*
Lehnhoff, Eugene E.
Levitt, Herbert A.
Lindsley, A. J.*
Logan, Wilford W.
Lohrig, Charles W.
Louis, Laurence G.
Mabry, Jacob P.
Madson, Quentin C.
Maher, Arthur L.
Mahlandt, Melvin H.
Manista, Anton
Marinos, M. M.
Manion, T.*
Martin, Robert I.
Martwick, Philip W.
May, Earl V.
McFadden, Elmer L.
McGarvey, Albert E.
McManus, Harold E.
McManus, O. C.
McMasters, Samuel T.
Miles, William R.
Minton, Olen C.
Morris, Ralph E.
Musto, J. W.*
Neiderhouse, George
Neitsch, Alfred R.
Nelson, John B.
Netter, Jack G.
Nickle, Henry
O'Brien, Robert L.
Oliver, William M.

Omoth, R. E.*
Orth, Eugene R.
Papish, Paul E.
Paquin, James O.
Parham, Eugene
Parish, B. H.*
Parker, Claude E.
Payne, Thomas B.
Peters, Irving E.
Peterson, L. O.*
Pistole, F. L.*
Pitchon, Salvatore
Polidoro, Vincent
Porter, John J.
Price, Fred D.
Pullen, R. H.*
Pye, G. E.*
Ranger, John W.
Reas, John C.
Reed, C. O.*
Reese, Sheldon D.
Reilly, John D.
Reynolds, James E.
Rhodes, Frank
Roberts, Valdon
Rody, Leo
Rogers, Leon W.
Rose, Guy M.
Ross, R. B.
Ross, William
Roszell, L. T.*
Roth, J. T.*
Rushing, Robert C.
Russell, Milton B.
Schertz, Joseph W.
Schilperoort, Clarence
Schneck, Walter K.
Schram, Theodore
Schuelke, J. H.*
Schulz, Richard P.
Schwarz, Otto C.
Seidel, A. G.*
Shearer, James M.
Shettlesworth, Clenton
Sizemore, Marvin

Smith, Harold P.
Smith, Jack D.
Smith, Jack L.
Smith, James A.
Smith, Wilbur G.
Snyder, Earl J.
Snyder, Samuel E.
Soule, I. G.*
Sparks, Raymond L.
Spencer, M. D.*
Sprinkle, Kenneth
Stanczak, John
Starr, Melvin C.
Stefanek, John B.
Stevens, Norman E.
Stewart, William J.
Stivers, John B.
Stoddard, George D.
Stone, Harry H.
Strickland, H. S.
Su, Marco
Suomi, Sulo W.
Swanson, Dorsey G.

Swartz, Lowell W.
Tanberg, A. N.*
Templeman, Edward J.
Terry, Archie H.
Tetterton, William E.
Thew, Henry P.
Thomas, Charley L.
Tiefel, Dale J.
Trim, D. P.*
Tsoa, Chu L.
Tucker, W. E.*
Usher, Rexford D.
Vogt, LaVerne
Wampler, Carl A.
Warcken, August N.
Ward, F. C.*
Wargowsky, Lawrence
Washburn, Claude
Weeks, Roy S.
Weiler, F. B.*
Weissinger, William J.
Welfelt, Edward A.
Whaley, Joseph H.

White, J. H.*
Widmeyer, H. C.*
Wilder, Robert L.
Wilhite, Herman L.
Wilker, Max W.
Wilkinson, Eugene T.
Willerton, R. P.*
Williams, D. M.*
Williams, John M.
Williams, Roy O.
Willis, D. W.*
Winn, M. A.*
Winslow, Walter G.
Wisecup, John W.
Wittkop, Lawrence H.
Wolf, Joseph W.
Wolos, Alex J.
Woody, Stanley D.
Yarbro, Robert L.
Yates, D. R.*
Ynclan, Eugene P.
Young, K. A.*
Zabler, Wallace E.

U.S. Marine Corps Personnel**

Aust, Richard J.
Barrett, Edward M.
Battles, Lawrence F.
Bukowsky, Emil G.
Charles, H. Robert
Cray, Hampton R.
Dupler, Harold H.*
Faulk, Joseph H.
Gallagher, Frank E.
Gee, James W.
Grice, Walter L.

Hill, D. W.*
Holsinger, F. O.*
King, F. W.
Lusk, J. M.*
McCone, James
McFarland, Thomas J.
Miller, William D.
O'Brien, Johnny F.
Owens, Floyd I.
Page, Bert E.
Pryor, Charles L.

Quick, Fred B.
Robinson, Marvin
Rochford, Eugene D.
Shaw, Kenneth R.
Shuster, John F.
Trice, Earnest M.
Willey, Lloyd V.
Williams, Carl H.
Wilson, J. R.*
Winters, Jack

Notes

Chapter 1

1. On Point: The Newsletter of the Army Historical Foundation 6 (Summer 2000): 6.

2. Ronald E. Marcello, "Lone Star POWs: Texas National Guardsmen and the Building of the Burma-Thailand Railroad, 1942–1944," Southwestern Historical Quarterly 95, no. 3 (January 1992): 295.

3. Ilo Hard to Ronald E. Marcello, March 26, 1980, interview transcript (OH 510), 2–3. All oral history interviews cited hereafter are housed in the University of North Texas Archives, Willis Library, Denton, Texas.

4. Huddleston Wright to Ronald E. Marcello, November 2, November 14, 1989, interview transcript (OH 794), 3.

5. Luther Prunty to Ronald E. Marcello, October 20, October 27, 1986, interview transcript (OH 689), 3.

6. Clark Taylor to Ronald E. Marcello, September 14, 1979, interview transcript (OH 491), 2.

7. Jess Stanbrough to Ronald E. Marcello, April 15, 1985, interview transcript (OH 658), 3.

8. Frank Ficklin to Ronald E. Marcello, January 16, 1987, interview transcript (OH 691), 2.

9. Uell Carter and George Killian to Ronald E. Marcello, September 19, 1970, interview transcript (OH 56), 3.

10. Edward Fung to Ronald E. Marcello, December 21, 1977, interview transcript (OH 404), 3–4.

11. Kelly Bob Bramlett to Ronald E. Marcello, November 2, 1976, interview transcript (OH 345), 2.

12. Roy M. Offerle to Ronald E. Marcello, August 14, 1978, interview transcript (OH 457), 2.

13. Roger White to Ronald E. Marcello, January 7, January 8, 1997, interview

transcript (OH 1167), 3; Dan Buzzo to Ronald E. Marcello, February 11, February 16, 1998, interview transcript (OH 1245), 5.

14. Crayton Gordon to Ronald E. Marcello, January 31, 1977, interview transcript (OH 383), 2.

15. Lester Rasbury to Ronald E. Marcello, June 10, June 15, 1978, interview transcript (OH 438); Alf Brown Jr. to Ronald E. Marcello, March 26, 1974, interview transcript (OH 188), 2–3.

16. Houston Wright to Ronald E. Marcello, August 15, 1978, interview transcript (OH 466), 2–3.

17. Thurman Capps to Ronald E. Marcello, July 8, 1997, interview transcript (OH 1196), 4.

18. Stanbrough (OH 658), 4.

19. Hard (OH 510), 4–6; Fung (OH 404), 5–7; Gordon (OH 383), 3.

20. Bramlett (OH 345), 2.

21. Fung (OH 404), 7; Gordon (OH 383), 3.

22. Prunty (OH 689), 2–3.

23. Taylor (OH 491), 2–3.

24. Huddleston Wright (OH 794), 3–4; Hard (OH 510), 3–4. The Ten Series and Twenty Series referred to by Lieutenant Hard were similar to the Army's Reserve Officer Training Corps but pertained only to noncommissioned officers in the National Guard. After completing the more basic Ten Series, which included a number of tests and other exercises, a candidate moved on to the more advanced Twenty Series. After successfully completing both series, the candidate became part of a war pool reserve, indicating that should the United States go to war and mobilize the National Guard, the candidate would become an officer in the U.S. Army.

25. Offerle (OH 457), 2–3.

26. Executive Order Number 8594, "Ordering Certain Units and Members of the National Guard of the United States into the Active Military Service of the United States," November 16, 1940.

27. For a general history of the 36th Division, see Bruce L. Brager, *The Texas 36th Division: A History* (Austin, Tex.: Eakin Press, 2002), especially chap. 6, "Between the Wars," 78–95, and chap. 7, "Getting Ready for War Again," 96–120.

28. Buzzo (OH 1245), 5–6; Hard (OH 510), 8; White (OH 1167), 7.

29. Hard (OH 510), 8.

30. Carter (OH 56), 4.

31. Offerle (OH 457), 4.

32. Lawrence Brown to Ronald E. Marcello, March 13, 1974, interview transcript (OH 178), 4; Rasbury (OH 438), 5–6.

33. Webb (OH 1181), 21.

34. Gordon (OH 383), 4.

35. Killian (OH 56), 5.

36. Gordon (OH 383), 4; Rasbury (OH 438), 6; P. J. Smallwood to Ronald E. Marcello, October 25, 1973, interview transcript (OH 166), 4; Fung (OH 404), 9–10.

37. George Burns to Ronald E. Marcello, March 12, 1974, interview transcript (OH 176), 6–8; Alf Brown (OH 188), 9; Offerle (OH 457), 7.

38. Kyle Thompson, *A Thousand Cups of Rice: Surviving the Death Railway* (Austin, Tex.: Eakin Press, 1994), 8–9.

39. Offerle (OH 457), 4.

40. White (OH 1167), 10; Rasbury (OH 438), 8; Roy G. Armstrong to Ronald E. Marcello, October 15, 1980, interview transcript (OH 530), 7–8; Huddleston Wright (OH 794), 7; Stanbrough (OH 658), 8.

41. Wade Webb to Ronald E. Marcello, February 7, 1997, interview transcript (OH 1181), 8.

42. White (OH 1167), 9.

43. *Brownwood Bulletin*, December 1940 through January 1941; *Fort Worth Star-Telegram*, December 17, 1940.

44. Ficklin (OH 691), 5–6; Houston Wright (OH 466), 6; Rasbury (OH 438), 8.

45. Hard (OH 510), 15–16.

46. Fung (OH 404), 10; White (OH 1167), 10; Alf Brown (OH 188), 5; Gordon (OH 383), 4–6; Armstrong (OH 530), 7–8.

47. White (OH 1167), 12; Alf Brown (OH 188), 6; Webb (OH 1181), 18.

48. Smallwood (OH 166), 8.

49. Burns (OH 176), 6.

50. Thaddeus Holt, "Relax—It's Only a Maneuver," *Military History Quarterly* 4, no. 2 (Winter 1992): 30–41. For a full discussion of the Louisiana Maneuvers, see Christopher R. Gabel, *The U.S. Army G.H.Q. Maneuvers of 1941* (Washington, D.C.: Center of Military History, United States Army, 1991).

51. Holt, "Relax—It's Only a Maneuver," 34–35.

52. Fred L. Walker, *From Texas to Rome* (Dallas: Taylor Publishing, 1969), 1; Headquarters, 36th Division, "Memorandum on Age-in-Grade Regulations, September 10, 1941," in Claude V. Birkhead Collection, Box E, File I, at Camp Mabry, Austin, Texas; "General Birkhead Retires from 36th Command," *Fort Worth Star-Telegram*, September 16, 1941.

53. Smallwood (OH 166), 9–10.

54. Prunty (OH 689), 8–10.

55. Cecil Minshew to Ronald E. Marcello, February 18, 1983, interview transcript (OH 597), 8–9; Stanbrough (OH 658), 13–16; Armstrong (OH 530), 8–9; Buzzo (OH 1245), 9–10; White (OH 1167), 13–16; Hard (OH 510), 16–21.

56. Kent R. Greenfield et al., *The Army Ground Forces: The Organization of Ground Combat Troops*, The United States Army in World War II (Washington, D.C.: Historical Division, Department of the Army, 1947), 12–14, 271–78.

57. Hard (OH 510), 21; Huddleston Wright (OH 794), 11; Capps (OH 1196), 7; Houston Wright (OH 466), 8; Burns (OH 176), 5; Lawrence Brown (OH 178), 7; Ficklin (OH 691), 7; Prunty (OH 689), 10.

58. Stanbrough (OH 658), 17.

59. Minshew (OH 597), 10.

60. Webb (OH 1181), 19.

61. Other units of the 36th Division were also assigned to duty in various places outside Texas. For example, a number of companies from the 143rd Infantry

Regiment were assigned to duty in Tucson and Phoenix, Arizona, to guard airfields and railroad tunnels. See Fred Walker, Daily Journal of the Commander of the 36th Division, Camp Mabry Archives, Austin, Texas.

62. This is based on biographical information drawn from the oral history interviews upon which most of this work is based. Commissioned and noncommissioned officers were naturally older than the enlistees. Volunteers from A Battery transferred to D Battery; those from B Battery went to E Battery; and those from C Battery transferred to F Battery.

63. Hard (OH 510), 22.

64. Fung (OH 404), 8.

65. Ficklin (OH 691), 8.

66. Buzzo (OH 1245), 11–14; Smallwood (OH 166), 11; Webb (OH 1181), 12–13; White (OH 1167), 17–18; Huddleston Wright (OH 794), 16.

67. Eldridge Rayburn to Ronald E. Marcello, January 16, 1980, interview transcript (OH 499), 17. At least one member of C Battery, however, was not so willing to go. M. L. Rea got married after returning to Camp Bowie and asked to remain in Brownwood. His lieutenant told him, "'Thank you for volunteering.'" Rea wanted it known that he did not volunteer but that he followed his orders anyway. M. L. Rea to Ronald E. Marcello, April 14, 1980, interview transcript (OH 517), 12–13.

68. Prunty (OH 689), 6.

69. Offerle (OH 457), 8.

70. Rayburn (OH 499), 18; Alf Brown (OH 188), 11; Bramlett (OH 345), 7–8; Capps (OH 1196), 8; Houston Wright (OH 466); Killian (OH 56), 8; Stanbrough (OH 658), 21; Huddleston Wright (OH 794), 13; Hard (OH 510), 22–23.

71. Buzzo (OH 1245), 14–15; Armstrong (OH 530), 13; Houston Wright (OH 466), 8–9; Stanbrough (OH 658), 25–26; Rasbury (OH 438), 16; Minshew (OH 597), 112–13; Rea (OH 517), 15–16; "Personal Diary of Colonel Blucher S. Tharp," pt. I, 1, Lost Battalion Collection, Camp Mabry Archives, Austin, Texas.

72. Webb (OH 1181), 16.

73. Prunty (OH 689), 12.

Chapter 2

1. Huddleston Wright (OH 794), 19.

2. Hard (OH 510), 29; Prunty (OH 689), 13; Webb (OH 1181), 17; Taylor (OH 491), 12–13; White (OH 1167), 20–21.

3. Webb (OH 1181), 16–17; White (OH 1167), 22; Armstrong (OH 530), 13.

4. Houston Wright (OH 466), 9.

5. Stanbrough (OH 658), 27–28.

6. Taylor (OH 491), 13–14.

7. Fung (OH 404), 10.

8. Armstrong (OH 530), 14; Huddleston Wright (OH 794), 17.

9. Hard (OH 510), 30–32.

10. Buzzo (OH 1245), 16.

11. Louis Morton, *Fall of the Philippines* (Washington, D.C.: Office of the Chief of Military History, 1953), 145–46. See also "Personal Diary of Colonel Blucher S. Tharp," pt. I, 1.

12. Armstrong (OH 530), 15; Webb (OH 1181), 23–24; Huddleston Wright (OH 794), 20–21; Ficklin (OH 691), 10.

13. Thompson, *A Thousand Cups of Rice*, 18–19; Lawrence Brown (OH 178), 11; Burns (OH 176), 7–8; Capps (OH 1196), 8; J. W. Buck to Ronald E. Marcello, February 24, 1975, interview transcript (OH 279), 5; Gordon (OH 383), 11; Smallwood (OH 166), 12–13.

14. Ficklin (OH 691), 10.

15. Houston Wright (OH 466), 10–11.

16. Fung (OH 404), 11.

17. Offerle (OH 457), 10.

18. Houston Wright (OH 466), 11–12; Fung (OH 404), 12; Armstrong (OH 530), 17; Buzzo (OH 1245), 20; Gordon (OH 383), 12; Offerle (OH 457), 10–11; Taylor (OH 491), 16–17.

19. Stanbrough (OH 658), 33–34; Gordon (OH 383), 12; Carter (OH 56), 8; Webb (OH 1181), 25; Buck (OH 279), 5; Fung (OH 404), 13.

20. Offerle (OH 457), 11.

21. Thompson, *A Thousand Cups of Rice*, 19.

22. Smallwood (OH 166), 13.

23. Linda Mayo, *The Ordnance Department: On Beachhead and Battlefront* (Washington, D.C.: Office of the Chief of Military History, 1968), 34–35.

24. Thompson, *A Thousand Cups of Rice*, 20; Frank Fujita, *Foo: A Japanese-American Prisoner of the Rising Sun* (Denton: University of North Texas Press, 1993), 44–45.

25. Fujita, *Foo*, 45–46; Thompson, *A Thousand Cups of Rice*, 20; Ben Kelley to Ronald E. Marcello, March 26, 1982, interview transcript (OH 565), 17; Houston Wright (OH 466), 16; Webb (OH 1181), 29–30; Stanbrough (OH 658), 35–36; Prunty (OH 689), 17. Mayo describes this as having been "the largest Army shellback initiation up to that time" (*Ordnance Department*, 35).

26. Gordon (OH 383), 13.

27. Quoted in Mayo, *Ordnance Department*, 35.

28. Taylor (OH 491), 19; Webb (OH 1181), 26–27; Houston Wright (OH 466), 14–16; Prunty (OH 689), 18–19; Rasbury (OH 438), 21–22; Kelley (OH 565), 19–20; Herbert R. Morris to Ronald E. Marcello, May 8, 1989, interview transcript (OH 780), 23–25; Benjamin Dunn, *The Bamboo Express* (Chicago: Adams Press, 1979), 7; Fujita, *Foo*, 47; Mayo incorrectly attributes the manning of the artillery pieces to the 453rd Ordnance (Aviation) Bombardment Company (*Ordnance Department*, 35).

29. Mayo, *Ordnance Department*, 35–36.

30. Offerle (OH 457), 11–12.

31. Houston Wright (OH 466), 14.

32. Thompson, *A Thousand Cups of Rice*, 21.

33. Stanbrough (OH 658), 37; Lawrence Brown (OH 178), 13–14; Buzzo (OH 1245), 21; Alf Brown (OH 188), 18–20; Fujita, *Foo*, 47.

34. Killian (OH 56), 8–9; Carter (OH 56), 10.

35. Capps (OH 1196), 9.

36. Hard (OH 510), 39–40. He also uncharacteristically said that when the zig-zagging began, the Republic "took a heading right straight back toward the States, and I was hoping we would keep going that way."

37. Fung (OH 404), 13; Burns (OH 176), 12; Buck (OH 279), 6.

38. Hard (OH 510), 41.

39. Burns (OH 176), 12.

40. Garth Slate to Ronald E. Marcello, August 13, 1980, interview transcript (OH 528), 20; Morris (OH 780), 23; Buzzo (OH 1245), 23; Stanbrough (OH 658), 38; Houston Wright (OH 466), 17; Offerle (OH 457), 13; Taylor (OH 491), 19; Gordon (OH 383), 15; Huddleston Wright (OH 794), 24; Smallwood (OH 166), 14.

41. Fung (OH 404), 14–15.

42. See Fujita, Foo, for the autobiography of this Japanese American soldier. Lawrence Brown (OH 178), 14; Buck (OH 279), 6; Burns (OH 176), 12; Alf Brown (OH 188), 19; Crayton Gordon said that Fujita was teased a little but that Fujita "was very much a soldier" ([OH 383], 16).

43. Morton, Fall of the Philippines, 148. The Republic and the rest of the Pensacola convoy were originally to be sent to the Philippines from Brisbane to help U.S. defenses there. Japanese dominance of the air and sea lanes made this impracticable, however, and the men and materiel never reached the Philippines.

44. Slate (OH 528), 22; Morris (OH 780), 28; Buzzo (OH 1245), 24–26; Houston Wright (OH 466), 18–20; Prunty (OH 689), 20; Rasbury (OH 438), 28–31; White (OH 1167), 27–28; Smallwood (OH 166), 20–22; "Personal Diary of Colonel Blucher S. Tharp," pt. I, 6.

45. Garth Slate remembers that the Australians continually referred to the Texans as "Yanks," and that "we tried to tell them we was from Texas, that we wasn't from the North, but they still referred to us as the 'Yanks'" ([OH 528], 22–23).

46. Preston E. Stone to Ronald E. Marcello, February 20, 1980, interview transcript (OH 498), 23; Bramlett (OH 345), 13; Armstrong (OH 530), 22–23; Prunty (OH 689), 22; Fung (OH 404), 19; Stanbrough (OH 658), 44–45; Buzzo (OH 1245), 25; Thomas Spencer to Ronald E. Marcello, February 5, 1979, interview transcript (OH 484), 22.

47. Ficklin (OH 691), 14; White (OH 1167), 28; Huddleston Wright (OH 794), 28; Rasbury (OH 438), 30; Prunty (OH 689), 21–22; Stanbrough (OH 658), 46–47.

48. Smallwood (OH 166), 22.

49. At this point, the Americans still hoped to get relief to the Philippines, of which the soldiers and cargo on the Bloemfontein would be a part. Japanese naval and air superiority in the region precluded American relief efforts, however, and the Bloemfontein made its way to Surabaja, Java, instead. See Morton, Fall of the Philippines, 154.

50. Clyde J. Shelton to Ronald E. Marcello, July 27, 1987, interview transcript (OH 700), 20–21; Spencer (OH 484), 25; Slate (OH 528), 28; Taylor (OH 491), 24–26; Armstrong (OH 530), 24; Bramlett (OH 345), 15; Gordon (OH 383), 25–26; Alf Brown (OH 188), 24–26.

51. Smallwood (OH 166), 26.

52. Buck (OH 279), 9.

53. Prunty (OH 689), 23; Houston Wright (OH 466), 20–21.

54. Stanbrough (OH 658), 50–51.

55. Stone (OH 498), 25.

56. Thomas Whitehead to Ronald E. Marcello, February 2, 1977, interview transcript (OH 366), 27–28; Granville T. Summerlin to Ronald E. Marcello, June 9, 1981, interview transcript (OH 543), 19; Martin Chambers to Ronald E. Marcello, April 8, 1982, interview transcript (OH 575), 17–18; Minshew (OH 597), 31–32; Fung (OH 404), 22; Ficklin (OH 691), 16–18; White (OH 1167), 30–31; Rasbury (OH 438), 34–35; "Personal Diary of Colonel Blucher S. Tharp," pt. I, 9–10.

57. For a full discussion of the 19th Bomb Group and other army air forces units on Java, see Walter D. Edmonds, *They Fought with What They Had: The Story of the Army Air Forces in the Southwest Pacific, 1941–1942* (Boston: Little, Brown, 1951). For a more general treatment of the army air forces in the Pacific, see Wesley Frank Craven and James Lea Cate, eds., *The Army Air Forces in World War II: Plans and Early Operations, January 1939 to August 1942* (Chicago: University of Chicago Press, 1948).

58. Webb (OH 1181), 40; Huddleston Wright (OH 794), 30–32; White (OH 1167), 32–33; Lawrence Brown (OH 178), 24–25; Burns (OH 176), 18–19; Minshew (OH 597), 32–34; Whitehead (OH 366), 28; Stanbrough (OH 658), 58–59.

59. *Roster, Lost Battalion Association,* 2002, 46. The Lost Battalion Association was formed shortly after World War II, and its membership includes survivors of the 2nd Battalion, as well as survivors of the sinking of the heavy cruiser USS *Houston* and their families. The association publishes an annual roster, providing information on the group's members and detailed information concerning the disposition of those held prisoner by the Japanese. Thompson, *A Thousand Cups of Rice,* 30; Dunn, *The Bamboo Express,* 16; Fujita, *Foo,* 63; Rasbury (OH 438), 45; "Personal Diary of Colonel Blucher S. Tharp," pt. I, 11.

60. Thompson, *A Thousand Cups of Rice,* 30–34; Dunn, *The Bamboo Express,* 13–15; Hard (OH 510), 52–60; Webb (OH 1181), 42–47; Houston Wright (OH 466), 25–30; Buck (OH 279), 10–11; Smallwood (OH 166), 29–35; Taylor (OH 491), 32–37.

61. Ficklin (OH 691), 22.

62. Buzzo (OH 1245), 36; Ficklin (OH 691), 19.

63. Fujita, *Foo,* 63.

64. Gordon (OH 383), 35–36; Smallwood (OH 166), 34; Buck (OH 279), 11; Burns (OH 176), 23; Alf Brown (OH 188), 30–31; Whitehead (OH 366), 32; Bramlett (OH 345), 22–23; Fung (OH 404), 25.

65. Prunty (OH 689), 31; Huddleston Wright (OH 794), 34; Gordon (OH 383), 38; Fujita, *Foo,* 66; "Personal Diary of Colonel Blucher S. Tharp," pt. I, 11.

66. Summerlin (OH 543), 25; Minshew (OH 597), 44; Chambers (OH 575), 26; Whitehead (OH 366), 32.

67. Gordon (OH 383), 40; Rasbury (OH 438), 48; Taylor (OH 491), 39; Houston Wright (OH 466), 33; Huddleston Wright (OH 794), 38; Bramlett (OH 345), 25; Armstrong (OH 530), 38.

68. Capps (OH 1196), 15–16; Hard (OH 510), 64; Buzzo (OH 1245), 47; Gordon (OH 383), 40–41.

69. Ficklin (OH 691), 24.

70. Webb (OH 1181), 48; Summerlin (OH 543), 25.

71. Lawrence Brown (OH 178), 35; Huddleston Wright (OH 794), 38; Bramlett (OH 345), 25.

Chapter 3

1. By the end of February 1942, the Japanese had air and naval superiority, but their troops, numbering around forty thousand, were outnumbered by ABDA ground forces. However, the quality of the large Dutch Home Guard was very poor, as was the quality of their weapons. See Lionel Wigmore, *Australia in the War of 1939–1945*, vol. 4, *The Japanese Thrust*, 22 vols., Series 1 (Canberra: Australian War Memorial, 1957), 497–500.

2. Ibid.

3. Ibid., 199–202.

4. Ibid., 201. See also Charles Robert Anderson, *East Indies* (Washington, D.C.: U.S. Army Center of Military History, 1995), 6.

5. Wigmore, *Japanese Thrust*, 205.

6. Language problems also hampered the ABDA defense of Java, causing confusion in communications. Walter D. Edmonds, *They Fought with What They Had*, 265–75; E. F. Aitken, *The Story of the 2/2nd Australian Pioneer Battalion* (Melbourne: 2/2nd Pioneer Battalion Association, 1953), 120.

7. Wigmore, *Japanese Thrust*, 442.

8. Ibid., 502.

9. Aitken, *The Story of the 2/2nd Pioneer Battalion*, 120–23; Wigmore, *Japanese Thrust*, 499–500.

10. Wigmore, *Japanese Thrust*, 501.

11. J. L. Summers to Ronald E. Marcello, August 21, August 22, 1995, interview transcript (OH 1079), 36; Alvin Morgan to Ronald E. Marcello, February 17, February 24, March 3, 1997, interview transcript (OH 1183), 29–30; Rayburn (OH 499), 65; Hard (OH 510), 65; Stanbrough (OH 658), 73–74; Rasbury (OH 438), 49; Ficklin (OH 691), 24–25; Prunty (OH 689), 32; White (OH 1167), 37; "Personal Diary of Colonel Blucher S. Tharp," pt. I, 14–15.

12. Fung (OH 404), 33; Lawrence Brown (OH 178), 30; Prunty (OH 689), 34–35; Buzzo (OH 1245), 42–43; Houston Wright (OH 466), 37–38; Aitken, *The Story of the 2/2nd Australian Pioneer Battalion*, 121; Wigmore, *Japanese Thrust*, 501.

13. Aitken, *The Story of the 2/2nd Australian Pioneer Battalion*, 121.

14. "Personal Diary of Colonel Blucher S. Tharp," pt. I, 15; Wigmore, *Japanese Thrust*, 502–503.

15. Quote from Rasbury (OH 438), 47; Jack W. Kenner to Ronald E. Marcello, April 4, 1980, interview transcript (OH 513), 36.

16. Rasbury (OH 438), 46.

17. Armstrong (OH 530), 42.

18. Houston Wright (OH 466), 91–92.

19. Stensland arrived with several thousand dollars left from the Robenson Mission, and he later used this money to purchase much-needed food and supplies for the American prisoners. See Edmonds, *They Fought with What They Had*, 371–92; Special Orders in Java, "Special Order Number 3, February 5, 1942," located in "Lost Battalion" Files, Wise County Heritage Museum, Decatur, Texas; "Prisoner of War Report: Howard Robert Charles," September 21, 1945, National Archives, Record Group (hereafter NA, RG) 153, Box 1407, File 57-195-1.

20. Wigmore, *Japanese Thrust*, 498–99; Fujita, *Foo*, 74–84; White (OH 1167), 44–45; Killian (OH 56), 30; "Personal Diary of Colonel Blucher S. Tharp," pt. I, 15.

21. Due to faulty intelligence, the Dutch command erroneously believed the Japanese invasion force numbered some two hundred thousand troops, which was the primary reason for the surrender. The Allies' total forces, including the Dutch Home Guard, numbered no more than seventy-five thousand troops. According to General Imamura, however, the Japanese had no more than forty thousand troops participating in the Java campaign and only twenty-five thousand available for combat near Bandung. See a portion of Imamura's edited memoirs in Imamura Hitoshi, *Memoirs of General Imamura*, vol. 4, in *The Japanese Experience in Indonesia: Selected Memoirs of 1942–1945*, ed. Anthony Reid and Oki Akira (Athens: Ohio University Center for International Studies, Center for Southeast Asian Studies, 1986), 31–48.

The men of E Battery, who remained at the eastern end of Java to defend Surabaja, were also taken prisoner. The Japanese shipped this group of POWs to Japan in October 1942, where they remained for the duration of the war. These men, therefore, did not labor on the "Death Railway."

22. Hard (OH 510), 79; Stanbrough (OH 658), 79–81; Ficklin (OH 691), 27–28; Bramlett (OH 345), 27; Armstrong (OH 530), 44–46; Gordon (OH 383), 44; Prunty (OH 689), 36–37. Apparently, as many as four of the men did escape through Tjilatjap, with one, Milton ("Red") Lyon, eventually making his way to the safety of Australia. Lyon went on to serve with distinction in the war in the campaigns of the southwest Pacific.

23. Fujita, *Foo*, 87–92; Buck (OH 279), 13–14; White (OH 1167), 45–46; Carter (OH 56), 30.

24. See Imamura Hitoshi, *Memoirs of General Imamura*, 34–36; Prunty (OH 689), 42–44; Webb (OH 1181), 50; Buzzo (OH 1245), 62; Houston Wright (OH 466), 44–45; Offerle (OH 457), 67.

25. *Roster, Lost Battalion Association*, 2002, vii.

26. Prunty (OH 689), 37–38; Rasbury (OH 438), 54–55; Lawrence Brown (OH 178), 35; Smallwood (OH 166), 42; Burns (OH 176), 27–28; Alf Brown (OH 188), 43.

27. Taylor (OH 491), 41; Houston Wright (OH 466), 34; Prunty (OH 689), 36; Smallwood (OH 166), 40; Webb (OH 1181), 48.

28. Huddleston Wright (OH 794), 41–42; Houston Wright (OH 466), 34; Dunn, *The Bamboo Express*, 23–24; Thompson, *A Thousand Cups of Rice*, 42.

29. Frank Fujita to Ronald E. Marcello, November 9, 1970, interview transcript (OH 59), 45; Rasbury (OH 438), 57; Buzzo (OH 1245), 41; Prunty (OH 689), 32; Smallwood (OH 166), 37; Capps (OH 1196), 19.

30. Ficklin (OH 691), 18.

31. Hard (OH 510), 62.

32. Stanbrough (OH 658), 77.

33. George P. Lawley to William J. Teague, November 3, 1973, interview transcript (OH 164), 23; Webb (OH 1181), 50–51; Buck (OH 279), 14; Lawrence Brown (OH 178), 32; Fung (OH 404), 34; Bramlett (OH 345), 28; Buzzo (OH 1245), 52; Dunn, *The Bamboo Express*, 23.

34. Houston Wright (OH 466), 39.

35. Huddleston Wright (OH 794), 42.

36. Douglas F. Knight to Ronald E. Marcello, March 12, 1978, interview transcript (OH 413), 28; Houston Wright (OH 466), 40; Lawrence Brown (OH 178), 31; Smallwood (OH 166), 41; Hard (OH 510), 71; Fung (OH 404), 34; Fujita (OH 59), 28–29.

37. Fung (OH 404), 34.

38. Kelley (OH 565), 41.

39. Buck (OH 279), 15; Gordon (OH 383), 47; Taylor (OH 491), 46–48; Sidney C. Matlock to Ronald E. Marcello, September 9, 1981, interview transcript (OH 555), 50–51; Kenner (OH 513), 39–40; Knight (OH 413), 28; Morgan (OH 1183), 32–33; Offerle (OH 457), 35; Huddleston Wright (OH 794), 43–44.

40. Dunn, *The Bamboo Express*, 24–25; Thompson, *A Thousand Cups of Rice*, 44; Armstrong (OH 530), 47–50; Knight (OH 413), 29; Ficklin (OH 691), 36; Hard (OH 510), 77–78; Alf Brown (OH 188), 40–42; Burns (OH 176), 29; Rasbury (OH 438), 59–60; "Personal Diary of Colonel Blucher S. Tharp," pt. I, 15.

41. Matlock (OH 555), 53–54; Rasbury (OH 438), 63; Lawrence Brown (OH 178), 34; Taylor (OH 491), 47; Buzzo (OH 1245), 59; Webb (OH 1181), 56–57; Capps (OH 1196), 21–22.

42. Offerle (OH 457), 36; Burns (OH 176), 31; Ficklin (OH 691), 30; Bramlett (OH 345), 30; Buck (OH 279), 16; Prunty (OH 689), 40–41; Buzzo (OH 1245), 58; Webb (OH 1181), 54.

43. Buck (OH 279), 16; Prunty (OH 689), 41.

44. Rasbury (OH 438), 60.

45. Taylor (OH 491), 47; Gordon (OH 383), 48; Rasbury (OH 438), 59–60.

46. For discussion of early treatment of prisoners by the Japanese, see Huddleston Wright (OH 794), 45; Offerle (OH 457), 36–37; Taylor (OH 491), 47–48; Smallwood (OH 166), 45; Burns (OH 176), 31; Alf Brown (OH 188), 44, 48; Ficklin (OH 691), 33–34; Buck (OH 279), 16. For a discussion of racism as a factor in the Pacific War, see John W. Dower, *War without Mercy: Race and Power in the Pacific War* (New York: Pantheon Books, 1986).

47. Ikuhiko Hata, "From Consideration to Contempt: The Changing Nature of Japanese Military and Popular Perceptions of War throughout the Ages," in *Prisoners of War and Their Captors in World War II*, ed. Bob Moore and Kent Fedorowich (Oxford: Oxford International Publishers, 1996), 253–75; see also Philip A. Towle, "Japanese Treatment of Prisoners in 1904–1905: Foreign Officers' Reports," *Military Affairs* 39, no. 3 (October 1975): 115–17.

48. Ikuhiko Hata, "From Consideration to Contempt," 254.

49. Ibid., 254; Charles G. Roland, "Allied POWs, Japanese Captors and the Geneva Convention," *War & Society* 9 (1991): 83–101.

50. Roland, "Allied POWs," 84.

51. For a full discussion of the evolution of the culture of the Japanese military in the twentieth century, see Robert B. Edgerton, *Warriors of the Rising Sun: A History of the Japanese Military* (New York: Norton, 1997), especially chap. 9, "From Chivalry to Brutality," 305–24; see also Edward F. L. Russell, *The Knights of Bushido: The Shocking History of Japanese War Atrocities* (New York: Dutton, 1958), 55–56.

52. Russell, *Knights of Bushido*, 55–56.

53. John R. Pritchard and Sonia M. Zaide, eds., *The Tokyo War Crimes Trials: The Complete Transcripts of the Proceedings of the International Military Tribunal for the Far East* [cited hereafter as IMTFE] (New York: Garland Publishing, 1981), Exhibit 3043.

54. Ibid.

55. Ibid.

56. Ibid., Exhibit 1490; see also U.S. Department of State, *Foreign Relations of the United States: Diplomatic Papers, 1942* (Washington, D.C.: U.S. Government Printing Office, 1960), 1:796–800.

57. IMTFE, Exhibit 1493.

Chapter 4

1. Dunn, *The Bamboo Express*, 27; Thompson, *A Thousand Cups of Rice*, 45; Buzzo (OH 1245), 59; Rasbury (OH 438), 66; Prunty (OH 689), 43–44; "Personal Diary of Colonel Blucher S. Tharp," pt. I, 16.

2. Webb (OH 1181), 58–59; Prunty (OH 689), 44; Buzzo (OH 1245), 62–63; Dunn, *The Bamboo Express*, 27. For a short, general description of the conditions of railway transport of prisoners of war on Java, see "In the Matter of Transporting Prisoners of War under Improper Conditions: Perpetuation of Testimony of Ralph Rentz," January 1, 1946, NA, RG 153, Box 1377, File 52-46-1.

3. Houston Wright (OH 466), 49; Fung (OH 404), 60–61; Ficklin (OH 691), 26; Prunty (OH 689), 44.

4. B. D. Fillmore to Ronald E. Marcello, October 9, 1973, interview transcript (OH 162), 29; Horace Chumley to Ronald E. Marcello, April 3, 1974, interview transcript (OH 199), 30; Fung (OH 404), 39; Prunty (OH 689), 46–47; Rasbury (OH 438), 66–67; Houston Wright (OH 466), 51–52; "Statement of James E. Crum," September 26, 1945, NA, RG 153, Box 1400, File 57-8-32.

5. Buzzo (OH 1245), 64–65; Burns (OH 176), 41–42; Huddleston Wright (OH 794), 52; Stanbrough (OH 658), 86; Fillmore (OH 162), 30.

6. Hard (OH 510), 85; Fung (OH 404), 47; Houston Wright (OH 466), 56; Prunty (OH 689), 47; Armstrong (OH 530), 56; Huddleston Wright (OH 794), 69; "Statement of James E. Crum," September 26, 1945, NA, RG 153, Box 1400, File 57-8-32; "In the Matter of the Japanese Failure to Provide . . . American Prisoners of War

with Proper Food, Quarters, and Medical Care from April 1, 1942, to September 16, 1945: Perpetuation of Testimony of Horace E. Chumley," November 20, 1945, NA, RG 153, Box 1376, File 52-0-8.

7. Buzzo (OH 1245), 74.

8. Stanbrough (OH 658), 85.

9. Huddleston Wright (OH 794), 52; Prunty (OH 689), 47.

10. Buzzo (OH 1245), 61; Stanbrough (OH 658), 85.

11. Chumley (OH 199), 31; Stanbrough (OH 658), 88–89; Huddleston Wright (OH 794), 49–53; Armstrong (OH 530), 52; Houston Wright (OH 466), 65; Fung (OH 404), 42; Webb (OH 1181), 60–62; Rasbury (OH 438), 69.

12. Raymond D. Reed to Ronald E. Marcello, March 13, 1979, interview transcript (OH 486), 94.

13. Prunty (OH 689), 47; Houston Wright (OH 466), 55; Fung (OH 404), 41–42; Hard (OH 510), 94–95; Bramlett (OH 345), 36–38.

14. E. Benjamin Dunn to Ronald E. Marcello, November 16, 1999, interview transcript (OH 1329), 63–64; Arthur B. Clark to Ronald E. Marcello, September 29, 2000, interview transcript (OH 1371), 66–67; Bramlett (OH 345), 33; Webb (OH 1181), 65; Rasbury (OH 438), 70–71; Hard (OH 510), 104; Taylor (OH 491), 57; Buzzo (OH 1245), 71–72; Fillmore (OH 162), 33–34; "Statement of Fred Conrad Grass," March 14, 1946, NA, RG 153, Box 1376, File 52-0-10.

15. Hard (OH 510), 97–98; Buzzo (OH 1245), 71–72; Taylor (OH 491), 53, 59; Clark (OH 1371), 61–62; Dunn (OH 1329), 64; Fung (OH 404), 43; Rasbury (OH 438), 69–70; Webb (OH 1181), 64; "In the Matter of the Use of Woodrow Leon Starnes . . . on Japanese Military Works and Operations from March 8, 1942, to August 23, 1945: Perpetuation of Testimony of Woodrow Leon Starnes," October 30, 1945, NA, RG 153, Box 1376, File 52-3-51.

16. Hard (OH 510), 82, 103.

17. Fillmore (OH 162), 37; Clark (OH 1371), 68–69; Huddleston Wright (OH 794), 49–50; Armstrong (OH 530), 51; Webb (OH 1181), 61–62; Buzzo (OH 1245), 73–74; Taylor (OH 491), 55; "In the Matter of Improper Treatment of American Prisoners of War at the 10th Battalion Bicycle Camp, Batavia, Java: Perpetuation of Testimony of Blucher S. Tharp," November 20, 1945, NA, RG 153, Box 1376, File 52-3-44.

18. Dunn (OH 1329), 93–94.

19. Grover Reichle to Ronald E. Marcello, January 22, 1979, interview transcript (OH 495), 59.

20. Prunty (OH 689), 45–46; Webb (OH 1181), 61–62; Armstrong (OH 530), 51; Huddleston Wright (OH 794), 50; Hard (OH 510), 102; Clark (OH 1371), 68–69; Dunn (OH 1329), 65; "In the Matter of a Severe Beating of a Prisoner of War Named Moss . . . at Tanjhan Priok [sic], about April 8, 1942: Perpetuation of Testimony of Horace E. Chumley," November 20, 1945, NA, RG 153, Box 1377, File 52-22-1.

21. Prunty (OH 689), 45–46.

22. Stanbrough (OH 658), 89; Huddleston Wright (OH 794), 50–51; Armstrong (OH 530), 60–61; Webb (OH 1181), 63; Buzzo (OH 1245), 80; Dunn (OH 1329), 65–66; Clark (OH 1371), 67–68.

23. Fung (OH 404), 45.

24. Ibid.

25. Huddleston Wright (OH 794), 50.

26. Armstrong (OH 530), 59–60, 62–63.

27. Buzzo (OH 1245), 77–78.

28. Houston Wright (OH 466), 55; Buzzo (OH 1245), 70–71; Rasbury (OH 438), 76.

29. Houston Wright (OH 466), 34–35.

30. Stanbrough (OH 658), 80; Huddleston Wright (OH 794), 77; Buzzo (OH 1245), 104; Armstrong (OH 530), 80–81.

31. Hard (OH 510), 89–93.

32. Donald C. Brain to Ronald E. Marcello, March 11, 1981, interview transcript (OH 546), 99–100.

33. Armstrong (OH 530), 53–54; Buzzo (OH 1245), 75–76; Huddleston Wright (OH 794), 62–64.

34. Prunty (OH 689), 48; Webb (OH 1181), 66; Taylor (OH 491), 53; Stanbrough (OH 658), 99–100; Hard (OH 510), 104.

35. U.S. Department of the Army, American Prisoners of War Information Bureau, Liaison and Research Branch, "Prisoner-of-War Camps in Japan & Japanese Controlled Areas As Taken from Reports of Interned American Prisoners: Batavia, Java," July 31, 1946, Camp Mabry Archives, Austin, Texas.

36. Armstrong (OH 530), 57; Fung (OH 404), 48; Prunty (OH 689), 51.

37. Department of the Army, "Prisoner-of-War Camps," 2; "Perpetuation of Testimony of Lt. L. E. Biechlin," August 26, 1946, NA, RG 153, Box 1377, File 52-30-2; "In the Matter of . . . Testimony of Horace E. Chumley," NA, RG 153, Box 1376, File 52-0-8.

38. Ficklin (OH 691), 66–68; Capps (OH 1196), 31–32; Gordon (OH 383), 60–62; Offerle (OH 457), 49–50; Buck (OH 279), 19–21; Smallwood (OH 166), 53; Houston Wright (OH 466), 64–67; Lawrence Brown (OH 178), 45; "In the Matter of Inadequate Food and Quarters at Bicycle Camp in Batavia . . . : Perpetuation of Testimony of Harold A. Brinker," February 1, 1946, NA, RG 153, Box 1376, File 52-3-45.

39. Smallwood (OH 166), 47; Paul E. Papish to Ronald E. Marcello, January 30, 1989, interview transcript (OH 781), 111.

40. Department of the Army, "Prisoner-of-War Camps," 2.

41. "Prisoner of War Report: John H. Wisecup," September 24, 1945, NA, RG 153, Box 1376, File 52-3-48; "In the Matter of the Death of Lt. Ross, USN, at Bicycle Camp, Batavia, Java: Perpetuation of Testimony of Theodore Schram," October 5, 1945, NA, RG 153, Box 1376, File 52-3-11; "Statement of Lieutenant Charles D. Smith," September 1945, NA, RG 153, Box 1400, File 57-8-31.

42. Department of the Army, "Prisoner-of-War Camps," 2; Gordon (OH 383), 59; Lawrence Brown (OH 178), 46; Taylor (OH 491), 75.

43. Alf Brown (OH 188), 52; Webb (OH 1181), 70–72; Fung (OH 404), 49–51; Rasbury (OH 438), 79–80; Armstrong (OH 530), 66–68; Buzzo (OH 1245), 85–88; Dunn, The Bamboo Express, 33–34; Department of the Army, "Prisoner-of-War Camps," 2; Wigmore, Japanese Thrust, 534.

44. "Prisoner of War Report: Jack Winters," October 9, 1945, NA, RG 153, Box 1376, File 52-3-48; "Prisoner of War Report: John H. Wisecup," September 5, 1945, NA, RG 153, Box 1376, File 52-3-48; "Testimony of Edward J. Templeman," February 5, 1946, NA, RG 153, Box 1376, File 52-3-29; "Statement of Charles D. Smith," no date, NA, RG 153, Box 1376, File 52-3-4; "Testimony of George D. Stoddard," October 22, 1945, NA, RG 153, Box 1377, File 52-32-1; *Roster, Lost Battalion Association*, 2002, vii; Ronald E. Marcello, "Lone Star POWs," 297; Duane Schultz, *The Last Battle Station: The Story of the USS Houston* (New York: St. Martin's Press, 1985), 227; Wigmore, *Japanese Thrust*, 533. For a firsthand history of the fate of the USS Houston, see W. G. Winslow, *The Ghost That Died at Sunda Strait* (Annapolis, Md.: Naval Institute Press, 1984).

45. *Roster, Lost Battalion Association*, 2002, iv–v; Schultz, *The Last Battle Station*, 201–26; Robert S. LaForte and Ronald E. Marcello, eds., *Building the Death Railway: The Ordeal of American POWs in Burma, 1942–1945* (Wilmington, Del.: Scholarly Resources, 1993), xiii–xiv.

46. Webb (OH 1181), 67–68; Taylor (OH 491), 69–70; Rasbury (OH 438), 98–99; Armstrong (OH 530), 74; Buzzo (OH 1245), 86–87; Bramlett (OH 345), 49–51; Lawrence Brown (OH 178), 49; Houston Wright (OH 466), 60–61; "Prisoner of War Report: John H. Wisecup," September 5, 1945, NA, RG 153, Box 1376, File 52-3-48; "Prisoner of War Report: Howard Robert Charles," September 21, 1945, NA, RG 153, Box 1407, File 57-195-1; "Prisoner of War Report: Marvin Earle Robinson," September 18, 1945, NA, RG 153, Box 1400, File 57-8-34.

47. Prunty (OH 689), 51.

48. Stanbrough (OH 658), 117.

49. Dunn, *The Bamboo Express*, 34.

50. Quoted in LaForte and Marcello, *Building the Death Railway*, 50.

51. Department of the Army, "Prisoner-of-War Camps," 1.

52. Webb (OH 1181), 89–90; "In the Matter of Improper Treatment . . . Testimony of Blucher S. Tharp," November 10, 1945, NA, RG 153, Box 1376, File 52-3-44; "In the Matter of Mistreatment of American Prisoners of War at the Bicycle Camp, Batavia, Java, July to October 1942: Perpetuation of the Testimony of Jack Wayne Bailey," October 13, 1945, NA, RG 153, Box 1376, File 52-3-26; "In the Matter of Mistreatment of American Prisoners of War at the Bicycle Camp, Batavia, Java from May to October 1942: Perpetuation of Testimony of Millard Lee Baker," November 19, 1945, NA, RG 153, Box 1376, File 52-3-23.

53. Webb (OH 1181), 90.

54. Webb (OH 1181), 90–93; Bramlett (OH 345), 41; Houston Wright (OH 466), 76; Smallwood (OH 166), 48–51; Offerle (OH 457), 53; Stanbrough (OH 658), 127.

55. Gordon (OH 383), 72.

56. Armstrong (OH 530), 86–87.

57. Ibid.; Buzzo (OH 1245), 94–95; Buck (OH 279), 26–27; "In the Matter of the Beating and Torture of Sergeant Hiram J. Whatley . . . by the 'Brown Bomber' at Bicycle Camp, Java around August 6, 1942: Perpetuation of Testimony of Warren Thomas Atkinson," November 20, 1945, NA, RG 153, Box 1377, File 52-26-2; "In the Matter of the Beating and Torture of Seventeen American Prisoners of War . . . at Bicycle Camp, Batavia, Java by the 'Brown Bomber' and Other Japanese on or about

July, August, 1942: Perpetuation of Testimony of J. L. Summers," October 16, 1945, NA, RG 153, Box 1377, File 52-26-1.

58. Gordon (OH 383), 69–70.

59. "Beating of Sergeant Rogers and Sergeant Sisk . . . by the 'Brown Bomber' at Bicycle Camp about June 20–22, 1942: Perpetuation of Testimony of William J. Chapman," January 17–18, 1946, NA, RG 153, Box 1387, File 52-76-1.

60. Charley L. Pryor to Ronald E. Marcello, November 4, 1972, January 22, February 20, 1973, interview transcript (OH 139), pt. I, 42–43.

61. Stanbrough (OH 658), 124.

62. Huddleston Wright (OH 794), 67–68.

63. Bramlett (OH 345), 40; Burns (OH 176), 39; Gordon (OH 383), 71.

64. Taylor (OH 491), 56.

65. Jack O. Burge to Ronald E. Marcello, May 16,1978, interview transcript (OH 427), 52; Dunn, The Bamboo Express, 42; "In the Matter of the Wholesale Looting in Java of March 1942: Perpetuation of Testimony of Franklin B. Torp," February 16, 1946, NA, RG 153, Box 1377, File 52-42-1; "In the Matter of Wholesale Looting by the Japanese at Batavia, Java, from April 1942 to October 1942: Perpetuation of Testimony of Thurman L. Capps," November 7, 1945, NA, RG 153, Box 1377, File 52-44-1.

66. The Japanese paid the prisoners for their work, enlisted men receiving the equivalent of ten cents per day. See Department of the Army, "Prisoner-of-War Camps," 3; Webb (OH 1181), 84–87; Bramlett (OH 345), 43–45; Lawrence Brown (OH 178), 41; Houston Wright (OH 466), 68–72; Offerle (OH 457), 51–52; Alf Brown (OH 188), 60–61; Burns (OH 176), 46–47, 51; Gordon (OH 383), 65.

67. Taylor (OH 491), 73; Stanbrough (OH 658), 121; Dunn, The Bamboo Express, 43.

68. Dunn, The Bamboo Express, 45.

69. Ibid., 41; Rasbury (OH 438), 82; Buzzo (OH 1245), 105.

70. Ficklin (OH 691), 75–76; Fung (OH 404), 59–62; Capps (OH 1196), 36; Taylor (OH 491), 73; Alf Brown (OH 188), 63; Rasbury (OH 438), 100.

71. Buzzo (OH 1245), 107–108; Lawrence Brown (OH 178), 48–49; Taylor (OH 491), 73.

72. Alf Brown (OH 188), 63; Rasbury (OH 438), 100; Capps (OH 1196), 36.

73. Buzzo (OH 1245), 66; Fung (OH 404), 62; Lawrence Brown (OH 178), 44; Houston Wright (OH 466), 80.

74. Hard (OH 510), 116.

75. Offerle (OH 457), 43.

76. Huddleston Wright (OH 794), 193.

77. Ibid., 98–99; Fung (OH 404), 62; Lawrence Brown (OH 178), 44; Offerle (OH 457), 43.

78. Stanbrough (OH 658), 97–98.

79. Ibid., 103–104; Ficklin (OH 691), 50–51.

80. Stanbrough (OH 658), 95–101; Ficklin (OH 691), 44; Bramlett (OH 345), 47; Papish (OH 781), 114–15; Offerle (OH 457), 57–58; Webb (OH 1181), 94–95; Armstrong (OH 530), 90; Huddleston Wright (OH 794), 86–87.

81. Ficklin (OH 691), 68; Lawrence Brown (OH 178), 39, 45; Capps (OH 1196),

31; Huddleston Wright (OH 794), 75; Hard (OH 510), 118–19; Taylor (OH 491), 58, 63–64.

82. Taylor (OH 491), 63–64; Webb (OH 1181), 73; Rasbury (OH 438), 88; Buzzo (OH 1245), 100–101; Bramlett (OH 345), 36–38; Houston Wright (OH 466), 61–63; Gordon (OH 383), 75–76; Ficklin (OH 691), 66–68.

83. "In the Matter of the Torture and Beating of a Number of American Prisoners of War at Bicycle Camp, Batavia, Java in August, 1942: Perpetuation of the Testimony of Herbert R. Morris," November 1, 1945, NA, RG 153, Box 1376, File 52-3-21.

84. Some of the enlisted men claim that Sgt. Jack Shaw was court-martialed at Bicycle Camp because he threatened to expose the officers' practice. Smallwood (OH 166), 53; Ficklin (OH 691), 68–69; Lawrence Brown (OH 178), 47; Bramlett (OH 345), 37; Buzzo (OH 1245), 101; Webb (OH 1181), 75.

85. Taylor (OH 491), 65.

86. Armstrong (OH 530), 85–86; Huddleston Wright (OH 794), 82–84; Stanbrough (OH 658), 128–30; Ficklin (OH 691), 77–78; Taylor (OH 491), 70–72; Hard (OH 510), 109–11; Gordon (OH 383), 66–67; "In the Matter of Improper Treatment of American Prisoners of War at the Bicycle Camp, Batavia, Java on July 4, 1942: Perpetuation of Testimony of Charles G. Slavens," November 17, 1945, NA, RG 153, Box 1376, File 52-3-40; "In the Matter of the Beating of a Number of American Prisoners of War at Bicycle Camp, Batavia, Java on July 4, 1942: Perpetuation of Testimony of Herbert R. Morris," November 1, 1945, NA, RG 153, Box 1376, File 52-3-20; "In the Matter of Physical Cruelties Being Inflicted on Allied and American Prisoners of War by the Japanese at Bicycle Camp, Batavia, Java, on July 4, 1942, in the Forced Signing of a Declaration Not to Try to Escape: Perpetuation of Testimony of Otho C. Casey," October 23, 1945, NA, RG 153, Box 1376, File 52-3-19.

87. Hard (OH 510), 92.

88. Rasbury (OH 438), 97.

89. According to the Americans, this was not the case among British POWs they encountered later in Singapore. British officers required proper military etiquette from all enlisted men, which included saluting superiors and addressing them formally. The British also required that the enlisted personnel perform calisthenics on a regular basis, and they received inferior rations. See Buzzo (OH 1245), 121; Burns (OH 176), 57–58; Alf Brown (OH 188), 72; Buck (OH 279), 31–32; Smallwood (OH 166), 70–71; Rasbury (OH 438), 122–23.

90. Prunty (OH 689), 45–46; Webb (OH 1181), 93; Offerle (OH 457), 53; Rasbury (OH 438), 77.

91. Alf Brown (OH 188), 58–59; Burns (OH 176), 44–47; Lawrence Brown (OH 178), 46; Huddleston Wright (OH 794), 74–75; Buck (OH 279), 19; Armstrong (OH 530), 79; Rasbury (OH 438), 90.

92. Papish (OH 781), 111; Hard (OH 510), 124; Alf Brown (OH 188), 53–54; Burns (OH 176), 48–49; Buzzo (OH 1245), 109–10; Bramlett (OH 345), 35–36.

93. Rasbury (OH 438), 104; Burns (OH 176), 99; Hard (OH 510), 137–38; Taylor (OH 491), 119; Fung (OH 404), 52; Lawrence Brown (OH 178), 65, 103; Houston Wright (OH 466), 55; Offerle (OH 457), 58–59.

94. Huddleston Wright (OH 794), 70; Houston Wright (OH 466), 60.

95. Buzzo (OH 1245), 112.

96. Bramlett (OH 345), 48–49; Burns (OH 176), 52–53; Lawrence Brown (OH 178), 52–53.

97. Offerle (OH 457), 64.

98. Gordon (OH 383), 83.

Chapter 5

1. "Personal Diary of Colonel Blucher S. Tharp," pt. I, 17. Prior to this, the Japanese separated some twenty-five to thirty of the American prisoners from the main group. Those who were deemed to have important technical skills were segregated from the rest of the POWs and sent to the Japanese home islands to labor in the mines and factories there. Capt. Lundy Zeigler was senior officer of this group. See William J. Stewart to Ronald E. Marcello, June 11, 1981, interview transcript (OH 544), 71–72; Jack Feliz to Ronald E. Marcello, February 28, 2000, interview transcript (OH 1373), 99–100; Stanbrough (OH 658), 133–35; Huddleston Wright (OH 794), 92; Rasbury (OH 438), 110–11.

2. Typically, the prisoners left Bicycle Camp with a blanket, a canteen, mosquito netting, some extra clothes, and a mess kit. See the following interviews: Brain (OH 546), 117–18; Griff L. Douglas to Ronald E. Marcello, April 18, 1978, interview transcript (OH 425), 69–70; Taylor (OH 491), 81; Rasbury (OH 438), 114; Fung (OH 404), 68–70.

3. Howard Robert Charles to Ronald E. Marcello, March 25, 1998, interview transcript (OH 1243), 86.

4. Lawrence Brown (OH 178), 53; Burns (OH 176), 53.

5. Armstrong (OH 530), 95–96; Fung (OH 404), 68–69; Ficklin (OH 691), 80–81; "Personal Diary of Colonel Blucher S. Tharp," pt. I, 17; "Case Files on Shipping, Transport Cases," NA, RG 331, Box 983, Folder TR-O Misc. For a discussion of Japanese transport of POWs during World War II, see Gregory F. Michno, *Death on the Hellships: Prisoners at Sea in the Pacific War* (Annapolis, Md.: Naval Institute Press, 2001), as well as Raymond Lamont-Brown, *Ships from Hell: Japanese War Crimes on the High Seas* (Stroud, Gloucestershire, U.K.: Sutton Publishing, 2002).

6. Armstrong (OH 530), 97.

7. Michno, *Death on the Hellships*, 60.

8. Fung (OH 404), 70; Houston Wright (OH 466), 82–89.

9. Fung (OH 404), 76.

10. Brain (OH 546), 120–21; "In the Matter of the Transportation of American Prisoners of War under Improper Conditions from Java to Singapore in May [sic] 1942: Perpetuation of Testimony of Salome G. Arroyo," November 13, 1945, NA, RG 153, Box 1450, File 76-152-5.

11. Fung (OH 404), 70–71.

12. Ibid., 70.

13. Armstrong (OH 530), 99; "Statement of Jose J. Garcia," October 19, 1945, NA, RG 331, Box 989, File TR-29-15.

14. Houston Wright (OH 466), 85–86; "Statement of Jose J. Garcia," October 19, 1945, NA, RG 153, Box 989, File TR-29-15; "In the Matter of the Transportation . . . Testimony of Salome G. Arroyo," November 13, 1945, NA, RG 153, Box 1450, File 76-152-5.

15. Julius B. Heinen to Ronald E. Marcello, October 29, 1973, interview transcript (OH 174), 64–65.

16. James W. Huffman to Ronald E. Marcello, April 11, 1990, interview transcript (OH 818), 80; Gordon (OH 383), 83–85; Rasbury (OH 438), 114–19; Buzzo (OH 1245), 113–14; Webb (OH 1181), 103; "In the Matter of the Improper Transportation of American Prisoners of War from Java to Singapore, November 1942: Perpetuation of Testimony of Buster H. Spann," October 31, 1945, NA, RG 153, Box 1450, File 67-138-5.

17. Hard (OH 510), 127.

18. Morris (OH 780), 132–33; Buzzo (OH 1245), 114; Hard (OH 510), 126–30; Smallwood (OH 166), 65–66; Alf Brown (OH 188), 68; "In the Matter of Transportation of 2nd Battalion, 131st Field Artillery Regiment under Improper Conditions . . . from Bicycle Camp, Batavia, Java to Singapore: Perpetuation of Testimony of Lester C. Rasbury," October 25, 1945, NA, RG 331, Box 989, Folder TR-29 *Daimichi Maru*, File TR-29-35; "In the Matter of Improper Transportation of Roy Luther Morrow . . . from 1942–1944: Perpetuation of Testimony of Roy Luther Morrow," December 6, 1945, NA, RG 153, Box 1450, File 67-152-13.

19. Heinen (OH 780), 65–66.

20. Alf Brown (OH 188), 70.

21. Thompson, *A Thousand Cups of Rice*, 58.

22. "In the Matter of Transportation of American Prisoners of War under Improper Conditions: Perpetuation of Testimony of Blucher S. Tharp," November 30, 1945, NA, RG 153, Box 1450, File 67-152-10; "In the Matter of the Transportation of Ray Olen Singleton . . . under Improper Conditions from Java to Singapore, October 11, 1942 to October 16, 1942: Perpetuation of Testimony of Ray Olen Singleton," November 13, 1945, NA, RG 153, Box 1450, File 67-152-9; "Statement of Fred Conrad Grass," March 4, 1946, NA, RG 153, Box 1450, File 67-152-7.

23. Papish (OH 781), 119–21.

24. Offerle (OH 457), 71.

25. Seldon D. Reese to Ronald E. Marcello, June 21, 1978, interview transcript (OH 426), 73–74.

26. Rasbury (OH 438), 118; approximately eight Allied prisoners died within a week of disembarking from the *Dai Nichi Maru*, most likely due to the conditions aboard ship. "Statement of Eric William Wright," January 24, 1946, NA, RG 331, Box 989, File TR-29-20; "In the Matter of Transportation of United States Prisoners of War under Improper Conditions: Perpetuation of Testimony of Blucher S. Tharp," November 30, 1945, NA, RG 331, Box 989, File TR-29-43; "In the Matter of the Transportation of United States Prisoners of War under Improper Conditions . . . about October 20, 1942 to October 25, 1942: Perpetuation of Testimony of Lawrence Edgar Ladwig," November 15, 1945, NA, RG 331, Box 989, File TR-29-24.

27. U.S. Department of the Army, American Prisoners of War Information Bureau, Liaison and Research Branch, "Prisoner-of-War Camps in Areas Other Than the Four Principal Islands of Japan: Changi Prisoner-of-War Camps, Singapore Island, Malay States," July 31, 1946, Camp Mabry Archives, Austin, Texas.

28. Ibid.

29. "Personal Diary of Colonel Blucher S. Tharp," pt. I, 19; "Statement of John E. Rogers, Jr.," April 11, 1946, NA, RG 153, Box 1401, File 57-69; "Perpetuation of Testimony of Albert Elmo Kennedy," September 25, 1946, NA, RG 153, Box 1401, File 57-69-A.

30. Morris (OH 780), 135–36.

31. Webb (OH 1181), 107–108; Gordon (OH 383), 88; Rasbury (OH 438), 120; Buzzo (OH 1245), 116–17; Fung (OH 404), 73.

32. Morris (OH 780), 135–36.

33. Gordon (OH 383), 88.

34. Ficklin (OH 691), 90–91; Gordon (OH 383), 97–98; Morris (OH 780), 137–40; "Prisoner of War Report: Marvin Earle Robinson," September 18, 1945, NA, RG 153, Box 1400, File 57-8-34; "Statement of James E. Crum," September 28, 1945, NA, RG 153, Box 1400, File 57-8-32; "Statement of Lieutenant Charles D. Smith," September 1945, NA, RG 153, Box 1400, File 57-8-31.

35. Fung (OH 404), 74; Gordon (OH 383), 92; Hard (OH 510), 133; Rasbury (OH 438), 121; Huddleston Wright (OH 794), 101.

36. Wigmore, *Japanese Thrust*, 518.

37. Papish (OH 781), 147.

38. Ibid., 114.

39. Burns (OH 176), 59; Webb (OH 1181), 108–109; Buzzo (OH 1245), 117–18; Offerle (OH 457), 73; Lawrence Brown (OH 178), 59; Bramlett (OH 345), 53; "Statement of Floyd Roy Lamb, Melvin Lee Clay, and Alton James Blackwelder," no date, NA, RG 153, Box 1400, File 57-8-29.

40. Papish (OH 781), 145; Houston Wright (OH 466), 90; Buzzo (OH 1245), 122.

41. Rasbury (OH 438), 129.

42. Smallwood (OH 166), 79; Taylor (OH 491), 88; Buzzo (OH 1245), 119–20; Burns (OH 176), 59.

43. Wigmore, *Japanese Thrust*, 512. See also Burns (OH 176), 58; Webb (OH 1181), 108; Buzzo (OH 1245), 121; Offerle (OH 457), 74–75; Lawrence Brown (OH 178), 59–60; "Statement of Floyd Roy Lamb, Melvin Lee Clay, and Alton James Blackwelder," no date, NA, RG 153, Box 1400, File 57-8-29. For firsthand accounts of British POWs in Changi and their attitudes toward the Americans, see Thomas Pounder, *Death Camps of the River Kwai* (St. Ives, Cornwall, U.K.: United Writers, 1977), and Tom Kitching, *Life and Death in Changi: The Diary of Tom Kitching* (Perth, Australia: Private publisher, 1998). For a firsthand account of a New Zealander in Changi, see David Nelson, *The Story of Changi Singapore* (Singapore: Changi Museum P.T.E., 1974). For a compilation of the Scottish experience, see Tom McGowran, ed., *Beyond the Bamboo Screen: Scottish Prisoners of War under the Japanese* (Dunfermline, Fife, Scotland: Cualann Press, 1999). For a

more humorous view of life in Changi from an Australian's perspective, see George Sprod, *Bamboo Round My Shoulder: Changi: The Lighter Side* (Kenthurst, Australia: Kangaroo Press, 1981).

44. Smallwood (OH 166), 70.

45. Buck (OH 279), 32.

46. Hard (OH 510), 131.

47. Rasbury (OH 438), 122.

48. Alf Brown (OH 188), 75; Hard (OH 510), 134; Armstrong (OH 530), 103.

49. Houston Wright (OH 466), 93; Hard (OH 510), 132; Alf Brown (OH 188), 74–75; Papish (OH 781), 131; Armstrong (OH 530), 106–107.

50. Lawrence Brown (OH 178), 63; Burns (OH 176), 58; Bramlett (OH 345), 56; Offerle (OH 457), 76; Rasbury (OH 438), 131; Morris (OH 780), 140.

51. Rasbury (OH 438), 131; Offerle (OH 457), 76–77; Gordon (OH 383), 90; Houston Wright (OH 466), 99; Ficklin (OH 691), 90.

52. Offerle (OH 457), 76; Morris (OH 780), 142; Huffman (OH 818), 84–85; Smallwood (OH 166), 71; Rasbury (OH 438), 130; Houston Wright (OH 466), 94; Burns (OH 176), 56–57.

53. Hard (OH 510), 135.

54. Buzzo (OH 1245), 121.

55. Houston Wright (OH 466), 93; Offerle (OH 457), 74–75; Buck (OH 279), 34; Armstrong (OH 530), 109.

Chapter 6

1. For a detailed account of various aspects of the construction of the Burma-Thailand railway, see Paul H. Kratoska, ed., *The Thailand-Burma Railway, 1942–1946: Documents and Selected Writings*, 6 vols. (New York: Routledge, 2006). See also Clifford Kinvig, *River Kwai Railway: The Story of the Burma-Siam Railroad* (London: Biddles, 1992).

2. Wigmore, *Japanese Thrust*, 545; LaForte and Marcello, *Building the Death Railway*, 113–15.

3. Wigmore, *Japanese Thrust*, 546.

4. Ibid., 545–46; LaForte and Marcello, *Building the Death Railway*, 115.

5. The Allied POWs who worked on the railway were a mixture of Australians and British captured during the fall of Singapore; British taken prisoner in Malaya; and Australians, Dutch, and Americans captured in the Dutch East Indies. See Arnold Brackman, *The Other Nuremberg: The Untold Story of the Tokyo War Crimes Trials* (New York: William Morrow, 1987), 253; Wigmore, *Japanese Thrust*, 588. See also Aiko Utsumi, "Prisoners of War in the Pacific War: Japan's Policy," in *The Burma-Thailand Railway: Memory and History*, ed. Gavan McCormack and Hank Nelson, (Chiang Mai, Thailand: Silkworm Books, 1993), 68–84.

6. Kinvig, *River Kwai Railway*, 40. See also Yoshinori Murai, "Asian Forced Labour (romusha) on the Burma-Thailand Railway," in *Burma-Thailand Railway*, ed. McCormack and Nelson, 59–67; Paul H. Kratoska, ed., *Southeast Asian Minorities in the Wartime Japanese Empire* (New York: Routledge Curzon, 2002).

7. "Personal Diary of Colonel Blucher S. Tharp," pt. I, 19. The numbers of POWs cited here are close approximations. Because there were no records kept of the exact number of Americans in each group, the researcher must rely on other historians' calculations, most of which are conflicting, as well as interviews with the former prisoners. Predictably, the former prisoners often disagree as to the number of men in their groups. It is clear, however, that a total of 668 Americans labored on the railway in Burma and Thailand.

8. James Gee to Ronald E. Marcello, March 24, 1997, interview transcript (OH 110), pt. II, 4–5.

9. Fung (OH 404), 80–81.

10. Kinvig, *River Kwai Railway*, 54–55.

11. "Speech Delivered by Lieutenant Colonel Yoshitida Nagatomo to Allied Prisoners of War at Thanbyuzayat, Burma, on October 28, 1942," quoted in LaForte and Marcello, *Building the Death Railway*, 287–88. See also "Instructions to Be Given to War Prisoners Who Are Quartered in the New No. 3 Branch Office of the Thai War Prisoners' Camp at Thanbyuzayat," Australian War Memorial (AWM), 54 544/2/4, in Kratoska, *Thailand-Burma Railway*, vol. 3, *POW Labour: Allied Prisoners of War on the Railway*, 16–18. The Japanese posted copies of this speech all along the railway, so numerous copies fell into the hands of the POWs.

12. For the regulations imposed by the Japanese and Col. Yoshitida Nagatomo, see "House Rules for War Prisoners: No. 3 Branch Office of Thai War Prisoners' Camp at Thanbyuzayat," AWM, 54 554/2/4, in Kratoska, *Thailand-Burma Railway*, 3:9–15.

13. Fung (OH 404), 91–92.

14. Ibid., 91–92; Houston Wright (OH 466), 115; Gee (OH 110), pt. II, 10–12; "Statement of Jose J. Garcia," October 19, 1945, NA, RG 331, Box 989, File TR-29-15; "In the Matter of the Transportation . . . Testimony of Salome G. Arroyo," November 13, 1945, NA, RG 331, Box 989, File TR-29-2.

15. Huddleston Wright (OH 794), 118; "Statement of Jack Gordon Netter," December 14, 1945, NA, RG 153, Box 1450, File 67-138-14; "In the Matter of Transportation of American Prisoners of War under Improper Conditions by Boat from Singapore to Rangoon in about November 1942: Perpetuation of Testimony of Gerald Leon Agin," December 5, 1945, NA, RG 331, Box 989, File TR-29-1; "In the Matter of the Transportation of Chester Lawrence Wood . . . under Improper Conditions by the Japanese from October 17 to 29, 1942 en route from Singapore to Rangoon to Moulmein, Burma: Perpetuation of the Testimony of Chester Lawrence Wood," October 30, 1945, NA, RG 331, Box 989, File TR-29-51.

16. Huddleston Wright (OH 794), 75–77; Houston Wright (OH 466), 101; Gee (OH 110), pt. II, 2–3. For the overall conditions on the Burma-Thailand railway, including food, work, medical facilities, punishment, and other various aspects of the project, see "Report on Conditions, Life and Work of POW in Burma and Siam 1942–1945," AWM, 54 554/2/1C, in Kratoska, *Thailand-Burma Railway*, 3:35–113.

17. Thompson, *A Thousand Cups of Rice*, 61; "Personal Diary of Colonel Blucher S. Tharp," pt. I, 19; "In the Matter of the Exposure by the Japanese of John C. Hensley . . . to Bombing by Allied Planes While on a Japanese Transport between Penang, Malay States to Moulmein, Burma on or about January 15, 1943: Perpetuation of

Testimony of John C. Hensley," November 16, 1945, NA, RG 153, Box 1450, File 67-138-4.

18. Chambers (OH 575), 95–96; Rasbury (OH 438), 135–36; Webb (OH 1181), 110–11; Offerle (OH 457), 81; Dunn, *The Bamboo Express*, 66; "In the Matter of Transporting American Prisoners of War under Improper Conditions by the Japanese on or about October 21, 1942 from Java to Singapore: Perpetuation of Testimony of Frank W. Ficklin," January 14, 1946, NA, RG 331, Box 989, File TR-29-11.

19. Thompson, *A Thousand Cups of Rice*, 62.

20. Slate (OH 528), 130; Hard (OH 510), 141–42; Taylor (OH 491), 91–92; "Personal Diary of Colonel Blucher S. Tharp," pt. I, 19; "In the Matter of the Transfer of American Prisoners of War under Improper Conditions from Batavia, Java, to Singapore in October 1942: Perpetuation of Testimony of Herman W. Barash," October 18, 1945, NA, RG 331, Box 989, File TR-29-6; "In the Matter of Transportation of Woodrow Leon Starnes . . . by the Japanese under Improper Conditions in Singapore, Burma, and French Indo-China: Perpetuation of Testimony of Woodrow Leon Starnes," October 30, 1945, NA, RG 331, Box 989, File TR-29-41.

21. Slate (OH 528), 131.

22. Rasbury (OH 438), 138–39; Webb (OH 1181), 112–13; Offerle (OH 457), 85–86; "Personal Diary of Colonel Blucher S. Tharp," pt. I, 19–20; "In the Matter of Improper Transportation of American Prisoners of War . . . from Penang to Burma January 1943: Perpetuation of Testimony of Charles O. Slavens," November 17, 1945, NA, RG 331, Box 989, File TR-29-38; "In the Matter of Transportation of American Prisoners of War . . . from Penang to Burma December 1942 [sic]: Perpetuation of Testimony of Millard Lee Baker," November 19, 1945, NA, RG 331, Box 989, File TR-29-5. See also Michno, *Death on the Hellships*, 96–97.

23. Offerle (OH 457), 85–86; Chambers (OH 575), 100–101; Slate (OH 528), 132; Huddleston Wright (OH 794), 106–107; Taylor (OH 491), 94–95; "In the Matter of the Exposure of American Prisoners of War to Bombing and Strafing and Other Hazards . . . en Route from Penang, Malay States to Moulmein, Burma on January 15, 1943: Perpetuation of Testimony of Roy Luther Morrow," December 6, 1945, NA, RG 331, Box 965, File SEA-2-10; "In the Matter of the Exposure by the Japanese of John C. Hensley . . . to Bombing by Allied Planes While on a Japanese Transport . . . on or about January 15, 1943: Perpetuation of Testimony of John C. Hensley," November 9, 1945, NA, RG 153, Box 1450, File 67-138-4.

24. Reese (OH 426), 89.

25. Rasbury (OH 438), 141.

26. Bramlett (OH 345), 59.

27. Buck (OH 279), 38.

28. Webb (OH 1181), 115.

29. Buzzo (OH 1245), 128.

30. Thompson, *A Thousand Cups of Rice*, 63–64.

31. Pryor (OH 139), pt. II, 79.

32. Buzzo (OH 1245), 127; Reese (OH 426), 88.

33. Reese (OH 426), 90; Buck (OH 279), 38; Huddleston Wright (OH 794), 108.

34. Rasbury (OH 438), 143.

35. Douglas (OH 425), 89–90.

36. Thompson, *A Thousand Cups of Rice*, 65.

37. Huddleston Wright (OH 794), 109–10; Webb (OH 1181), 118–19; Buzzo (OH 1245), 130–31; Buck (OH 279), 40; Bramlett (OH 345), 60–61; Rasbury (OH 438), 144–46; "Personal Diary of Colonel Blucher S. Tharp," pt. I, 20; "Affidavit of Henry Andrew Allen," no date, NA, RG 331, Box 965, File SEA-9-1; "Prisoner of War Report: Howard Robert Charles," September 21, 1945, NA, RG 153, Box 1407, File 57-195-1; "Affidavit of John E. Rogers," April 11, 1946, NA, RG 153, Box 1401, File 57-69.

38. Alf Brown (OH 188), 87–89; Lawrence Brown (OH 178), 73–74; Smallwood (OH 166), 92–93; Burns (OH 176), 70–71; Capps (OH 1196), 50–51; Offerle (OH 457), 93; Taylor (OH 491), 100–101; "In the Matter of the Cruel Beating of American Prisoners of War by Six Guards at the 18 Kilo Camp in Burma in February 1943: Perpetuation of Testimony of Clark Lewis Taylor," November 13, 1945, NA, RG 153, Box 1405, File 57-148-1. For firsthand accounts of Japanese soldiers on the railway, see Kazuo Tamayama, ed., *Railwaymen in the War: Tales by Japanese Railway Soldiers in Burma and Thailand, 1941–1947* (New York: Palgrave Macmillan, 2005).

39. Hard (OH 510), 152–53, 159; Taylor (OH 491), 107; Dunn, *The Bamboo Express*, 75–76; "In the Matter of the Beating of Cpl. Bert F. Jones, 18 Kilo Camp, February 1943: Perpetuation of Testimony of Bert F. Jones," October 5, 1945, NA, RG 153, Box 1404, File 57-84-1.

40. Although erratic in carrying out their policy, the Japanese paid the POWs for their labor on the railway. Officers received the equivalent of $85 to $170 per month, although the Japanese deducted the cost of room and board from this amount, and held about 33 percent of the pay in reserve, leaving officers between $30 and $50 each month. Noncommissioned officers received fifteen cents per working day, and enlisted men received ten cents. The POWs were to be paid once a month, but the Japanese often neglected to pay them for months at a time. See Taylor (OH 491), 109; Fung (OH 404), 96; Buck (OH 279), 56; Huddleston Wright (OH 794), 136; "Report on Conditions, Life and Work of POW in Burma and Siam 1942–1945," AWM, 54 554/2/1C, in Kratoska, *Thailand-Burma Railway*, 3:35–113; Wigmore, *Japanese Thrust*, 543, 560.

41. Thompson, *A Thousand Cups of Rice*, 72–73; Buzzo (OH 1245), 139–40; Buck (OH 279), 47, 53; Rasbury (OH 438), 155; Alf Brown (OH 188), 102.

42. Taylor (OH 491), 112; Burns (OH 176), 77.

43. Thompson, *A Thousand Cups of Rice*, 73.

44. "In the Matter of the Conditions at the 18 Kilo Camp, Burma: Perpetuation of Testimony of William A. Epstein," September 5, 1945, NA, RG 153, Box 1400, File 57-8-92; "In the Matter of the Imprisonment under Improper Conditions of American Prisoners of War in the Kilometer Camps in Burma: Perpetuation of Testimony of Blucher S. Tharp," November 30, 1945, NA, RG 153, Box 1400, File 57-8-57; Allan Walker, *Australia in the War of 1939–1945*, vol. 2, *Middle East and Far East*, 7 vols., Series 5 (Canberra: Australian War Memorial, 1953), 584–88.

45. Buzzo (OH 1245), 171; Bramlett (OH 345), 64; Alf Brown (OH 188), 99–101; "Check List: 18 Kilo Camp, William A. Epstein," no date, NA, RG 389, Box 2120A, File 18-Kilo, Bur-Thai R.R.

46. Smallwood (OH 166), 103.

47. Walker, *Middle East and Far East*, 584.

48. Thompson, *A Thousand Cups of Rice*, 69; Buzzo (OH 1245), 176; "Check List: 18 Kilo Camp, William A. Epstein," no date, NA, RG 389, Box 2120A, File 18-Kilo, Bur-Thai R.R.

49. Thompson, *A Thousand Cups of Rice*; Wright (OH 466), 118–20, 153; see also H. Robert Charles, *Last Man Out* (Austin: Eakin Press, 1988), for an account of an American prisoner who became close to Hekking throughout the war.

50. Webb (OH 1181), 139; Rasbury (OH 438), 167; Alf Brown (OH 188), 105; Huddleston Wright (OH 794), 143; Armstrong (OH 530), 148; Hard (OH 510), 175; "Check List: 18 Kilo Camp, Howard Robert Charles," no date, NA, RG 389, Box 2120A, File 18-Kilo, Bur-Thai R.R.; "Prisoner of War Report: Charley L. Pryor," September 26, 1945, NA, RG 153, Box 105, File 101-215-8.

51. Dunn, *The Bamboo Express*, 76; Huddleston Wright (OH 794), 144; Fung (OH 404), 112.

52. Whitehead (OH 366), 126.

53. Huddleston Wright (OH 794), 127–29; Webb (OH 1181), 124–25; Buck (OH 279), 44; Bramlett (OH 345), 63; Dunn, *The Bamboo Express*, 76; "Prisoner of War Report: Charley L. Pryor," September 26, 1945, NA, RG 153, Box 105, File 101-215-8; "Prisoner of War Report: Joseph H. Faulk, October 2, 1945, NA, RG 153, Box 105, File 101-215-7.

54. These devices earned their names from the chants uttered by the Asian conscripts who used them. The Asian workers hauled dirt with these devices, walking and chanting rhythmically, "yo-ho, yo-ho," as the load bounced up and down in rhythm with their steps. Keeping rhythm with the bouncing of the load made carrying the load easier upon the laborer. See Bramlett (OH 345), 63; Webb (OH 1181), 124; Lawrence Brown (OH 178), 75; Rasbury (OH 438), 154; Fung (OH 404), 86–87.

55. Rasbury (OH 438), 151–54; Alf Brown (OH 188), 95–97; Lawrence Brown (OH 178), 75, 85; Offerle (OH 457), 94–95.

56. Armstrong (OH 530), 119.

57. Capps (OH 1196), 59–60; Offerle (OH 457), 96; Hard (OH 510), 154–56; Taylor (OH 491), 103; Burns (OH 176), 74–75; "Check List: 18 Kilo Camp, William A. Epstein," no date, NA, RG 389, Box 2120A, File 18-Kilo, Bur-Thai R.R.; "Check List: 18 Kilo Camp, Howard Robert Charles," no date, NA, RG 389, Box 2120A, File 18-Kilo, Bur-Thai R.R.

58. Webb (OH 1181), 127–28; Buzzo (OH 1245), 143–44; Alf Brown (OH 178), 76–77; Hard (OH 510), 160–61; "In the Matter of the Use of Prisoners of War on Military Installations on the Moulmein to Bangkok Railway: Perpetuation of the Testimony of Claude W. Washburn, Jr.," December 1, 1945, NA, RG 153, Box 105, File 101-214-31.

59. Kinvig, *River Kwai Railway*, 67–68.

60. Smallwood (OH 166), 109; Huddleston Wright (OH 794), 130–32; Buzzo (OH 1245), 146–48; Hard (OH 510), 157–58; Armstrong (OH 530), 142–43.

61. Dunn, *The Bamboo Express*, 87; Webb (OH 1181), 136–37.

62. Huddleston Wright (OH 794), 120–22, 133; Buzzo (OH 1245), 150–51; Buck (OH 279), 45–48; Taylor (OH 491), 102; Webb (OH 1181), 135.

63. Fung (OH 404), 89; see also "Prisoner of War Report: Eugene David Rochford," October 3, 1945, NA, RG 153, Box 1396, File 56-46-1; "In the Matter of the Cruel Beating . . . Testimony of Clark Lewis Taylor," November 13, 1945, NA, RG 153, Box 1405, File 57-148-1; "In the Matter of the Beating and Torture of Kelly Bob Bramlett and Henry C. Drake, Jr. . . . at 18 Kilo Camp on or about February 1, 1943: Perpetuation of Testimony of Kelly Bob Bramlett," December 11, 1945, NA, RG 153, Box 1400, File 57-8-85; "In the Matter of the Beating of Lt. Robert Wade Hampton at the 18 Kilo Camp, Burma: Perpetuation of Testimony of Jack T. Cellum," November 29, 1945, NA, RG 153, Box 1401, File 57-67-2.

64. Lloyd Willey to Ronald E. Marcello, March 3, 1999, interview transcript (OH 1295), 164–65; "Prisoner of War Report: Lloyd W. Willey," September 18, 1945, NA, RG 153, Box 1400, File 57-8-27.

65. Offerle (OH 457), 126.

66. Huddleston Wright (OH 794), 116; Lawrence Brown (OH 178), 78; Alf Brown (OH 188), 99; Houston Wright (OH 466), 15, 134; Thompson, *A Thousand Cups of Rice*, 73.

Chapter 7

1. Kinvig, *River Kwai Railway*, 103–104.

2. Ibid., 108–109; LaForte and Marcello, *Building the Death Railway*, 119.

3. Kinvig, *River Kwai Railway*, 100.

4. *Roster, Lost Battalion Association*, 2002; Wigmore, *Japanese Thrust*, 560–61; Kinvig, *River Kwai Railway*, 102.

5. Taylor (OH 491), 110; Buzzo (OH 1245), 156; Bramlett (OH 345), 75; Alf Brown (OH 188), 105; Lawrence Brown (OH 178), 91; "Personal Diary of Colonel Blucher S. Tharp," pt. I, 20.

6. Hard (OH 510), 173.

7. Chambers (OH 575), 140; "Prisoner of War Report: Howard Robert Charles," September 21, 1946, NA, RG 153, Box 1407, File 57-195-1; "Testimony of Warren Thomas Atkinson," November 20, 1945, NA, RG 153, Box 1400, File 57-8-2.

8. Heinen (OH 174), 90–91.

9. Hard (OH 510), 162; Buzzo (OH 1245), 152.

10. Houston Wright (OH 466), 147–50; Buzzo (OH 1245), 157–58; Alf Brown (OH 188), 108; Huddleston Wright (OH 794), 140; Offerle (OH 457), 100; "Extract from SEATIC Publication 193," July 20, 1945, NA, RG 153, Box 1400, File 57-8-30; "Prisoner of War Report: Lloyd V. Willey," September 18, 1945, NA, RG 153, Box 1400, File 57-8-27.

11. Slate (OH 528), 170; Burns (OH 176), 86; Prunty (OH 689), 143; Whitehead (OH 366), 107–108.

12. Chambers (OH 575), 136–37.

13. Matlock (OH 555), 160.

14. Armstrong (OH 530), 149; Huddleston Wright (OH 794), 144; Buzzo (OH 1245), 152; Burns (OH 176), 89; Alf Brown (OH 188), 118; "In the Matter of Conditions Prevailing at the 100 Kilo Camp, Burma: Perpetuation of the Testimony of Ira H. Fowler," April 9, 1946, NA, RG 153, Box 1400, File 57-8-155.

15. Fung (OH 404), 107; Rasbury (OH 438), 167; Taylor (OH 491), 122–23; Webb (OH 1181), 139–40; Buzzo (OH 1245), 153; "Ill Treatment of Allied Prisoners of War Working on the Burma-Siam Railroad," NA, RG 153, Box 1400, File 57-8-17.

16. Fung (OH 404), 105; "Ill Treatment of Allied Prisoners of War . . . ," NA, RG 153, Box 1400, File 57-8-17.

17. Dunn, *The Bamboo Express*, 95.

18. Slate (OH 528), 177.

19. Buzzo (OH 1245), 160–61; Huddleston Wright (OH 794), 141; Armstrong (OH 530), 155; Rasbury (OH 438), 178; Slate (OH 528), 177; "In the Matter of Using American Prisoners of War . . . to Build an Enemy Railroad for the Japanese: Perpetuation of Testimony of Paul Chesnutt Jones," November 1, 1945, NA, RG 153, Box 1400, File 57-8-160; "Affidavit of Theodore Schram," NA, RG 389, Box 2120, General File: Thailand, Burma, Etc.

20. Offerle (OH 457), 107; Bramlett (OH 345), 79–80; Fung (OH 404), 110; Hard (OH 510), 164; "In the Matter of the Failure of the Japanese to Provide Proper Food, Quarters, and Medical Care for American Prisoners of War at 100 Kilo Camp, Burma: Perpetuation of Testimony of Jose F. Vallejo," January 31, 1946, NA, RG 153, Box 1400, File 57-8-102; "In the Matter of the Conditions at the 18 Kilo Camp, Burma: Perpetuation of Testimony of William A. Epstein," September 5, 1945, NA, RG 153, Box 1400, File 57-8-92; Wigmore, *Japanese Thrust*, 553.

21. Houston Wright (OH 466), 151.

22. Bramlett (OH 345), 78; Smallwood (OH 166), 136; Capps (OH 1196), 67; Webb (OH 1181), 145; Alf Brown (OH 188), 112; Burns (OH 176), 88; "In the Matter of the Failure of the Japanese to Provide . . . American Prisoners of War with Proper Food, Quarters, and Medical Care: Perpetuation of Testimony of Drew Wyatt Crain," November 30, 1945, NA, RG 153, Box 1400, File 57-8-101.

23. Huddleston Wright (OH 794), 147–48.

24. Whitehead (OH 366), 68.

25. Huffman (OH 818), 116–17.

26. Houston Wright (OH 466), 134; Dunn, *The Bamboo Express*, 90.

27. *Roster, Lost Battalion Association*, 2002, vii.

28. Huffman (OH 818), 118.

29. Houston Wright (OH 466), 129–31.

30. Offerle (OH 457), 118–19; "Death Records, Japanese POW Information Bureau," NA, RG 407, Box 172, File J.A.-250-5.

31. Buzzo (OH 1245), 182; Taylor (OH 491), 122; Rasbury (OH 438), 169–70; Gordon (OH 383), 119–21; Huddleston Wright (OH 794), 150–53; Houston Wright (OH 466), 127; Bramlett (OH 345), 83–84.

32. Lawrence Brown (OH 178), 89.

33. Reed (OH 486), 166–67.

34. Marvin E. Robinson to Ronald E. Marcello, May 25, 1982, interview transcript (OH 580), 124; Offerle (OH 457), 108; Capps (OH 1196), 69–71; Fung (OH 404), 104; Huddleston Wright (OH 794), 150–53; Roster, Lost Battalion Association, 2002, 45.

35. Houston Wright (OH 466), 129–30; Hard (OH 510), 172; Bramlett (OH 345), 79–80; Armstrong (OH 530), 153–54.

36. Pryor (OH 139), pt. III, 7.

37. Ibid., 9–11; Offerle (OH 457), 110–11; Dunn, The Bamboo Express, 101–104; "Check List for 80 Kilo Camp: Huddleston W. Wright," "Check List for 80 Kilo Camp: Charley L. Pryor," NA, RG 389, Box 2120A, File 80-Kilo, Bur-Thai R.R.

38. Buzzo (OH 1245), 160.

39. Burns (OH 176), 87–88, 98.

40. Taylor (OH 491), 115–18, 125–27.

41. Gordon (OH 383), 118–19.

42. Taylor (OH 491), 118–20.

43. Buzzo (OH 1245), 175; Burns (OH 176), 88; Bramlett (OH 345), 92; Hard (OH 510), 170; Offerle (OH 457), 130; Rasbury (OH 438), 176; "Personal Diary of Colonel Blucher S. Tharp," pt. I, 21; "Affidavit of John E. Rogers, Jr.," April 11, 1946, NA, RG 153, Box 1401, File 57-69. Many Australian POWs also expressed their admiration for Lumpkin in letters to his widow, Mary Jean Lumpkin, following the war. See File "Letters about Lumpkin," Collection 74 of the "Lost Battalion Collection," Camp Mabry Archives, Austin, Texas.

44. Pryor (OH 139), pt. III, 7; "Letter to Captain Willard A. Smith from Charley L. Pryor, Jr.," May 24, 1946, NA, RG 389, Box 2120, General File, Thailand, Burma, Etc.; "Check List for 80 Kilo Camp: Huddleston W. Wright," "Check List for 80 Kilo Camp: Charley L. Pryor," NA, RG 389, Box 2120A, File 80-Kilo, Bur-Thai R.R.

45. Pryor (OH 139), pt. III, 6; "In the Matter of the Failure of the Japanese to Provide Proper Food, Quarters, and Medical Care for American Prisoners of War at 100 Kilo Camp, Burma: Perpetuation of Testimony of Jack Richard Speece," November 5, 1945, NA, RG 153, Box 1401, File 57-62-1; "In the Matter of Mistreatment of Captured American Soldiers at the 100 Kilo Camp, Burma: Perpetuation of Testimony of James M. Ballinger," December 6, 1945, NA, RG 153, Box 1401, File 57-69-4.

46. Roster, Lost Battalion Association, 2002, 46; Marcello, "Lone Star POWs," 293–321.

47. Huddleston Wright (OH 794), 165–67; Capps (OH 1196), 74–75; Webb (OH 1181), 157–59; Armstrong (OH 530), 163; Buck (OH 279), 62–63.

48. Buzzo (OH 1245), 179–80; Bramlett (OH 345), 87–88; Burns (OH 176), 93; Hard (OH 510), 171; Offerle (OH 457), 119–29; "Prisoner of War Cemeteries," NA, RG 389, Box 2120, General File: Thailand, Burma, Etc.

49. Dunn, The Bamboo Express, 97.

50. Bramlett (OH 345), 86.

51. Rasbury (OH 438), 171–73; Webb (OH 1181), 150; Capps (OH 1196), 74; Huddleston Wright (OH 794), 158–59.

52. Rea (OH 517), 119.

53. Hard (OH 510), 171–72; "Prisoner of War Report: James McCone," September 28, 1945, NA, RG 153, Box 1400, File 57-8-167; "Prisoner of War Report: Eugene David Rochford," October 3, 1945, NA, RG 153, Box 1396, File 56-46-1.

54. Huddleston Wright (OH 794), 158–59.

55. Reed (OH 486), 172.

56. Heinen (OH 174), 117.

57. Buzzo (OH 1245), 171.

58. Gordon (OH 383), 125.

59. Fung (OH 404), 123.

60. Smallwood (OH 166), 59.

61. Webb (OH 1181), 181.

62. Hard (OH 510), 130.

63. Charles A. Cates to Ronald E. Marcello, March 14, 1974, interview transcript (OH 185), 54.

64. Gee (OH 110), pt. II, 52–53.

65. Fung (OH 404), 106.

66. Armstrong (OH 530), 165; Fung (OH 404), 113; Offerle (OH 457), 77, 130; Taylor (OH 491), 123; Buzzo (OH 1245), 182–88; Hard (OH 510), 163.

67. Reed (OH 486), 160.

68. Buzzo (OH 1245), 154; Huddleston Wright (OH 794), 146; Armstrong (OH 530), 149; Bramlett (OH 345), 89.

69. Burns (OH 176), 97; Rasbury (OH 438), 183–84.

70. Hard (OH 510), 176.

71. Gordon (OH 383), 127.

72. Dunn, The Bamboo Express, 86.

73. Fung (OH 404), 109–10.

74. George E. Detre to Ronald E. Marcello, August 17, 1978, interview transcript (OH 475), 149–50.

75. Buzzo (OH 1245), 172.

76. Thompson, A Thousand Cups of Rice, 94.

77. Offerle (OH 457), 115.

78. Ibid., 116.

79. Taylor (OH 491), 118–19, 130.

80. Clyde Fillmore, Prisoners of War: History of the Lost Battalion (Wichita Falls, Tex.: Nortex Offset Publications, 1973), 97.

81. Roster, Lost Battalion Association, 2002, 45–46.

Chapter 8

1. Roster, Lost Battalion Association, 2002, 47–50. Altogether, 133 Americans—or 19.9 percent of those on the railway—died as a result of their experiences building the railway. Although most prisoners left the jungle upon completion of the railway, an additional 39 prisoners died in subsequent camps while trying to recover from their diseases, wounds, and nutritional problems associated with the Speedo campaign.

2. Weldon O. Western to Ronald E. Marcello, February 16, 1987, interview transcript (OH 693), 104; Lawrence Brown (OH 178), 112; Ficklin (OH 691), 93–94; Alf Brown (OH 188), 119; "Personal Diary of Colonel Blucher S. Tharp," pt. I, 21.

3. Melford L. Forsman to Ronald E. Marcello, July 28, 1980, interview transcript (OH 521), 193; Marvin E. Tilghman to Ronald E. Marcello, September 6, 1978, interview transcript (OH 478), 120–21; Taylor (OH 491), 131; Alf Brown (OH 188), 119; Lawrence Brown (OH 178), 112; Rasbury (OH 438), 192.

4. Dunn, *The Bamboo Express*, 110–11; "In the Matter of the Inadequacies of Food and Quarters at Tammacan [sic]—April 1944: Perpetuation of Testimony of Bert F. Jones," October 5, 1945, NA, RG 153, Box 105, File 101-214-21; "Statement of Lt. Cmdr. Harold S. Hamlin," October 4, 1945, NA, RG 389, Box 2120, General File, Thailand, Burma, Etc.; "Letter from Preston R. Clark to Captain Norwood," May 20, 1946, NA, RG 389, Box 2120, General File, Thailand, Burma, Etc.; "Check List: Camp Tamarkan, Kanchanaburi, Thailand, J. L. Summers," no date, NA, RG 389, Box 2120, General File, Thailand, Burma, Etc.

5. Summers, August 22, 1995 (OH 1079), 158–59; Buzzo (OH 1245), 204; Armstrong (OH 530), 174; Dunn, *The Bamboo Express*, 111; "Check List: Camp Tamarkan, Kanchanaburi, Thailand, J. L. Summers," no date, NA, RG 389, Box 2120, File Thai Makam (Tamarkan) Bur-Thai R.R.; "Telegram from the International Committee of the Red Cross," regarding conditions in Thailand camps, September 21, 1945, NA, RG 389, Box 2120, File Thai Camps.

6. Armstrong (OH 530), 178–79; Forsman (OH 521), 201; Western (OH 693), 105; Taylor (OH 491), 137.

7. Summerlin (OH 543), 121–22; "In the Matter of Group Punishments of Allied Prisoners of War at Tamerkan [sic] Prisoner of War Camp, between September 1944 and December 1944: Perpetuation of Testimony of Albert Emery McGarvey," March 12, 1946, NA, RG 153, Box 1396, File 56-33-1; "In the Matter of the Beating of Sgt. Ben C. Keith by a Japanese 1-Bar Private Named Alliya at Kanburi, Thailand about July 6–7, 1943 [sic]: Perpetuation of the Testimony of Frank W. Ficklin," January 14, 1946, NA, RG 153, Box 1405, File 57-110-1.

8. Forsman (OH 521), 196–97; Lawrence Brown (OH 178), 113; Western (OH 693), 104–105; Burns (OH 176), 106; Buzzo (OH 1245), 201; Summers (OH 1079), 173–75; Gordon (OH 383), 143; "Statement of J. L. Summers," October 16, 1945, NA, RG 153, Box 105, File 101-214-39; "In the Matter of the Use of American Prisoners of War to Carry Ammunition and Dig Fox Holes for the Japanese: Perpetuation of Testimony of Salome G. Arroyo," November 13, 1945, NA, RG 153, Box 105, File 101-214-10.

9. Taylor (OH 491), 134–35; Cates (OH 185), 93–96; Armstrong (OH 530), 172–73; Dunn, *The Bamboo Express*, 112; "Perpetuation of the Testimony of Chester Lawrence Wood," October 30, 1945, NA, RG 153, Box 105, File 101-214-47; "Statement of J. L. Summers," October 16, 1945, NA, RG 153, Box 105, File 101-214-39; "Statement of Edward J. Templeman," February 6, 1946, NA, RG 153, Box 1396, File 56-38-1; Kinvig, *River Kwai Railway*, 174–83.

10. Armstrong (OH 530), 174–76; Cates (OH 185), 90–91; Western (OH 693), 106; Summers (OH 1079), 169–70.

11. Pryor (OH 139), pt. III, 71; Fung (OH 404), 135–37; Dunn, *The Bamboo Express*, 115–16; "Statement of Clark Lewis Taylor," November 29, 1945, NA, RG 153, Box 105, File 101-214-42; "In the Matter of the Exposure of American Prisoners of War to the Danger of Gunfire, Bombings and Other Hazards of War at Camp 1, Canburry [sic], Thailand: Perpetuation of Testimony of Lawrence Henry Wittkop," December 28, 1945, NA, RG 153, Box 105, File 101-214-29; "In the Matter of Prisoners of War Being Exposed to Bombings and Gunfire at Tamarkan-Kanburi Camp on the Moulmein to Bangkok Railway: Perpetuation of Testimony of Claude E. Washburn," December 1, 1945, NA, RG 153, Box 105, File 101-214-27.

12. Fung (OH 404), 140–41; Buck (OH 279), 69–70; Buzzo (OH 1245), 199; Taylor (OH 491), 134–35; "Perpetuation of Testimony of Chester Lawrence Wood," October 30, 1945, NA, RG 153, Box 105, File 101-214-47; "In the Matter of the Improper Use of American Prisoners of War . . . to Build AA Emplacement at Camp Tamarkan, Thailand Occurring on or about June 15, 1944: Perpetuation of Testimony of Oscar W. Keithly," November 5, 1945, NA, RG 153, Box 105, File 101-214-34; "In the Matter of the Use of American Prisoners of War . . . Perpetuation of Testimony of Salome G. Arroyo," November 13, 1945, NA, RG 153, Box 105, File 101-214-10; Kinvig, *River Kwai Railway*, 182–83.

13. Rasbury (OH 438), 198–99; Dunn, *The Bamboo Express*, 113; Thompson, *A Thousand Cups of Rice*, 100.

14. Bramlett (OH 345), 117; Buzzo (OH 1245), 195; Rasbury (OH 438), 201; Thompson, *A Thousand Cups of Rice*, 111; "Personal Diary of Colonel Blucher S. Tharp," pt. I, 21–22; "Telegram from the International Committee of the Red Cross" regarding conditions in Thailand camps, September 21, 1945, NA, RG 389, Box 2120, File Thai Camps; "In the Matter of Misappropriation of International, American and British Red Cross Supplies to American Prisoners of War at Kanburi, Thailand: Perpetuation of Testimony of Homero L. Martinez," January 23, 1946, NA, RG 153, Box 105, File 101-214-38.

15. Whitehead (OH 366), 136–51; Alf Brown (OH 188), 130–34; "Statement of Grover W. Reichle," November 27, 1945, NA, RG 153, Box 105, File 101-214-45.

16. Willey (OH 1295), 191–94; Frank H. King to Ronald E. Marcello, December 12, 1978, interview transcript (OH 468), 147–48; Summers (OH 1079), 175–82; Reed (OH 486), 202–207; Prunty (OH 689), 196–98; Matlock (OH 555), 178–79.

17. Huffman (OH 818), 148–55.

18. Forsman (OH 521), 208–14.

19. Ibid., 216–34.

20. Ibid., 233–34.

21. A total of eighteen Americans were killed when the ships carrying them were sunk en route to Japan by American submarines operating in the southwest Pacific. Fifteen of these Americans were killed on June 24, 1944, and three others died on September 18, 1944. See *Roster, Lost Battalion Association*, 2002, 47–50; Untitled document, NA, RG 407, Box 147, File SS/330/120/misc./24-2.

22. Spencer (OH 484), 140; Robert Gregg to Ronald E. Marcello, March 24, 1971, interview transcript (OH 69), 89–90; Albert E. Kennedy to Ronald E. Marcello, April 15, 1987, interview transcript (OH 699), 132–36; John H. Owen to Ronald E.

Marcello, February 7, 1977, interview transcript (OH 362), 114; Tilghman (OH 478), 130–31; Western (OH 693), 110–11; "In the Matter of the Beating of S/Sgt Warren Thomas Atkinson . . . at Saigon Airport, French Indo-China in February 1945: Perpetuation of the Testimony of Roy Luther Morrow," December 6, 1945, NA, RG 153, Box 1396, File 56-24-3; "In the Matter of the Beating of 19 American Prisoners of War at Japanese Prison Camp, Saigon, Indochina in January 1945: Perpetuation of Testimony of Theodore Schram," October 5, 1945, NA, RG 153, Box 1396, File 56-24-1.

23. Otto C. Schwarz to Ronald E. Marcello, August 7, 1979, interview transcript (OH 497), 133.

24. W. L. Starnes to Ronald E. Marcello, April 2, 1974, interview transcript (OH 186), 91–93; Spencer (OH 484), 140–41; Rea (OH 517), 145–47; Kennedy (OH 699), 132–34; Schwarz (OH 497), 131–32; "In the Matter of the Use of Roy Luther Morrow . . . by the Japanese on Military Works and Operations at . . . Saigon Camp, Tuy-Hoa and Dalat, French Indo-China from 1942 to 1945: Perpetuation of the Testimony of Roy Luther Morrow," December 6, 1945, NA, RG 331, Box 965, File SEA-2-10; "In the Matter of the Use of Woodrow Leon Starnes and Other American Prisoners of War on Japanese Military Works and Operations from about March 8, 1942 to August 23, 1945: Perpetuation of the Testimony of Woodrow Leon Starnes," October 30, 1945, NA, RG 153, Box 1376, File 52-3-51.

25. Schwarz (OH 497), 142–43; Rea (OH 517), 153–55; Spencer (OH 484), 149–50; Starnes (OH 186), 105; Tilghman (OH 478), 145–47; Smallwood (OH 166), 184–89; "In the Matter of the Use of Roy Luther Morrow . . . Perpetuation of the Testimony of Roy Luther Morrow," December 6, 1945, NA, RG 331, Box 965, File SEA-2-10; "In the Matter of the Use of Woodrow Leon Starnes . . . Perpetuation of the Testimony of Woodrow Leon Starnes," October 30, 1945, NA, RG 153, Box 1376, File 52-3-51.

26. Tilghman (OH 478), 146.

27. Gordon (OH 383), 170; Papish (OH 781), 169.

28. Huddleston Wright (OH 794), 197; Cates (OH 185), 97–98.

29. Hard (OH 510), 177–80; Detre (OH 475), 181–82; Houston Wright (OH 466), 166; "Personal Diary of Colonel Blucher S. Tharp," pt. II, 2.

30. Summerlin (OH 543), 132; Summers (OH 1079), 186–87; Fung (OH 404), 141–42; Offerle (OH 457), 159; "Letter from U.S. Department of State to the Swiss Government," protesting Japanese use of American prisoners of war on military installations in Thailand, June 23, 1945, NA, RG 153, Box 105, File 101-214-5; "In the Matter of the Use of American Prisoners of War . . . Perpetuation of Testimony of Salome G. Arroyo," November 13, 1945, NA, RG 153, Box 105, File 101-214-10.

31. Rasbury (OH 438), 205; Lawrence Brown (OH 178), 118; Cleon Stewart to Ronald E. Marcello, March 18, 1993, interview transcript (OH 911), 115–16; Dunn, *The Bamboo Express*, 138.

32. Buzzo (OH 1245), 206; Summers (OH 1079), 188–89; Offerle (OH 457), 143; Thompson, *A Thousand Cups of Rice*, 120; Dunn, *The Bamboo Express*, 138.

33. Tilghman (OH 478), 142–43.

34. Hard (OH 510), 186–87.

35. Dunn, *The Bamboo Express*, 139.

36. Rasbury (OH 438), 213–14, 217; Alf Brown (OH 188), 133–34; Huddleston Wright (OH 794), 191–92; Chambers (OH 575), 189; Fung (OH 404), 143–44; Reichle (OH 495), 136–37; Clark (OH 1371), 184; "Prisoner of War Report: Charley L. Pryor," September 26, 1945, NA, RG 153, Box 105, File 101-215-8.

37. Taylor (OH 491), 144; Cates (OH 185), 99.

38. Owen (OH 362), 131; Rea (OH 517), 165; Kennedy (OH 699), 140–41; Smallwood (OH 166), 203; Armstrong (OH 530), 106–107; Western (OH 693), 120–21; Tilghman (OH 478), 150.

39. Dunn, *The Bamboo Express*, 139; Chambers (OH 575), 191.

40. Taylor (OH 491), 144–45.

41. Fung (OH 404), 144.

42. Schwarz (OH 497), 147–48.

43. Offerle (OH 457), 160.

44. Dunn, *The Bamboo Express*, 139.

45. Offerle (OH 457), 160–61; Lawrence Brown (OH 178), 140; Bramlett (OH 345), 128; Spencer (OH 484), 154; Dunn, *The Bamboo Express*, 141. Ilo Hard remembered that a British POW, who had survived all the hardships of the railroad and the prison camps, drank a lethal amount of Japanese whiskey during the celebration and died of alcohol poisoning before he could get out of camp ([OH 510], 191).

46. Armstrong (OH 530), 209; Hard (OH 510), 190; Reichle (OH 495), 138.

47. Dunn, *The Bamboo Express*, 140.

48. Armstrong (OH 530), 207; Reichle (OH 495), 138–39; Hard (OH 510), 187; Chambers (OH 575), 191–93; Gordon (OH 383), 170; Buzzo (OH 1245), 219; Clark (OH 1371), 185–86; Thompson, *A Thousand Cups of Rice*, 124.

49. Offerle (OH 457), 163.

50. Prunty (OH 689), 211.

51. Hard (OH 510), 189; Rasbury (OH 438), 227; Pryor (OH 139), 98; Alf Brown (OH 188), 145; Offerle (OH 457), 162.

52. Prunty (OH 689), 212; Huddleston Wright (OH 794), 200–203; Armstrong (OH 530), 210; Reichle (OH 495), 140; Taylor (OH 491), 145–46; Chambers (OH 575), 195.

53. Western (OH 693), 122; Tilghman (OH 478), 151–52; Bramlett (OH 345), 128–29; Lawrence Brown (OH 178), 140–43.

54. Owen (OH 362), 133.

55. Tilghman (OH 478), 151–52; Lawrence Brown (OH 178), 141–42; Owen (OH 362), 132–33; Schwarz (OH 497), 152–53; Bramlett (OH 345), 127–28; Rea (OH 517), 166.

56. Schwarz (OH 497), 153–54.

57. Gordon (OH 383), 171.

58. John Wisecup to Ronald E. Marcello, July 28, 1987, interview transcript (OH 704), 117; Papish (OH 781), 171–73; Morris (OH 789), 189–90; Gordon (OH 383), 172–73; Ficklin (OH 691), 144–46.

59. Morris (OH 789), 189.

60. American OSS officers and troops parachuted into some camps, taking power from the defeated Japanese, and presided over the evacuation of the liberated

prisoners. Rea (OH 517), 172–73; Bramlett (OH 345), 130–31; Schwarz (OH 497), 154–55; Owen (OH 362), 133–34; Thompson, *A Thousand Cups of Rice*, 125–26; Dunn, *The Bamboo Express*, 142.

61. Taylor (OH 491), 150.

62. Clark (OH 1371), 188.

63. Wisecup (OH 704), 119.

64. Kennedy (OH 699), 145.

65. Prunty (OH 689), 219–20; Armstrong (OH 530), 211–13; Reichle (OH 495), 144; Hard (OH 510), 192–93; Taylor (OH 491), 152; Chambers (OH 575), 201; Offerle (OH 457), 164–65; "Report on Prisoners-of-War Treated at 142nd General Hospital," no date, NA, RG 389, Box 2120, File Lists, 142nd General Hospital; "Statement of James McCone," September 26, 1945, NA, RG 153, Box 1400, File 57-8-167.

66. Offerle (OH 457), 164; Taylor (OH 491), 152; Wisecup (OH 704), 121; Kennedy (OH 699), 148–49; Pryor (OH 139), 108–109; Chambers (OH 575), 201; Rasbury (OH 438), 230.

67. Western (OH 693), 128; Rea (OH 517), 174; Fung (OH 404), 147–48; Morris (OH 789), 190.

68. Buzzo (OH 1245), 219; Chambers (OH 575), 198–99; Rasbury (OH 438), 229.

69. Prunty (OH 689), 216.

70. Schwarz (OH 497), 155; Bramlett (OH 345), 132; Clark (OH 1371), 193–94; Tilghman (OH 478), 154; Ficklin (OH 691), 147–48.

71. Dunn, *The Bamboo Express*, 146.

72. Chambers (OH 575), 202; Buzzo (OH 1245), 223; Owen (OH 362), 135–36; Armstrong (OH 530), 213; Papish (OH 781), 175–76.

Chapter 9

1. Fujita, *Foo*, 342.

2. *Amarillo Daily News*, October 15, 1945. Fujita, a member of E Battery, spent most of the war as a POW in the Japanese home islands.

3. *Wise County Messenger*, November 29, 1945; *Fort Worth Star-Telegram*, October 25, 1945.

4. *Wichita Falls Daily Times*, October 28, 1945. The first reference to the 2nd Battalion, 131st Field Artillery Regiment, as the "Lost Battalion" appeared in the *Fort Worth Star-Telegram*, June 5, 1942.

5. *Wichita Falls Record News*, October 30, 1945; Coke R. Stevenson, Governor of Texas, Proclamation of "Lost Battalion" Day, October 2, 1945. Papers of Coke R. Stevenson, Files as Governor of Texas; Miscellaneous Proclamations; Box 4-14/159.

6. Tilghman (OH 478), 156.

7. Shelton (OH 700), 137.

8. Buzzo (OH 1245), 223.

9. Huddleston Wright (OH 794), 222–23; Hard (OH 510), 196.

10. Cleon Stewart (OH 911), 133.

11. Sister Dianna Ortiz, "The Survivor's Perspective: Voices from the Center," in

The Mental Health Consequences of Torture, ed. Ellen Gerrity, Terence M. Keane, and Farris Tuma (New York: Kluwer Academic/Plenum Publishers, 2001), 24. Ortiz believes that although denial can help a survivor cope with his trauma temporarily, it is not likely to be a successful form of coping.

12. Houston Wright (OH 466), 200–201.

13. Prunty (OH 689), 224–25.

14. Kennedy (OH 699), 150–51; Ficklin (OH 691), 156–58; Chambers (OH 575), 204–206; Gordon (OH 383), 179; Stanbrough (OH 658), 212; Webb (OH 1181), 179; William A. Visage to Ronald E. Marcello, July 15, July 16, 1987, interview transcript (OH 698), 154.

15. Pryor (OH 139), pt. III, 109–10.

16. Clark (OH 1371), 199–200.

17. Gordon (OH 383), 69. Reliance on humor while under extreme stress has long been accepted by authorities as a successful coping mechanism, especially for POWs. See Linda D. Henman, "Humor as a Coping Mechanism: Lessons from POWs," *Humor* 14, no. 1 (2001), 83–94.

18. White (OH 1167), 156; Cates (OH 185), 106; Summers (OH 1079), 194; Offerle (OH 457), 129; Buzzo (OH 1245), 227–28; *Abilene Reporter-News*, August 13, 1982.

19. Offerle (OH 457), 165.

20. Minshew (OH 597), 202–203. Minshew was a member of E Battery and spent most of the war as a prisoner in Japan.

21. Rasbury (OH 438), 232. See also Gordon (OH 383), 179; Tilghman (OH 478), 156; Paul D. Stein to Ronald E. Marcello, March 11, 1998, interview transcript (OH 1242), 131.

22. Fujita (OH 59), 130.

23. Stein (OH 1242), 94. Stein was also a member of E Battery.

24. *Roster, Lost Battalion Association*, 2002, 34–44.

25. Cates (OH 185), 102–103.

26. Visage (OH 698), 152.

27. Fung (OH 404), 47.

28. See Charles, *Last Man Out*.

29. B. M. Cohen and M. Z. Cooper, *A Follow-Up Study of World War II Prisoners of War* (Washington, D.C.: U.S. Department of Veterans Affairs, 1954).

30. *Roster, Lost Battalion Association*, 2002, 34–44.

31. G. W. Beebe, "Follow-Up Studies of World War II and Korean War Prisoners, II: Morbidity, Disability, and Maladjustments," *American Journal of Epidemiology* 101, no. 5 (May 1975): 400–422. See also Brian Engdahl and John A. Fairbank, "Former Prisoners of War: Highlights of Empirical Research," in *Mental Health Consequences of Torture*, ed. Gerrity, Keane, and Tuma, 133–42.

32. Guy J. Kelnhofer and Amy Lindgren, *Understanding the Former Prisoner of War: Life after Liberation* (St. Paul, Minn.: Banfill Street Press, 1992), 40.

33. Visage (OH 698), 151.

34. Burns (OH 176), 118; White (OH 1167), 156–57; Visage (OH 698), 152; Gordon (OH 383), 178.

35. Evans (OH 624), 143.

36. Gordon (OH 383), 79.

37. Taylor (OH 491), 130.

38. Offerle (OH 457), 115.

39. Hard (OH 510), 138.

40. *Bridgeport Index*, November 11, 1990.

41. Gavan Daws, *Prisoners of the Japanese: POWs of World War II in the Pacific* (New York: Morrow, 1994), 53.

42. Houston Wright (OH 466), 2–4.

43. Hard (OH 510), 22, 138.

44. Armstrong (OH 530), 221.

45. *Roster, Lost Battalion Association*, 2002, vii, 47–50. Ten percent of the "Jacksboro Boys" died while prisoners. Two of those who died were killed when the ship carrying them to Japan was sunk by an American submarine on September 18, 1944. This brings the number of F Battery dead on the railway to nine men, or 8 percent of those taken prisoner.

46. For a more detailed discussion of this coping mechanism, see Edna J. Hunter, "Prisoners of War: Readjustment and Rehabilitation," in *Handbook of Military Psychology*, ed. Reuven Gal and A. David Manglesdorff (New York: Wiley, 1991), 741–57.

47. Chambers (OH 575), 142.

48. Webb (OH 1181), 181.

49. *Lubbock Avalanche-Journal*, March 8, 1982. See also Julius Segal, Edna J. Hunter, and Zelda Segal, "Universal Consequences of Captivity: Stress Reactions among Divergent Populations of Prisoners of War and Their Families," *International Social Science Journal* 28, no. 3 (1976): 593–609. According to these authors, "While a man may be subjugated and destroyed by the strange and threatening environment of captivity, he can also attempt to work within it, to mould it, and to rise above it as a vehicle for survival," and describing one POW's attitude toward survival, "[He] pointed out that the one major decision he made during captivity was the decision to live, and that was made during the first few months following his capture, or he would never have survived" (605).

50. Houston Wright (OH 466), 128–29.

51. Fung (OH 404), 117.

52. Armstrong (OH 530), 220.

53. Gee (OH 110), 27.

54. The 36th Division suffered tremendous casualties at the Battle of the Rapido River. Formerly an exclusively Texas division, the 36th experienced such extensive casualties that it received hundreds of replacements after the battle, ending its long history as a purely Texas division. See Bruce L. Brager, *The Texas 36th Division: A History* (Austin, Tex.: Eakin Press, 2002). See also Walker, *From Texas to Rome*.

55. Cates (OH 185), 107.

56. Fung (OH 404), 148.

57. Detre (OH 475), 174.

58. Pryor (OH 139), pt. III, 103–104.

59. *Roster, Lost Battalion Association*, 2002, vii.

Bibliography

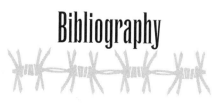

Primary Sources

Official Documentary Sources

Executive Order Number 8594. "Ordering Certain Units and Members of the National Guard of the United States into the Active Military Service of the United States." November 16, 1940.

Kratoska, Paul H., ed. The Thailand-Burma Railway, 1942–1946: Documents and Selected Writings. 6 vols. New York: Routledge, 2006.

National Archives, Record Group 59. College Park, Maryland.

National Archives, Record Group 153. College Park, Maryland.

National Archives, Record Group 331. College Park, Maryland.

National Archives, Record Group 389. College Park, Maryland.

National Archives, Record Group 407. College Park, Maryland.

Pritchard, R. John, and Sonia M. Zaide, eds. The Tokyo War Crimes Trials: The Complete Transcripts of the Proceedings of the International Military Tribunal for the Far East. New York: Garland Publishing, 1981.

U.S. Department of the Army, American Prisoners of War Information Bureau, Liaison and Research Branch. "Prisoner-of War-Camps in Areas Other Than the Four Principal Islands of Japan: Changi Prisoner of War Camps, Singapore Island, Malay States." July 31, 1946. Camp Mabry Archives. Austin, Texas.

———. "Prisoner-of-War Camps in Japan & Japanese Controlled Areas As Taken from Reports of Interned American Prisoners: Batavia, Java." July 31, 1946. Camp Mabry Archives. Austin, Texas.

U.S. Department of State. Foreign Relations of the United States: Diplomatic Papers, 1942. Vol. 1. Washington, D.C.: U.S. Government Printing Office, 1960.

Personal Papers

Stevenson, Coke R. Papers. Files as Governor of Texas. Texas State Archives. Austin, Texas.

Walker, Fred. Daily Journal of the Commander of the 36th Division. Camp Mabry
    Archives. Austin, Texas.

Archival Collections
Birkhead, Claude V., Collection. Camp Mabry Archives. Austin, Texas.
"Lost Battalion" Files. Wise County Heritage Museum. Decatur, Texas.
"Personal Diary of Blucher S. Tharp." Lost Battalion Collection. Camp Mabry Ar-
    chives. Austin, Texas.

Published Memoirs
Allen, Hollis. *The Lost Battalion.* Jacksboro, Tex.: Herald Publishing, 1963.
Charles, H. Robert. *Last Man Out.* Austin, Tex.: Eakin Press, 1988.
Dunn, Benjamin. *The Bamboo Express.* Chicago: Adams Press, 1979.
Fillmore, Clyde. *Prisoners of War: History of the Lost Battalion.* Wichita Falls, Tex.: Nortex
    Offset Publications, 1973.
Fujita, Frank. *Foo: A Japanese-American Prisoner of the Rising Sun.* Denton: University of
    North Texas Press, 1993.
Imamura Hitoshi. *Memoirs of General Imamura,* vol. 4. In *The Japanese Experience in Indone-
    sia: Selected Memoirs of 1942–1945,* ed. Anthony Reid and Oki Akira. Athens: Ohio
    University Center for International Studies, Center for Southeast Asian Studies,
    1986.
Kitching, Tom. *Life and Death in Changi: The Diary of Tom Kitching.* Perth, Australia: Private
    publisher, 1998.
Nelson, David. *The Story of Changi Singapore.* Singapore: Changi Museum P.T.E., 1974.
Pounder, Thomas. *Death Camps of the River Kwai.* St. Ives, Cornwall, U.K.: United Writ-
    ers, 1977.
Sprod, George. *Bamboo Round My Shoulder: Changi: The Lighter Side.* Kenthurst, Australia:
    Kangaroo Press, 1981.
Thompson, Kyle. *A Thousand Cups of Rice: Surviving the Death Railway.* Austin, Tex.: Eakin
    Press, 1994.
Walker, Fred L. *From Texas to Rome.* Dallas: Taylor Publishing, 1969.
Winslow, W. G. *The Ghost That Died at Sunda Strait.* Annapolis, Md.: Naval Institute Press,
    1984.

Oral History Interviews (University of North Texas Oral History Collection, Denton)
Armstrong, Roy G. Interview by Ronald E. Marcello, OH 530. October 15, 1980.
Brain, Donald C. Interview by Ronald E. Marcello, OH 546. March 11, 1981.
Bramlett, Kelly Bob. Interview by Ronald E. Marcello, OH 345. November 2, 1976.
Brown, Alf, Jr. Interview by Ronald E. Marcello, OH 188. March 26, 1974.
Brown, Lawrence. Interview by Ronald E. Marcello, OH 178. March 13, 1974.
Buck, J. W. Interview by Ronald E. Marcello, OH 279. February 24, 1975.
Burge, Jack O. Interview by Ronald E. Marcello, OH 427. May 16, 1978.
Burns, George. Interview by Ronald E. Marcello, OH 176. March 12, 1974.

Buzzo, Dan. Interview by Ronald E. Marcello, OH 1245. February 11, 1998; February 12, 1998.

Capps, Thurman. Interview by Ronald E. Marcello, OH 1196. July 8, 1997.

Carter, Uell. Interview by Ronald E. Marcello, OH 56. September 19, 1970.

Cates, Charles A. Interview by Ronald E. Marcello, OH 185. March 14, 1974.

Chambers, Martin. Interview by Ronald E. Marcello, OH 575. April 8, 1982.

Charles, Howard Robert. Interview by Ronald E. Marcello, OH 1243. March 25, 1998.

Chumley, Horace. Interview by Ronald E. Marcello, OH 199. April 3, 1974.

Clark, Arthur B. Interview by Ronald E. Marcello, OH 1371. September 29, 2000.

Detre, George E. Interview by Ronald E. Marcello, OH 475. August 17, 1978.

Douglas, Griff L. Interview by Ronald E. Marcello, OH 425. April 18, 1978.

Dunn, E. Benjamin. Interview by Ronald E. Marcello, OH 1329. November 16, 1999.

Evans, Peter. Interview by Ronald E. Marcello, OH 624. February 15, 1984; February 29, 1984; March 7, 1984.

Feliz, Jack. Interview by Ronald E. Marcello, OH 1373. February 28, 2000.

Ficklin, Frank W. Interview by Ronald E. Marcello, OH 691. January 16, 1987.

Fillmore, Benjamin D. Interview by Ronald E. Marcello, OH 162. October 9, 1973.

Forsman, Melford L. Interview by Ronald E. Marcello, OH 521. July 28, 1980.

Fujita, Frank. Interview by Ronald E. Marcello, OH 59. November 9, 1970.

Fung, Edward. Interview by Ronald E. Marcello, OH 404. December 21, 1977.

Gee, James. Interview by Ronald E. Marcello, OH 110. March 24, 1997.

Gordon, Crayton R. Interview by Ronald E. Marcello, OH 383. January 31, 1977.

Gregg, Robert. Interview by Ronald E. Marcello, OH 69. March 24, 1971.

Hard, Ilo. Interview by Ronald E. Marcello, OH 510. March 26, 1980.

Harrelson, M. T. Interview by Ronald E. Marcello, OH 666. May 9, 1985.

Heinen, Julius B. Interview by Ronald E. Marcello, OH 174. October 29, 1973.

Huffman, James W. Interview by Ronald E. Marcello, OH 818. April 11, 1990.

Kelley, Ben. Interview by Ronald E. Marcello, OH 565. March 26, 1982.

Kennedy, Albert E. Interview by Ronald E. Marcello, OH 699. April 15, 1987.

Kenner, Jack W. Interview by Ronald E. Marcello, OH 513. April 4, 1980.

Killian, George. Interview by Ronald E. Marcello, OH 56. September 19, 1970.

King, Frank H. Interview by Ronald E. Marcello, OH 468. December 12, 1978.

Knight, Douglas F. Interview by Ronald E. Marcello, OH 413. March 12, 1978.

Lawley, George P. Interview by William J. Teague, OH 164. November 3, 1973.

Matlock, Sidney C. Interview by Ronald E. Marcello, OH 555. September 9, 1981.

Minshew, Cecil T. Interview by Ronald E. Marcello, OH 597. February 18, 1983.

Morgan, Alvin. Interview by Ronald E. Marcello, OH 1183. February 17, 1997; February 24, 1997; March 3, 1997.

Morris, Herbert R. Interview by Ronald E. Marcello, OH 780. May 8, 1989.

Offerle, Roy M. Interview by Ronald E. Marcello, OH 457. August 14, 1978.

Owen, John H. Interview by Ronald E. Marcello, OH 362. February 7, 1977.

Papish, Paul E. Interview by Ronald E. Marcello, OH 781. January 30, 1989.

Prunty, Luther G. Interview by Ronald E. Marcello, OH 689. October 20, 1986; October 27, 1986.

Pryor, Charley L. Interview by Ronald E. Marcello, OH 139. November 4, 1972; January 22, 1973; February 20, 1973.

Rasbury, Lester C. Interview by Ronald E. Marcello, OH 438. June 10, 1978; June 15, 1978.

Rayburn, Eldridge. Interview by Ronald E. Marcello, OH 499. January 16, 1980.

Rea, M. L. Interview by Ronald E. Marcello, OH 517. April 14, 1980.

Reed, Raymond D. Interview by Ronald E. Marcello, OH 486. March 13, 1979.

Reese, Seldon D. Interview by Ronald E. Marcello, OH 426. June 21, 1978.

Reichle, Grover. Interview by Ronald E. Marcello, OH 495. January 22, 1979.

Robinson, Marvin E. Interview by Ronald E. Marcello, OH 580. May 25, 1982.

Robinson, Ray F. Interview by Ronald E. Marcello, OH 503. June 25, 1979; June 28, 1979.

Schwarz, Otto C. Interview by Ronald E. Marcello, OH 497. August 7, 1979.

Shelton, Clyde J. Interview by Ronald E. Marcello, OH 700. July 27, 1987.

Slate, Garth W. Interview by Ronald E. Marcello, OH 528. August 13, 1980.

Smallwood, P. J. Interview by Ronald E. Marcello, OH 166. October 25, 1973.

Spencer, Thomas. Interview by Ronald E. Marcello, OH 484. February 5, 1979.

Stanbrough, Jess. Interview by Ronald E. Marcello, OH 658. April 15, 1985.

Starnes, W. L. Interview by Ronald E. Marcello, OH 186. April 2, 1974.

Stein, Paul D. Interview by Ronald E. Marcello, OH 1242. March 11, 1998.

Stewart, Cleon. Interview by Ronald E. Marcello, OH 911. March 18, 1993.

Stewart, William J. Interview by Ronald E. Marcello, OH 544. June 11, 1981.

Stone, Preston E. Interview by Ronald E. Marcello, OH 498. February 20, 1980.

Summerlin, Granville T. Interview by Ronald E. Marcello, OH 543. June 9, 1981.

Summers, J. L. Interview by Ronald E. Marcello, OH 1079. August 21, 1995; August 22, 1995.

Taylor, Clark. Interview by Ronald E. Marcello, OH 491. September 14, 1979.

Tilghman, Marvin E. Interview by Ronald E. Marcello, OH 478. September 6, 1978.

Visage, William A. Interview by Ronald E. Marcello, OH 698. July 15, 1987; July 16, 1987.

Webb, Wade. Interview by Ronald E. Marcello, OH 1181. February 7, 1997.

Western, Weldon O. Interview by Ronald E. Marcello, OH 693. February 16, 1987.

White, Roger. Interview by Ronald E. Marcello, OH 1167. January 7, 1997; January 8, 1997.

Whitehead, Thomas A. Interview by Ronald E. Marcello, OH 366. February 2, 1977.

Willey, Lloyd. Interview by Ronald E. Marcello, OH 1295. March 3, 1999.

Wisecup, John. Interview by Ronald E. Marcello, OH 704. July 28, 1987.

Wright, Houston T. Interview by Ronald E. Marcello, OH 466. August 15, 1978.

Wright, Huddleston W. Interview by Ronald E. Marcello, OH 794. November 2, 1989; November 14, 1989.

Newspapers

Abilene Reporter-News
Amarillo Daily News
Bridgeport Index
Brownwood Bulletin
Fort Worth Star-Telegram
Lubbock Avalanche-Journal
Wichita Falls Daily Times
Wichita Falls Record News
Wise County Messenger

Secondary Sources

Books

Aitken, *The Story of the 2 / 2nd Australian Pioneer Battalion.* Melbourne: 2 / 2nd Pioneer Battalion Association, 1953.

Anderson, Charles Robert. *East Indies.* Washington, D.C.: U.S. Army Center of Military History, 1995.

Brackman, Arnold. *The Other Nuremberg: The Untold Story of the Tokyo War Crimes Trials.* New York: William Morrow, 1987.

Brager, Bruce L. *The Texas 36th Division: A History.* Austin, Tex.: Eakin Press, 2002.

Cohen, B. M., and M. Z. Cooper. *A Follow-Up Study of World War II Prisoners of War.* Washington, D.C.: U.S. Department of Veterans Affairs, 1954.

Craven, Wesley Frank, and James Lea Cate, eds. *The Army Air Forces in World War II: Plans and Early Operations, January 1939 to August 1942.* Chicago: University of Chicago Press, 1948.

Daws, Gavan. *Prisoners of the Japanese: POWs in World War II in the Pacific.* New York: Morrow, 1994.

Dower, John. *War without Mercy: Race and Power in the Pacific War.* New York: Pantheon Books, 1986.

Edgerton, Robert B. *Warriors of the Rising Sun: A History of the Japanese Military.* New York: Norton, 1997.

Edmonds, Walter D. *They Fought with What They Had: The Story of the Army Air Forces in the Southwest Pacific, 1941–1942.* Boston: Little, Brown, 1951.

Gabel, Christopher R. *The U.S. Army G.H.Q. Maneuvers of 1941.* Washington, D.C.: Center of Military History, United States Army, 1991.

Greenfield, Kent R., et al. *The Army Ground Forces: The Organization of Ground Combat Troops.* The United States Army in World War II. Washington, D.C.: Historical Division, Department of the Army, 1947.

Kazuo Tamayama. *Railwaymen in the War: Tales by Japanese Railway Soldiers in Burma and Thailand, 1941–1947.* New York: Palgrave Macmillan, 2005.

Kelmhofer, Guy J., and Amy Lindgren. *Understanding the Former Prisoner of War: Life after Liberation.* St. Paul, Minn.: Banfill Street Press, 1992.

Kinvig, Clifford. *River Kwai Railway: The Story of the Burma-Siam Railroad*. London: Biddles, 1992.

Kratoska, Paul H., ed. *Southeast Asian Minorities in the Wartime Japanese Empire*. New York: Routledge Curzon, 2002.

LaForte, Robert S., and Ronald E. Marcello, eds. *Building the Death Railway: The Ordeal of American POWs in Burma, 1942–1945*. Wilmington, Del.: Scholarly Resources, 1993.

Lamont-Brown, Raymond. *Ships from Hell: Japanese War Crimes on the High Seas*. Stroud, Gloucestershire, U.K.: Sutton Publishing, 2002.

McGowran, Tom, ed. *Beyond the Bamboo Screen: Scottish Prisoners of War under the Japanese*. Dunfermline, Fife, Scotland: Cualann Press, 1999.

Mayo, Linda. *The Ordnance Department: On Beachhead and Battlefront*. Washington, D.C.: Office of the Chief of Military History, 1968.

Michno, Gregory F. *Death on the Hellships: Prisoners at Sea in the Pacific War*. Annapolis, Md.: Naval Institute Press, 2001.

Moore, Bob, and Kent Fedorowich, eds. *Prisoners of War and Their Captors in World War II*. Oxford: Oxford International Publishers, 1996.

Morton, Louis. *Fall of the Philippines*. Washington, D.C.: Office of the Chief of Military History, 1953.

Russell, Edward F. L. *The Knights of Bushido: The Shocking Story of Japanese War Atrocities*. New York: Dutton, 1958.

Schultz, Duane. *The Last Battle Station: The Story of the USS Houston*. New York: St. Martin's Press, 1985.

Walker, Allan. *Australia in the War of 1939–1945*. Vol. 2, *Middle East and Far East*. 7 vols. Series 5. Canberra: Australian War Memorial, 1953.

Wigmore, Lionel. *Australia in the War of 1939–1945*. Vol. 4, *The Japanese Thrust*. 22 vols. Series 1. Canberra: Australian War Memorial, 1957.

Journal Articles

Beebe, G. W. "Follow-Up Studies of World War II and Korean War Prisoners, II: Morbidity, Disability, and Maladjustments." *American Journal of Epidemiology* 101 (1975): 400–422.

Henman, Linda D. "Humor as a Coping Mechanism: Lessons from POWs." *Humor* 14, no. 1 (2001): 83–94.

Holt, Thaddeus. "Relax—It's Only a Maneuver." *Military History Quarterly* 4, no. 2 (Winter 1992): 30–41.

Marcello, Ronald E. "Lone Star POWs: Texas National Guardsmen and the Building of the Burma-Thailand Railroad, 1942–1944." *Southwestern Historical Quarterly* 95, no. 3 (January 1992): 293–321.

Roland, Charles G. "Allied POWs, Japanese Captors and the Geneva Convention." *War & Society* 9 (1991): 83–101.

Segal, Julius, Edna J. Hunter, and Zelda Segal. "Universal Consequences of Captivity: Stress Reactions among Divergent Populations of Prisoners of War and Their Families." *International Social Sciences Journal* 28, no. 3 (1976): 593–609.

Towle, Philip A. "Japanese Treatment of Prisoners in 1904–1905: Foreign Officers' Reports." *Military Affairs* 39, no. 3 (October 1975): 115–17.

Essays

Aiko Utsumi. "Prisoners of War in the Pacific War: Japan's Policy." In *The Burma-Thailand Railway: Memory and History*, edited by Gavan McCormack and Hank Nelson, 68–84. Chiang Mai, Thailand: Silkworm Books, 1993.

Engdahl, Brian, and John A. Fairbank. "Former Prisoners of War: Highlights of Empirical Research." In *The Mental Health Consequences of Torture*, edited by Ellen Gerrity, Terrence M. Keane, and Farris Tuma, 133–42. New York: Kluwer Academic / Plenum Publishers, 2001.

Hunter, Edna J. "Prisoners of War: Readjustment and Rehabilitation." In *Handbook of Military Psychology*, edited by Reuven Gal and A. David Manglesdorff, 741–57. New York: Wiley, 1991.

Ikuhiko Hata. "From Consideration to Contempt: The Changing Nature of Japanese Military and Popular Perceptions of War throughout the Ages." In *Prisoners of War and Their Captors in World War II*, edited by Bob Moore and Kent Fedorowich, 253–75. Oxford: Oxford International Publishers, 1996.

Ortiz, Sister Dianna. "The Survivors' Perspective: Voices from the Center." In *The Mental Health Consequences of Torture*, edited by Ellen Gerrity, Terence M. Keane, and Farris Tuma, 13–34. New York: Kluwer Academic / Plenum Publishers, 2001.

Yoshinori Murai. "Asian Forced Labour (*romusha*) on the Burma-Thailand Railway." In *The Burma-Thailand Railway: Memory and History*, edited by Gavan McCormack and Hank Nelson, 59–67. Chiang Mai, Thailand: Silkworm Books, 1993.

Newsletters

On Point: The Newsletter of the Army Historical Foundation 6 (Summer 2000). Arlington, Va.: National Museum of the U.S. Army.

Roster, Lost Battalion Association, 2002.

Index

ISBN-13: 978-1-58544-635-3
ISBN-10: 1-58544-635-1

52995